PAPERS IN MEDIAEVAL STUDIES 17

Charters, Cartularies, and Archives: The Preservation and Transmission of Documents in the Medieval West

Proceedings of a Colloquium
of the
Commission Internationale de Diplomatique
(Princeton and New York, 16-18 September 1999)

edited by

Adam J. Kosto and Anders Winroth

Pontifical Institute of Mediaeval Studies

National Library of Canada Cataloguing in Publication

Charters, cartularies and archives : the preservation and transmission of documents in the medieval west : proceedings of the Commission internationale de diplomatique (Princeton and New York, 16-18 September 1999) / edited by Adam J. Kosto and Anders Winroth.

(Papers in mediaeval studies 17)
ISBN 0-88844-817-1

1. Cartularies–Congresses. 2. Charters–History–To 1500–Congresses. 3. Europe–History–476-1492–Sources–Congresses. 4. Middle Ages–History–Sources–Congresses. I. Kosto, Adam J. II. Winroth, Anders III. Pontifical Institute of Mediaeval Studies IV. Commission internationale de diplomatique V. Series

D113.C48 2002 940.1 C2002-903308-X

Pontifical Institute of Mediaeval Studies
59 Queen's Park Crescent East
Toronto, Ontario, Canada M5S 2C4

www.pims.ca

Manufactured in Canada

Contents

Abbreviations vii
Participants viii
Foreword
Giles Constable and Robert Somerville ix

Les ambitions d'origine et les positions actuelles de la Commission internationale de diplomatique
Walter Prevenier 1

Originale, authenticum, publicum: Una sciarada per il documento diplomatico
Giovanna Nicolaj 8

Monastic Cartularies: Organizing Eternity
Constance B. Bouchard 22

The Transmission of Lombard Documents (to 774)
Herbert Zielinski 33

Towards an Archaeology of the Medieval Charter: Textual Production and Reproduction in Northern French *Chartriers*
Brigitte Bedos-Rezak 43

The Contribution of Diplomatics to the Identification of an Early-Eleventh-Century Aquitanian Narrative
George T. Beech 61

La tradition de l'ombre: Les actes sous le regard des archivistes médiévaux (Saint-Denis, XIIe-XVe siècle)
Olivier Guyotjeannin 81

Originaux et copies: La reproduction des éléments graphiques des actes des Xe et XIe siècles dans le cartulaire de Cluny
Hartmut Atsma and Jean Vezin 113

Étienne de Gallardon and the Cartulary of Bourges (Abstract)
John Baldwin 127

The Earliest Comital Cartulary from Champagne
Theodore Evergates 128

Cartularies and the Preservation of Documents in the Archives of the Bohemian Crown before the Hussite Revolution
Ivan Hlaváček 137

Documenting the Ordinary: The *Actes de la Pratique* of Late Medieval Douai
Martha C. Howell 151

Observations on Entry and Copying in the Cartularies with Charters of the Province of North Brabant (Abstract)
Geertrui Van Synghel 174

Papal Letters to Scandinavia and Their Preservation
Anders Winroth 175

Abbreviations

AD Archives départementales
AfD *Archiv für Diplomatik*
BEC *Bibliothèque de l'École des chartes*
BnF Bibliothèque nationale de France
JL Philipp Jaffé, *Regesta pontificum Romanorum*, 2d ed. (Leipzig, 1885-88)
MGH Monumenta Germaniae historica

Participants

*Hartmut Atsma (Deutsches Historisches Institut, Paris)
John Baldwin (The Johns Hopkins University)
Brigitte Bedos-Rezak (University of Maryland)
George T. Beech (Western Michigan University)
Thomas N. Bisson (Harvard University)
Constance Bouchard (University of Akron)
Elizabeth A. R. Brown (Brooklyn College, City University of New York)
*Giles Constable (Institute for Advanced Study, Princeton)
Theodore Evergates (Western Maryland College)
Paul Freedman (Yale University)
*Olivier Guyotjeannin (École nationale des chartes, Paris)
*Ivan Hlaváček (Univerzita Karlova, Prague)
Martha C. Howell (Columbia University)
*Hermann Jakobs (Ruprecht-Karls-Universität, Heidelberg)
William Chester Jordan (Princeton University)
*Walter Koch (Ludwig-Maximilians-Universität, Munich)
Adam J. Kosto (Columbia University)
John Mundy (Columbia University)
Giovanna Nicolaj (Università degli studi di Roma "La Sapienza")
*Walter Prevenier (Universiteit Gent)
*Robert Somerville (Columbia University)
Geertrui Van Synghel (Instituut voor Nederlandse Geschiedenis, The Hague)
*Jean Vezin (École pratique des hautes études, Paris)
Anders Winroth (Yale University)
*Herbert Zielinski (Justus-Liebig-Universität, Gießen)
*Patrick Zutshi (Cambridge University)

*Member of the Commission

Foreword

Giles Constable and Robert Somerville

It is a pleasure for both of us, as the American members of the Commission internationale de diplomatique, to introduce the publication of the papers delivered at the meeting of the Commission held at the Institute for Advanced Study in Princeton and at Columbia University in New York City on Thursday to Saturday, 16-18 September 1999. The appearance of this volume also gives us an opportunity formally to thank the participants and contributors, the president of the Commission, Professor Walter Prevenier, and especially the two editors of this collection, Professors Adam Kosto of Columbia and Anders Winroth of Yale. We also offer our deep thanks to those who made the meetings possible: Dr. Philipp Griffiths, director of the Institute, and at Columbia, Dr. Elaine Sloan, former Vice President for Information Services and University Librarian, and Kris Kavanaugh, Assistant Vice President for Library Finance and Administration. The Institute and the Columbia Libraries also generously subsidized the publication of these proceedings.

The 1999 meeting of the Commission internationale de diplomatique was the first to be held in the United States, and it brought together scholars from nine countries. The conference was memorable not only for the papers that were presented and the discussions, but also for the fact that it coincided with Hurricane Floyd, which flooded parts of Princeton and made transportation from one place to another difficult if not impossible on the first day of the conference. The next day the weather cleared, and the group was able to go to New York for morning meetings and lunch at Columbia, followed by an afternoon visit to the Cloisters (the branch of the Metropolitan Museum of Art devoted to medieval Europe). The meetings on the final day were held, again, at Princeton. The libraries of both Princeton and Columbia Universities mounted special exhibitions to coincide with the conference.

Charters, Cartularies, and Archives is the latest in the series of published proceedings of the meetings of the Commission. All of the papers delivered at the Princeton–New York conference are represented in this volume, in the order and the language in which they were delivered. Two papers that have been published elsewhere are not reprinted in full, but abstracts are included. In addition, the former president of the Commission, Professor Walter Prevenier, has kindly agreed to provide an introductory essay especially for this volume. In this essay, Professor Prevenier situates the Princeton–New York meeting in the context of the Commission's history and highlights the significance of convening in North America. The scholarly study of *diplomata* has flourished in Europe for centuries, but only in recent decades has this "auxiliary science" found serious practitioners and teachers in scholarly centers in the United States and Canada. The meeting in the United States, the editing of the volume by two young medievalists teaching here, plus the publication of those papers by a distinguished North American press are clear signs, as Professor Prevenier writes, of a true interest in the United States and Canada in "la science de la diplomatique."

The organizing themes behind the Princeton–New York meeting were the notions of transmission and preservation of medieval documents. The participants' papers interpreted those ideas in various ways. One issue was the actual preservation of an original charter. But the content of originals was transmitted and saved in other ways too, and thus several papers discussed questions relating to recopied originals, cartularies, and a range of archival practices for retaining *diplomata*, their copies, and cartularies. The volume's subtitle points to the wide chronological and geographical scope of the meeting, with contributions spread across Europe and the Middle Ages from the eighth-century Lombard Kingdom to late medieval Douai. A number of papers are concerned with institutions in medieval France, but both Scandinavia and Bohemia also are represented. No brief summary here of the book's contents will substitute for the richness of issues presented in the papers themselves; and it is especially gratifying to note, in conclusion, that while our distinguished European colleagues are well represented among the contributors, the preponderance of essays in *Charters, Cartularies, and Archives* are by North Americans.

Les ambitions d'origine et les positions actuelles de la Commission internationale de diplomatique

Walter Prevenier

Les sciences auxiliaires classiques de l'histoire, la paléographie, la chronologie, la diplomatique, sont des techniques rigoureuses et ardues. Elles sont depuis longtemps les servantes méticuleuses de la «grande histoire», celle des grandes synthèses. Elles ont connu leurs heures de gloire au dix-neuvième siècle, avec la création, à Paris et à Vienne, d'écoles prestigieuses, où l'on enseignait leurs raffinements. Au vingtième siècle des nouvelles disciplines, non moins utiles, sont venues s'y ajouter: la statistique, la prosopographie, la dendrochronologie, la cliométrie. Et à l'aube de ce nouveau millénaire aucun historien n'échappera plus à l'initiation aux secrets prodigieux et tellement utiles de l'approche digitalisée ni à la richesse des banques de données.

D'ailleurs la vieille dame qu'on appelle «diplomatique» n'a pas raté cette voie royale du futur digitalisé. Toutes les chartes des anciens Pays-Bas méridionaux d'avant 1200 se retrouvent depuis 1997 sous des formes multiples (analyses critiques, transcription intégrale, et photos des originaux) en un seul CD-ROM, produit par les efforts du CETEDOC à Louvain-la-Neuve et de la Commission royale d'histoire à Bruxelles, et distribué par la maison d'édition Brepols.[1] Une mise à jour prochaine élargira bientôt le dossier jusqu'en 1250. Des chantiers pareils sont en train de produire des dossiers analogues pour plusieurs autres pays d'Europe.

Les diplomatistes et les paléographes accomplissent une autre lourde tâche, celle de conserver, dans le bon sens du terme, l'enseignement au niveau universitaire et le renouvellement permanent de la recherche fondamentale dans ce secteur sophistiqué. Il existe pour cet entêtement une bien simple raison. Il est inconcevable qu'un véritable historien, qui mérite ce vocable, ne serait pas en mesure de déchiffrer, à l'aide de la paléographie,

[1] Philippe Demonty et al., eds., *Thesaurus diplomaticus*, CD-ROM (Turnhout, 1997).

les mots et les lettres des chartes, des comptes, des correspondances, des journaux intimes, dans leur forme originale, qu'il ne serait pas capable d'en décoder le sens, qu'il ne pourrait pas émettre un jugement solide sur l'authenticité, la véracité et la fonction juridique et sociale de ces documents, à l'aide de la diplomatique.

En 1965 d'audacieux historiens, comme Jindřich Šebánek, ont pris l'initiative de rassembler les spécialistes de la science du vénérable Jean Mabillon dans une «Commission internationale de diplomatique» (C.I.D.), une initiative qui a été formalisée en 1970 au Congrès international des sciences historiques (C.I.S.H.) tenu à Moscou. L'ambition en était double. D'une part on voulait faire acte de présence au forum le plus important du monde scientifique des historiens, les congrès quinquennaux du C.I.S.H., pour y révéler aux confrères-historiens que les diplomatistes sont des historiens à part entière et qu'ils sont utiles. D'autre part on voulait remédier à un mal invétéré de tant de chercheurs individualistes. Au coeur du positivisme s'était niché non seulement le nationalisme comme idéologie, mais surtout une variante curieuse de ce nationalisme, qui prétendait que l'érudition n'avait point besoin de comparer les résultats et les méthodes disponibles dans d'autres pays, dans d'autres langues. La création de la C.I.D. fut donc le manifeste d'une volonté de comparatisme bien compris, et d'internationalisme bien fructueux.

La C.I.D. voulait en effet créer un instrument de la méthodologie des actes universellement applicable, par l'acheminement d'un nombre incroyable d'approches spécifiques dans chacun des pays européens. Au coeur du problème se situait non seulement la difficulté de la diversité des langues, mais encore et surtout des contradictions dans la définition des termes techniques. On peut considérer comme la pièce maîtresse des prestations de la C.I.D. la publication en 1994 (avec une réédition en 1997) du *Vocabulaire international de la diplomatique*, sous la direction de madame María Milagros Cárcel Ortí, mais préparé lors de nombreux colloques techniques par un grand nombre de membres de la C.I.D. sous la baguette efficace et enthousiaste de Robert-Henri Bautier.[2]

L'autre handicap de la science diplomatique était qu'un nombre significatif de spécialistes, pas tous et toutes évidemment, étaient convaincus que déjà au Moyen Âge les scribes et les rédacteurs d'actes travaillaient en vase clos, produisant des types de chartes, des systèmes d'enregistrement

[2] Ma. Milagros Cárcel Ortí, éd., *Vocabulaire international de la diplomatique* (Valencia, 1994; 2e éd., 1997).

et des méthodes de falsification spécifiques pour chaque région, et en tout cas uniques au monde. Pas mal d'articles érudits avaient l'air de suggérer que chaque document était une pièce unique, que chaque année on réinventait les mêmes techniques perfides de falsification. Le colloque de la C.I.D. à Madrid, en 1990, «Falsos y falsificaciones», a fait table rase de ce curieux malentendu bien enraciné.[3] Et le colloque de la C.I.D. à Heidelberg en 1996, sur «Der Einfluss der päpstlichen Kanzlei auf das Urkundenwesen Europas»,[4] était une autre belle réfutation. Sans oublier cependant les congrès qui situaient la production de documents dans le contexte également international des facteurs culturels et conditions intellectuelles et matérielles (à Stuttgart en 1985, et à Oslo en 2000), ni le congrès qui a eu lieu à Bologne en 2001 sur l'impact du droit dans la production des actes, ni les deux colloques tenus, à l'initiative de feu Carlrichard Brühl, en ce temps là président de la C.I.D., à Porto et Coïmbra en 1991, et à Olomouc (République tchèque) en 1992, sur la typologie des actes en Europe au Moyen Âge. L'utilité des résultats, publiés en deux volumes parus en 1996 et 1998, pour une réstructuration essentielle de la recherche comparative est sans pareille.[5] En plus chacun des grands types de chancelleries et de centres de production de chartes a eu les devants de la scène au cours d'un congrès ad hoc, et d'un volume publié: la diplomatique pontificale (en 1971),[6] les chancelleries souveraines (en 1973 et en 1977),[7] les chancelleries des prin-

[3] Ángel Cañellas López, éd., *Falsos y falsificaciones de documentos diplomáticos en la Edad Media* (Zaragoza, 1991).

[4] Peter Herde et Hermann Jakobs, éd., *Papsturkunde und europäisches Urkundenwesen: Studien zu ihrer formalen und rechtlichen Kohärenz vom 11. bis 15. Jahrhundert*, AfD, Beiheft 7 (Cologne, 1999).

[5] José Marques, éd., *Diplomatique royale du Moyen Âge, XIIIe-XIVe siècles* (Porto, 1996); Jan Bistřický, éd., *Typologie der Königsurkunden: Kolloquium de[r] Com[m]ission internationale de diplomatique in Olmütz 30.8.-3.9.1992* (Olomouc, 1998).

[6] Le congrès de Rome n'a pas donné lieu à une publication de ses actes. Voir la liste de tous les congrès et autres réunions de la C.I.D. (avec les publications qui en sont découlées): Walter Prevenier, *La Commission internationale de diplomatique, 1965-2000, présentée à l'occasion du XIXe Congrès international des sciences historiques (Oslo, 6-13 août 2000)* (Turnhout, 2000), 14-21.

[7] Budapest 1973: publication partielle dans *Folia Budapestina*, Publicaciones de la Institución "Fernando el Católico" 900 (Zaragoza, [1983]). Paris 1977, "Les chancelleries souveraines de l'Europe médiévale du début du XIIIe au milieu du XVe siècle": publication partielle dans *Folia Parisiensia* 1-2, Publicaciones de la Institución "Fernando el Católico" 915, 970 (Zaragoza, 1983-84). Cf. aussi *Documents*

cipautés territoriales (en 1983),[8] le notariat (en 1986 et 1994),[9] les chancelleries épiscopales (en 1993),[10] la diplomatique urbaine (en 1998).[11]

Y a-t-il un avenir pour les diplomatistes au vingt et unième siècle? Je perçois des signaux divergents. Négatifs, d'une part, comme dans certaines universités allemandes, où un nombre de chaires en sciences auxiliaires, pourtant vénérables, dès les débuts du dix-neuvième siècle, est supprimé ou fortement réduit par des administrateurs qui préfèrent des secteurs plus à la mode, comme si les deux ne pouvaient être utilement juxtaposés. Par contre en Espagne la plupart des universités semblent pouvoir conserver la continuation de cet enseignement et de cette recherche, comme en témoignent les multiples publications et congrès. L'aperçu si utile de madame María Milagros Cárcel Ortí sur *La enseñanza de la paleografía y diplomática: Centros y cursos* (Valencia, 1996) prouve que c'est vrai un peu partout dans le monde. Mais à deux conditions.

Une, que les diplomatistes sortent plus souvent de leurs tours d'ivoire, pour montrer au monde des historiens que leur travaux sont compréhensibles et «utiles». Les comptes-rendus des historiens traditionnels du Vieux Monde sur des travaux parus dans le Nouveau Monde se plaignent souvent du manque d'érudition dans l'interprétation des sources, tout en louant l'originalité du discours scientifique. Et dans le Nouveau Monde on se plaint de l'inverse. Il y a certainement des jalousies de métier sous-jacentes. Mais il

---

impériaux et royaux de l'Europe médieval: Catalogue de l'exposition: Commission internationale de diplomatique: Ve Congrès international de diplomatique, Paris, 12-16 septembre 1977 (Paris, 1977).

[8] *Landesherrliche Kanzleien im Spätmittelalter: Referate zum VI. Internationalen Kongress für Diplomatik, München 1983,* 2 t., Münchener Beiträge zur Mediävistik und Renaissance-Forschung, 35:1-2 (Munich, 1984). Publication partielle aussi dans *Folia Munichensia*, Publicaciones de la Institución "Fernando el Católico" 1025 (Zaragoza, 1985).

[9] *Notariado público y documento privado: De los orígenes al siglo XIV: Actas del VII Congreso Internacional de Diplomática, Valencia, 1986*, Papers i documents 7 (Valencia, 1989). Pilar Ostos Salcedo et María Luisa Pardo Rodríguez, éd., *Estudios sobre el notariado europeo (siglos XIV-XV)* (Sevilla, 1997).

[10] Christoph Haidacher et Werner Köfler, éd., *Die Diplomatik der Bischofsurkunde vor 1250: La diplomatique épiscopale avant 1250: Referate zum VIII. Internationalen Kongress für Diplomatik, Innsbruck, 27. September-3. Oktober 1993* (Innsbruck, 1995).

[11] Walter Prevenier et Thérèse de Hemptinne, éd., *La diplomatique urbaine en Europe au Moyen Âge: Actes du congrès de la Commission internationale de diplomatique, Gand, 25-29 août 1998* (Leuven, 2000).

doit être possible de combiner les meilleurs aspects des deux traditions.

Deux, les diplomatistes doivent faire preuve de flexibilité pédagogique et intellectuelle en intégrant mieux leurs cours dans l'enseignement global de leurs institutions et en utilisant intensivement les moyens technologiques actuels de digitalisation et autres, dont disposent les historiens d'aujourd'hui. Au colloque de Gand en 1998 la C.I.D. a bien montré son intérêt pour les banques de données. L'École des chartes à Paris, et l'École des archivistes à La Haye, ont complètement remanié, il y a déjà quelques années, leur curriculum en ce sens.

Aux États-Unis et au Canada également, je perçois une persistance de l'intérêt pour les sciences auxiliaires. D'abord dans des centres où cette tradition fleurit depuis longtemps et où elle continue à se développer, comme aux Universités de Toronto et Notre Dame. Des diplomatistes tels Carlrichard Brühl, György Györffy, Theo Kölzer et moi-même ont séjourné à l'Institute for Advanced Study à Princeton. Là, sous la houlette de Giles Constable, membre de la C.I.D., ils ont pu présenter leurs plus récentes recherches aux médiévistes, membres de l'Institute, venus des États-Unis et d'un peu partout dans le monde. En outre Brühl et moi-même avons eu le plaisir d'enseigner aux États-Unis différents cours donnant une voix à la diplomatique et à la paléographie, aussi bien à Princeton University qu'à celle de Columbia à New York, où enseigne d'ailleurs un autre membre de la C.I.D., Robert Somerville. A The Johns Hopkins University à Baltimore Stephen Swisdak, un jeune et enthousiaste étudiant de John Baldwin, lui-même grand spécialiste de la chancellerie des rois de France et membre d'honneur de la C.I.D., entame une prometteuse recherche sur la chancellerie des évêques de Cambrai, en concertation avec des chercheurs en France et en Belgique. Le volume, que j'ai le plaisir de présenter ici, est édité par deux jeunes médiévistes-diplomatistes. D'une part, Adam Kosto, enseignant à Columbia, formé par Thomas Bisson de Harvard, grand éditeur de textes et spécialiste de la diplomatique catalane. D'autre part Anders Winroth de Yale University, un Suédois qui, dans son passé suédois, a profité des bons conseils des membres scandinaves de la C.I.D., et qui a eu Brühl, Somerville et moi-même comme professeurs à Columbia University. Je pourrais ajouter que depuis de longues années des éditions de textes critiques ont été produits aux États-Unis. Giles Constable est sans aucun doute l'érudit américain le plus actif et le plus complet en ce domaine; il a publié aussi bien des textes diplomatiques (*The Cartulary and*

Charters of Notre-Dame of Homblières, 1990),[12] que des textes normatifs ecclésiastiques (*Libellus de diversis ordinibus*, 1972; *Consuetudines Benedictinae*, 1975),[13] que des lettres (*The Letters of Peter the Venerable*, 1967),[14] et même des correspondences modernes (celle de Bernard Berenson, en 1993).[15] Robert Somerville a produit les *Scotia pontificia*, une édition des textes et regestes des bulles papales pour l'Écosse avant 1198.[16] Bryce Lyon, à Brown University, à édité aussi bien le *Wardrobe Book of William de Norwell*, 1338-1340,[17] que le *Journal de Guerre* de Henri Pirenne,[18] et les lettres de Marc Bloch et Lucien Febvre à Henri Pirenne.[19] Récemment plusieurs jeunes érudits américains ont enrichis ce patrimoine. Une édition des comptes de la ville de Gand au quatorzième siècle a été publiée par David Nicholas (Clemson University).[20] L'édition des actes des notaires flamands du treizième au quinzième siècle a été produite par James M. Murray (University of Cincinnati).[21] Ils ont, tous les deux, bien voulu m'associer à leur travaux pour des aspects techniques. A l'University of Maryland ma-

[12] William Mendel Newman, Theodore Evergates, et Giles Constable, éd., *The Cartulary and Charters of Notre-Dame of Homblières*, Medieval Academy Books 97 (Cambridge, Mass., 1990).

[13] Giles Constable et Bernard Smith, éd. et trad., *Libellus de diversis ordinibus et professionibus qui sunt in aecclesia* (Oxford, 1972); Giles Constable et Faustino Avagliano, éd., *Consuetudines Benedictinae variae (saec. XI-saec. XIV)*, Corpus consuetudinum monasticarum 6 (Siegburg, 1975).

[14] Giles Constable, éd., *The Letters of Peter the Venerable*, 2 t., Harvard Historical Studies 78 (Cambridge, Mass., 1967).

[15] Giles Constable avec la collaboration d'Elizabeth H. Beatson et Luca Dainelli, éd., *The Letters between Bernard Berenson and Charles Henry Coster* (Florence, [1993]).

[16] Robert Somerville, éd., *Scotia pontificia: Papal Letters to Scotland before the Pontificate of Innocent III* (Oxford, 1982).

[17] Mary Lyon, Bryce Lyon et Henry S. Lucas avec la collaboration de Jean de Sturler, éd., *The Wardrobe Book of William de Norwell, 12 July 1338 to 27 May 1340* (Bruxelles, 1983).

[18] Bryce Lyon et Mary Lyon, éd., *The Journal de Guerre of Henri Pirenne* (Amsterdam, 1976).

[19] Bryce Lyon et Mary Lyon, éd., *The Birth of Annales History: The Letters of Lucien Febvre and Marc Bloch to Henri Pirenne (1921-1935)* (Bruxelles, 1991).

[20] David Nicholas et Walter Prevenier, éd., *Gentse Stads- en Baljuwsrekeningen (1365-1376)* (Bruxelles, 1999).

[21] James M. Murray avec la collaboration de Walter Prevenier et Michel Oosterbosch, éd., *Notarial Instruments in Flanders between 1280 and 1452* (Bruxelles, 1995).

dame Brigitte Bedos-Rezak, ancienne étudiante, à l'École des chartes à Paris, de Robert-Henri Bautier, président d'honneur de la C.I.D., prouve à ses nouveaux compatriotes l'utilité de la sigillographie—dont elle est devenue une grande spécialiste—en tant que discipline technique, mais surtout par son apport à l'histoire culturelle et à l'histoire des mentalités.

Comme autre signe de l'intérêt incontestable dans le Nouveau Monde pour les problèmes de critique historique, je peux citer la parution chez Cornell University Press de *From Reliable Sources* par Martha Howell, de Columbia University, et moi-même.[22] Ce livre est une version fondamentalement adaptée, avec l'aide inestimable de mon co-auteur américain, d'un manuel de critique historique qui a accompagné un cours que j'ai enseigné à l'Université de Gand (Belgique). Il fallait en effet transférer ce discours très européen dans un contexte universitaire et social totalement différent. Il est fort significatif cependant que notre éditeur américain nous a vivement encouragé pour conserver dans la version anglaise les chapitres sur les sciences auxiliaires, qui commentent largement la fonction utile des techniques classiques et de l'érudition dans l'interprétation des sources.

On peut donc considérer l'organisation du colloque de la C.I.D. à l'Institute for Advanced Study à Princeton et à Columbia University en 1999, par Giles Constable et Robert Somerville, et la publication des exposés y tenus par des érudits aussi bien américains qu'européens, dans un volume, préparé soigneusement par Adam Kosto de Columbia University et par Anders Winroth de Yale University, et accepté par le Pontifical Institute of Mediaeval Studies dans ses collections prestigieuses, comme un geste et une preuve supplémentaire de l'intérêt véritable pour les aspects ardus, mais si utiles, de notre métier d'historien, que soigne depuis Mabillon la science de la diplomatique.

[22] Walter Prevenier et Martha C. Howell, *From Reliable Sources: An Introduction to Historical Methodology* (Ithaca, N.Y., 2001).

Originale, authenticum, publicum: Una sciarada per il documento diplomatico

Giovanna Nicolaj

Il tema della tradizione dei documenti diplomatici antichi e medievali deve muovere necessariamente dalla considerazione di due elementi fondamentali per quei testi, e cioè dai loro profili di originalità e di autenticità.

Dedico questa tesina, esposta in sintesi per sommi capi e punti chiave, solo a tracciare una prima pista alla questione dell'autenticità, perché ritengo che su essa gravino alcuni equivoci e qualche confusione: equivoci e confusione che derivano sia da uno studio degli scritti diplomatici di tipo eminentemente filologico[1]—e pertanto né sufficiente né adeguato, come dirò —, sia da una lontana nozione e definizione di documento diplomatico o d'età positivistica e ormai troppo ristretta, anche se lucida e coerente, ovvero d'uso contemporaneo e corrente e perciò d'uso instabile, impreciso e ambiguo per la tempesta che nasce da dilaganti, ultime novità quali quelle della comunicazione, della documentazione[2] e dell'impiego incalzante e indiscriminato del cosiddetto bene culturale sul piano scientifico e sul piano divulgativo e d'impresa.

Quello dell'autenticità «non è un concetto assoluto»:[3] se in senso generale esso significa la riferibilità o, più tecnicamente, l'imputabilità di un' opera al suo autore, in campi determinati (per tempi e luoghi storici o per

---

Ringrazio affettuosamente per l'aiuto la mia allieva Francesca Macino.

[1] V. per esempio, U. Eco, "Tipologia della falsificazione," in *Fälschungen im Mittelalter: Internationaler Kongreß der Monumenta Germaniae historica, München 16-19 Sept. 1986*, t. 1, *Kongreßdaten und Festvorträge: Literatur und Fälschung*, MGH Schriften 33.1 (Hannover, 1988), 69-82.

[2] Cf., per esempio, A. Baldazzi, "Le radici storiche della documentazione in Europa," in *La documentazione in Italia: Scritti in occasione del centenario della FID*, a cura di A. M. Paci (Milano, 1996), 44-73.

[3] G. Cencetti, "'Archivio': Progetto di 'voce' per vocabolario, di Charles Samaran: Traduzione e osservazioni" (1938), ora in Cencetti, *Scritti archivistici*, Fonti e studi di storia, legislazione e tecnica degli archivi moderni 3 (Roma, 1970), 34.

soggetti e materie) il concetto stesso assume significati peculiari. Per un esempio facile, in ambito ecclesiale e di fede sono autentiche le parole, orali o scritte, caricate di *auctoritas* divina (per esempio, secondo 1 Sam 3:19) e ufficialmente «recepite» dalla Chiesa e pertanto «vincolanti per la coscienza».[4]

Il punto di vista della indagine e della determinazione di un concetto di autenticità in riferimento ad un soggetto e ad un contesto dati va tanto più seguito nello specifico ambito della diplomatica.

*

* *

In via preliminare, qualche considerazione sul documento diplomatico. Sullo sfondo delle società storiche, considerate sotto l'aspetto dei loro ordinamenti giuridici (*ubi societas, ibi ius*)—regole, procedure e istituzioni di diritto privato e di diritto pubblico[5]—considero documento diplomatico qualunque scrittura svolga funzioni tipiche in forme peculiari (tipiche) nella vita e nel funzionamento di quegli ordinamenti giuridici.

Da qui discende che: (1) considero troppo angusto il tradizionale concetto di *Urkunde* o di documento definito come «testimonianza scritta di un fatto di natura giuridica, compilata coll'osservanza di certe determinate forme, le quali sono destinate a procurarle fede e a darle forza di prova»:[6] perché, «se è vero che il documento ha sempre, attuale o potenziale, una funzione di prova, è altrettanto vero che la formazione di esso può essere sollecitata da una diversa finalità»,[7] e questa finalità principale va considerata primariamente così per l'oggi come per i passati storici; (2) considero omologhi documenti e *gesta* o *acta*, poiché i secondi non sono altro che scritture seriali e continue di singole unità documentarie, scritture prodotte e ordinate dall'attività e dagli atti continuativi di una qualunque istituzione giu-

[4] E. Cortese, *Il diritto nella storia medievale*, t. 1, *L'alto medioevo* (Roma, 1995), 222.

[5] Nel senso terminologico espresso da F. Modugno, "Istituzione," in *Enciclopedia del diritto*, t. 22 (Milano, 1973), 69-96.

[6] H. Bresslau, *Manuale di diplomatica per la Germania e l'Italia*, trad. it. a cura di A. M. Voci-Roth, Pubblicazioni degli Archivi di Stato, Sussidi 10 (Roma, 1998), 9-10; C. Paoli, *Diplomatica*, nuova ed. aggiornata da G. C. Bascapè (Firenze, 1942), 18.

[7] A. Candian, "Documentazione e documento (teoria generale)," in *Enciclopedia del diritto*, t. 13 (Milano, 1964), 588, par. 23.

ridica, per esempio a funzione legislativa, di governo, giurisdizionale, fiscale, militare o amministrativa.

Da ciò viene che gli spazi del documento diplomatico sono molto più ampi di quelli considerati dalla diplomatica tradizionale e si possono disporre in uno spettro ricco di generi—che vanno per esempio dalla legge alle unità di un catasto—, mentre sono tutti connessi per procedimento analogico in un reticolato costituito da un sistema storico-giuridico dato, tradotto ed espresso nella prassi scritta in *Aktenwesen* o *Urkundenwesen*, secondo le chiare categorie indicate da Classen.[8]

A corollario di tutto ciò, in via un po' teorica e astratta se si vuole ma pregiudiziale per chiarezza di metodo, un documento diplomatico va considerato oggi secondo punti di vista differenziati: a) per la sua prima e originaria funzione nell'ordinamento storico di formazione; b) per la sua funzione probatoria, eventualmente secondaria, nell'ordinamento cui va riferito; c) per la sua funzione, *ex post*, di testimonianza storica.

Proprio per la natura e la funzionalità di questi scritti in ambito giuridico—e cioè in un ambito di regole prescrittive e vincolanti—, sono essenziali le forme con le quali essi vengono emessi e per le quali appunto risultino giuridicamente validi. Fra le tante forme, una posizione di spicco assumono nel corso storico quelle dell'autenticità: tali forme saranno mirate in particolare alla funzione degli scritti addotti in processo e ancor più specificatamente alla funzione di quelli prodotti come mezzi di prova (*instrumenta*): per l'uso appunto dei documenti in processo, sarà pregiudiziale la loro *fides*, o credibilità come i diplomatisti usano dire, ovvero la loro autenticità come diremmo oggi, al fondo di un secolare spostamento semantico. In altre parole l'autenticità legale del documento diplomatico non sarà solo la «corrispondenza fra autore apparente e autore reale» del documento stesso—intendendo per autore «colui per conto del quale il documento è formato, non chi materialmente lo forma»—, bensì la «certezza»[9]

[8] Per l'età romana e l'alto medioevo, v. P. Classen, *Kaiserreskript und Königsurkunden: Diplomatische Studien zum Problem der Kontinuität zwischen Altertum und Mittelalter* (Thessaloniki, 1977), 205-10. Su tutto quanto detto sopra v. G. Nicolaj, "Fratture e continuità nella documentazione fra tardo antico e alto medioevo: Preliminari di diplomatica e questioni di metodo," in *Morfologie sociali e culturali in Europa fra tarda antichità e alto medioevo*, t. 2, Settimane di studio del Centro italiano di studi sull'alto medioevo 45.2 (Spoleto, 1998), 954-69.

[9] F. Carnelutti, *La prova civile, Parte generale, Il concetto giuridico della prova (Milano, 1992), 150 e ss.*

di tale corrispondenza, vale a dire la capacità del documento stesso di certificare da sé e preventivamente la propria provenienza e formazione ad un giudice che ne possa quindi assumere e valutare il tenore.

La storia di questa autenticità, peculiare nel campo della diplomatica, è lunga e tortuosa.

*

* *

In età romana, come è noto, la prova per documento emerge relativamente tardi, si confronta con la prova principe per i Romani, quella per testimoni, e pertanto il problema della *fides* probatoria dello scritto si pone dapprima episodicamente.[10]

Si pone infatti per le *tabulae* testamentarie e altre di diritto privato e pubblico quando il senatoconsulto del 61 d.C. decreta la sigillatura sui legacci di lino a chiusura: questa *fides* però non è inerente al documento ma verrà a questo conferita dai testimoni che, prima dell'apertura dei legacci, riconosceranno i propri sigilli.[11]

Ma un problema di *fides certa* in processo si pone anche per i documenti sovrani, che siano prodotti come precedenti di riferimento o come scritti di introduzione al processo stesso. Infatti Plinio come governatore della Bitinia scrive a Traiano:

> recitabatur apud me edictum quod dicebatur divi Augusti, ad Andaniam pertinens; recitatae divi Vespasiani ad Lacedaemonios et divi Titi ad eosdem et Achaeos, et Domitiani ad Avidium Nigrinum et Armenium Brocchum proconsules item ad Lacedaemonios. Quae tibi non misi, quia et parum emendata et quaedam non certae fidei videbantur, et quia vera et emendata in scriniis tuis esse credebam.

E l'imperatore risponde:

> Quaestio ista...saepe tractata est, nec quicquam invenitur in commentariis eorum principum, qui ante me fuerunt, quod ad omnes provincias sit constitutum. Epistulae sane sunt Domitiani ad Avidium Nigri-

[10] G. Pugliese, "La prova nel processo romano classico," *Jus: Rivista di scienze giuridiche*, n.s., 11.1 (1960): 386-424; cf. Nicolaj, "Fratture," 956.

[11] Cf. G. Nicolaj, "Il documento privato italiano nell'alto medioevo," in *Libri e documenti d'Italia: Dai Longobardi alla rinascita delle città: Atti del Convegno nazionale dell'Associazione italiana dei paleografi e diplomatisti, Cividale, 5-7 ottobre 1994*, a cura di C. Scalon (Udine, 1996), 157.

num et Armenium Brocchum, quae fortasse debent observari; sed inter eas provincias, de quibus rescripsit, non est Bithynia.[12]

Peraltro, l'archiviazione della documentazione pubblica, anche se lacunosa e caotica come appare dalla risposta di Traiano, era «soprattutto un modo di assicurare l'autenticità» di tale documentazione, «e si comprende quindi come venisse considerata forma necessaria per la...validità» di essa a partire dal II sec. a.C.;[13] e la sicurezza rappresentata dall'archiviazione aumentò anche per l'influsso della mentalità del mondo ellenistico, se Ignazio, vescovo di Antiochia e padre della Chiesa, all'inizio del II sec. sente dire da alcuni «se non lo trovo negli archivi, non mi fido nemmeno del Vangelo» (ἐὰν μὴ ἐν τοῖς ἀρχείοις εὕρω, ἐν τῷ εὐαγγελίῳ οὐ πιστεύω).[14]

Il problema della *fides instrumentorum*, o della *fides scripturae* in funzione probatoria, dilaga dall'età dioclezianea e per tutto il tardoantico. Ma la norma romana continua a risolverlo ancora e sempre attraverso i testimoni che ne fanno un'*impositio apud iudices* (Nov. 73, a. 538); mentre la prassi, mossa da una costituzione dell'a. 414 (C. 7,52,6):

> gesta, quae sunt translata in publica monumenta, habere volumus perpetuam firmitatem. neque enim morte cognitoris perire debet publica fides,

introduce l'uso di una *insinuatio* di documenti privati in *monumenta* o *acta publica* giurisdizionali e amministrativi, che precostituisca per essi la copertura di una *publica fides.*[15]

D'altronde se fa fede piena in processo una scrittura *edita* e perciò doppiata ufficialmente dagli *acta* pubblici, il termine di *authenticus*, equivalente a *originalis*, come lo ritroviamo in una costituzione dell'a. 292 (C. 1,23,4):

> sancimus, ut authentica ipsa atque originalia rescripta et nostra manu subscripta, non exempla eorum, insinuentur,

[12] Plin., *Epp.*, 10.65.3; 10.66.1.

[13] G. Cencetti, "Gli archivi dell'antica Roma nell'età repubblicana" (1940), ora in Cencetti, *Scritti*, 184.

[14] Cito da Cencetti, "Gli archivi," 220n.

[15] G. Nicolaj, "Il 'signum' dei tabellioni romani: Simbologia o realtà giuridica?" in *Palaeographica, diplomatica et archivistica: Studi in onore di Giulio Battelli*, t. 2, Storia e letteratura 140 (Roma, 1979), 25-31.

dove si tratta dei processi per rescritto[16] nei quali lo stesso rescritto viene poi insinuato, e cioè doppiato, negli *acta* processuali, il termine di *authenticus* dunque sembra perciò restare divaricato da un ambito di *publica fides* e sembra inoltre legarsi ancora al significato di autorevole e autoritativo che spetta al principe, secondo la prima etimologia e il significato di partenza.[17]

A finire poi una storia secolare e ad accompagnare sia il precipizio di una civiltà con tutti i suoi ordinamenti giuridici sia l'alba di un'altra epoca sono assai significative due costituzioni giustinianee che trasferiscono agli archivi della Chiesa l'antica tutela di documenti pubblici e di Stato:

> Cum vero apud defensorem nominatio tutorum curatorumque fit, praesente etiam religiosissimo civitatis episcopo, gesta in ipsis sacrosanctae ecclesiae archivis deponi sancimus (C. 1,4,30,2, a. 531);
>
> Cumque lex publice proposita fuerit (in omni terra) et omnibus manifestata, tunc sumpta intus recondatur in sanctissima ecclesia cum sacris vasis, utpote et ipsa dicata deo et ad salutem ab eo factorum hominum scripta (*edictum post* Nov. 8, a. 535).

*
* *

Perché un cammino possa riprendere devono passare altri lunghi secoli e si deve arrivare al rinascimento giuridico dell'XI-XII secolo. Infatti, nell'alto medioevo la *charta*, che si sostituisce all'*instrumentum*, assume funzioni e caratteri nuovi, rappresenta un portato complesso romano-barbarico e il problema della *fides* sprofonda in un processo che si fa vieppiù schematico, rigidamente formalizzato e colorito di ordalico.[18] L'unica notazione da fare è che nell'alto medioevo anche per il documento privato il termine di *authenticus*, usato talvolta, equivale a *originalis*.

Come è noto, il rinascimento giuridico rappresenta un importante feno-

[16] N. Palazzolo, "Le modalità di trasmissione dei provvedimenti imperiali nelle province (II-III sec. d.C.)," *Iura: Rivista internazionale di diritto romano e antico* 28 (1977): 1-55.

[17] E. A. Sophocles, *Greek Lexicon of the Roman and Byzantine Periods (from B.C. 146 to A.D. 1100)* (Boston, 1870), s.v. ἀυθέντικον.

[18] Nicolaj, "Il documento privato," 163 e ss.; Nicolaj, "Formulari e nuovo formalismo nei processi del Regnum Italiae," in *La giustizia nell'alto medioevo (secc. IX-XI)*, t. 1, Settimane di studio del Centro italiano di studi sull'alto medioevo 44.1 (Spoleto, 1997), 347-84; Nicolaj, "Fratture," 975-86.

meno storico, centrale e di svolta nel lungo arco che usiamo chiamare età medievale. È inutile ricordare forse i fattori, tanti, coincidenti e contestuali, che muovono questa svolta: fattori economico-sociali, come per esempio l'aumento demografico, la riemersione delle città con mercati e commerci e ceti in ascesa (come quello dei giuristi, dal notaio al *legis doctor*), la più incisiva e intensiva organizzazione e amministrazione del territorio; fattori ecclesiologici e politico-istituzionali, con una lotta delle investiture che passa dalla ricerca di una «assoluta sacralizzazione della realtà ecclesiale e sociale» a una fase finale (1106-25, regno di Enrico V) di scontro sul terreno più mondano, giurisdizionale, patrimoniale e politico,[19] con insieme l'irrobustirsi dei Comuni e il costituirsi della monarchia meridionale e dei territori della Chiesa fino allo stato teocratico di Innocenzo III; fattori culturali, fortemente accelerati da nuove logiche, nuovi razionalismi e nuove scienze (arabo-aristotelica, teologica, giuridica) e rinnovati da grammatica e retorica rifiorenti (*dictamen*).

Quanto alla storia giuridica, il rinascimento significa in primo luogo ricerca di leggi e di codici normativi dopo il vuoto e il caos post-carolingi;[20] una ricerca certamente voluta e perseguita dalla prassi—notai, giudici, *causidici*, avvocati—, una prassi che appare coesa ed omogenea almeno fino ad Irnerio.[21]

Da ciò deriva, per la storia diplomatica, dapprima un fondamentale passaggio logico-culturale relativo al documento diplomatico, del quale si restaura il profilo probatorio razionale espresso con il termine di *instrumentum*. Con ciò non voglio dire che il documento diplomatico d'ora innanzi sarà solo e principalmente mezzo di prova; anzi, esso svolgerà molte, tipiche funzioni, circa le quali la diplomatica dovrebbe pur interrogarsi. Voglio dire solo che il rinascimento giuridico recupera e perciò rinnova radicalmente la considerazione della funzione probatoria della scrittura, insieme a un sempre più vivo interesse per la materia processuale tutta, come testi-

[19] V., per esempio, il lucidissimo O. Capitani, "Papato e Impero nei secoli XI e XII," in *Storia delle idee politiche, economiche e sociali,* dir. da L. Firpo (Torino, 1983), 117-63.

[20] G. Nicolaj, "Ambiti di copia e copisti di codici giuridici in Italia (secc. V-XII in.)," relazione tenuta al Convegno di Cluny del Comité international de paléographie (in corso di stampa), e soprattutto Cortese, *Il diritto nella storia medievale,* t. 2, *Il basso medioevo*, capp. 1-3.

[21] G. Nicolaj, *Cultura e prassi di notai preirneriani: Alle origini del rinascimento giuridico*, Ius nostrum 19 (Milano, 1991).

moniano i tanti *ordines iudiciarii* del XII secolo;[22] pertanto, ritorna in primo piano il problema della *fides* del documento in processo, che come sembra naturale e come infatti avverrà, punta a sboccare in *publica fides*.

Su questo sfondo, infatti, sembra snodarsi una lunga pista, a slalom e a gincana; una pista segnata, sembra, dai punti elencati di seguito.

(1) sec. XI/2, Bologna. La prassi notarile bolognese ripropone il termine di *instrumentum* al posto del termine altomedievale di *charta*, rilevando del documento il profilo probatorio;[23] peraltro il notariato bolognese è rappresentato da un'imponente massa di notai che rogano un'imponente massa di scritti.[24]

(2) sec. XI/2, Roma. La prassi romana recupera e ripropone la costituzione 6 di C. 7,52, citata sopra, relativa ai *publica monumenta* carichi di *publica fides*.[25]

(3) 1089, Arezzo. Un Pietro misterioso roga da quest'anno alcuni documenti «notarii functus officio»,[26] sollevando il sospetto (e v. punto 8) che con il termine di *officium* rispolveri il concetto tardoantico di funzione inerente a una carica pubblica.[27]

(4) 1116, Bologna. Esegesi di Irnerio, primo maestro dello *Studium* bolognese, alla *lex Iubemus* (C. 1,2,14,6-7), nella quale sono nominati di

[22] L. Fowler-Magerl, *Ordines iudiciarii and libelli de ordine iudiciorum*, Typologie des sources du Moyen Âge occidental 63 (Turnhout, 1994); Cortese, *Il diritto*, 2: 116 e ss.

[23] G. Cencetti, "La 'rogatio' nelle carte bolognesi: Contributo alla storia del documento notarile italiano nei secoli X-XIII," *Atti e memorie della Deputazione di storia patria per le provincie di Romagna*, n.s., 7 (1960): 17-150, ora in *Notariato medievale bolognese*, t. 1, *Scritti di Giorgio Cencetti*, Studi storici sul notariato italiano 3 (Roma, 1977), 217-352; Nicolaj, *Cultura e prassi*, 10-11.

[24] G. Feo, "Proposta per un piano di pubblicazione dei documenti bolognesi del secolo XI," *Atti e memorie della Deputazione di storia patria per le provincie di Romagna*, n.s., 43 (1992): 33-42; Feo, "Per l'edizione delle carte bolognesi del secolo XI: Il censimento dei notai," *Nuovi annali della Scuola speciale per archivisti e bibliotecari* 12 (1998): 7-47.

[25] Nicolaj, *Cultura e prassi*, 35-37.

[26] Nicolaj, *Cultura e prassi*, 75 e ss.; Nicolaj, "Ambiti," 140-41 e 491-92.

[27] G. Cervenca, "Sull'uso del termine 'officium' nella legislazione postclassico-giustinianea," in *Studi in onore di Giuseppe Grosso*, t. 3 (Torino, 1971), 207-43; F. Grelle, "Le categorie dell'amministrazione tardoantica: *Officia, munera, honores*," in *Società romana e impero tardoantico: Istituzioni, ceti, economie*, a cura di A. Giardina (Roma-Bari, 1986), 37-56.

seguito *tabelliones, iudices vel ius gestorum habentes*, quasi a provocare e a suggerire una omologia delle loro funzioni e posizioni.[28]

(5) secc. XI-XII, Italia centrale (e specificatamente, con le vicende altalenanti di Benevento, territori della Chiesa). Cartulari monastici di abbazie imperiali o principesche—Farfa, Santa Sofia di Benevento, San Vincenzo al Volturno, Casauria—, che suggeriscono il sospetto di un travaso archivistico pensato non solo per la conservazione ma soprattutto in funzione, più o meno consapevole, di «assicurare l'autenticità» degli scritti doppiati e riuniti «in uno volumine» (*Praef.* di Farfa). I vari *libri* che ne escono infatti sono ancorati ad archivi ecclesiastici, riecheggiano il fenomeno documentario dei cartulari ecclesiastici germanici già in uso dal IX secolo[29] e, forse non per caso, in un periodo di lotte e di definizioni politiche e patrimoniali, vengono da fondazioni imperiali o principesche tutte intorno alla Roma dei papi.

In seconda battuta, sospetto che questa pratica si trasferisca ai *libri iurium* delle città italiane,[30] che si vanno dotando di *sigillum*, *arca* e *clavarii*, *cancellarius;* questo genere documentario, che trova un contemporaneo riscontro nelle pratiche di città mercantili europee, in particolare d'area tedesca,[31] naturalmente per le città italiane, alla conquista di autonomie e giurisdizioni usurpate a Impero e Papato in lotta fra loro, viene garantito dal notariato, che nella seconda metà del XII secolo è in dirittura d'arrivo all'istituzione, come si vedrà.

(6) sec. XII. Diffusione dell'uso del sigillo, per esempio in città come Genova o Venezia o Roma, a incremento di una prassi altomedievale europea ed anche molto seguita dalla Chiesa.

[28] G. Orlandelli, "Petitionibus emphyteuticariis annuendo: Irnerio e l'interpretazione della legge Iubemus (C. 1,2,14)" (1983), ora in Orlandelli, *Scritti di paleografia e diplomatica*, a cura di R. Ferrara e G. Feo, Istituto per la Storia dell'Università di Bologna, Opere dei maestri, 7 (Bologna, 1994), 253-525; Nicolaj, "Il documento privato," 188-89.

[29] Bresslau, *Manuale*, 90 e ss.

[30] A. Rovere, "Tipologia documentale nei *Libri iurium* dell'Italia comunale," in *La diplomatique urbaine en Europe au Moyen Âge: Actes du congrès de la Commission internationale de diplomatique*, a cura di W. Prevenier e Th. de Hemptinne (Leuven, 2000).

[31] Bresslau, *Manuale*, 666 e ss.

(7) sec. XII, Italia meridionale. Rafforzamento della prassi, risalente, del giudice ai contratti, che sarà poi codificata da Federico II.[32]

Nel corso dell'affermazione travagliata dell'*instrumentum* e della sua *fides*, appaiono in Italia alcune varianti rispetto alla pista principale, che non avranno un gran sbocco:

(a) a Genova, la trovata di *publici testes* «in laudibus et in contractibus»,[33] per echi romanistici certo, ma poco perspicui;
(b) ancora a Genova, città marinara e di commerci, uso della *charta partita*, plausibilmente per importazione della pratica europea della chirografazione (*Chirographierung*), pratica che, diversamente da Bresslau,[34] è da ritenere non originale dell'alto medioevo, bensì originata da un fraintendimento altomedievale del passo biblico Tob. 5:3: lì infatti si parla di un chirografo, e cioè correttamente di un documento autografo, diviso in due parti; ma la miniatura allo stesso passo in un manoscritto parigino (Parigi, BnF, lat. 94, c. 18) rappresenta due uomini che tagliano un documento, riducendo appunto al taglio (senza più autografia) il formalismo di prova;
(c) 1135, Piacenza. Giuramento di notai piacentini prestato ad una assemblea del *populus Placentinus*, e «coram comite palatino»:[35] il giuramento ha un sapore antico («nichil falsitatis») e non comporta una nomina e soprattutto una legittimazione non ancora postasi e che peraltro il Comune non si sarebbe neanche potuto permettere.

Dalla metà del XII secolo le cose incalzano; e sembra che la pista si biforchi in due rami, forse in concorrenza, quello della prassi poi raccolto dalla canonistica, e quello della civilistica, più legata ai testi romani di riferimento.

[32] M. Amelotti, "Il giudice ai contratti," in *Civiltà del Mezzogiorno d'Italia: Libro, scrittura, documento in età normanno-sveva: Atti del Convegno dell'Associazione italiana dei paleografi e diplomatisti, Napoli–Badia di Cava dei Tirreni, 14-18 ott. 1991*, a cura di F. D'Oria (Salerno, 1994), 359-67.

[33] A. Rovere, "I 'publici testes' e la prassi documentale genovese (secc. XII-XIII)," *Serta antiqua et mediaevalia*, n.s., 1 (1997): 291-332.

[34] Bresslau, *Manuale*, 608 e ss.

[35] *Registrum magnum del comune di Piacenza*, t. 1, ed. crit. a cura di E. Falconi e R. Peveri (Milano, 1940), no. 40, pp. 73-74.

(8) 1149-52, Arezzo. Saraceno *iudex domni Heinrici imperatoris* roga qualche documento «huic etiam officio ab imperatore delegatus»,[36] con ripresa del termine e concetto di *officium*, questa volta chiaramente usato in senso pubblicistico e attribuito dal sovrano nello schema della *delegatio.*[37]

(9) 1164, Piacenza. Il conte palatino di Lomello investe un Pietro, che fa «sacramentum notarietatis in sua presentia..., de officio notarietatis a parte domini imperatoris».

(10) Pista civilistica circa un nuovo processo: si comincia con un trattatello generale sul processo di Bulgaro (*Excerpta legum*), precedente al 1141,[38] con lavoretti dedicati alle *actiones* e al libello introduttivo —l'*Arbor actionum* attribuito a Giovanni Bassiano,[39] il *Quicumque vult* di Giovanni Bassiano dedicato al libello[40] e ancora il *Cum essem Mantuae* attribuito a Piacentino del 1160 circa[41]—; nel 1158 a Roncaglia i quattro dottori definiscono i *regalia* per Federico I in termini fiscali o di *potestas constituendorum magistratuum;* 1160 circa, la *Summa Codicis*, XXII, *de fide instrumentorum* di Rogerio definisce gli *instrumenta publica* o in base alla *forma* o in base all'*utilitas publica* (per es., *de re publica, acta,* documento *forense*), proprio perché, per fedeltà e aderenza al testo romano, non arriva ad attribuire al *tabellio* redattore la *manus publica;* arrivo invece che, in contemporanea con la canonistica (v. punto seg.), è toccato dagli *ordines Si quis de re* e *Olim*, della seconda metà del secolo,[42] per i quali è valida l'equivalenza *tabellio-manus publica.*

(11) 1159-81, decretale di Alessandro III (2,X,22,2):

> scripta vero authentica, si testes inscripti decesserint, nisi per manum publicam (*gl.* idest per notarium) facta fuerint, ita quod appareant publica, aut authenticum sigillum habuerint, per quod possint probari, non videtur nobis alicuius firmitatis habere.

[36] Nicolaj, *Cultura e prassi*, 91; Nicolaj, "Alle origini della minuscola notarile italiana e dei suoi caratteri storici," *Scrittura e civiltà* 10 (1986): 49-82.

[37] M. Talamanca, "Delegazione (dir. rom.)," in *Enciclopedia del diritto*, t. 11 (Milano, 1962), 918 e ss.

[38] Cortese, *Il diritto*, 2:119-20.

[39] Cortese, *Il diritto*, 2:120-21.

[40] Cortese, *Il diritto*, 2:121.

[41] Fowler, *Ordines*, 216; Cortese, *Il diritto*, 2:121.

[42] Cortese, *Il diritto*, 2:129n.

La norma pontificia, straordinariamente, raccoglie la tradizione romanistica dei *testes*, la consuetudine altomedievale del *sigillum* (e si ricordi che *sigillum authenticum* per antonomasia è quello del vescovo, gl. *sigillum* a 2,X,22,2), e la nuova istituzione di una *manus publica* notarile, costruita dalla prassi dei notai e del sovrano e accompagnata, con qualche resistenza, dalla civilistica. Si noti anche, di passaggio, che nei punti elencati sopra, mentre la civilistica usa preferibilmente il termine giustinianeo di *tabellio*, la prassi e di seguito la canonistica usano preferibilmente i termini di *notarius* e *notarietas*, e la canonistica in particolare riprende il termine che le è familiare di *authenticus*.

(12) 1186, Medicina (presso Bologna). Enrico VI investe un fiorentino «de arte et officio notarie eo modo ut de hinc inantea sit publicus notarius» e il nuovo notaio «iuravit fidelitatem ipsi domino regi et patri suo Frederico invictissimo Romanorum imperatori augusto, ut est mos notariorum et vassallorum suo regi et imperatori iurare»;[43] la nomina è fatta, come si dichiara, nel profilo della *fidelitas* vassallatica, mentre negli stessi anni compaiono per la prima volta notai *auctoritate imperiali* ed anche *apostolica auctoritate*,[44] per i quali il titolo è legittimato da un'*auctoritas*, un tempo lontanissimo termine tecnico nel diritto pubblico (*auctoritas senatus, principis*), poi, secondo il testo gelasiano, supremo potere carismatico del pontefice,[45] ed ora fonte di legittimazione sia imperiale che pontificia.

(13) 1216, Tancredi, *Ordo iudiciarius*, P. III, tit. 13, par. 6:

> species autem probationis sunt sex; probatur videlicet per evidentiam facti, per famam, per praesumptionem, per iuramenti delationem, per testes et per instrumenta.

E tit. 13, par. 2:

> instrumentorum duae sunt species: aliud est publicum, aliud est privatum. Publicum est, quod publicam habet auctoritatem. Et

[43] Bologna, Archivio di Stato, Comune-Governo, Atti concernenti privati, b. I, c. 1.

[44] R. Hiestand, "*Notarius sedis apostolicae*: Ein Beitrag zum Verhältnis von Notariat und Politik," in *Tradition und Gegenwart: Festschrift zum 175jährigen Bestehen eines badischen Notarstandes*, a cura di P. J. Schuler (Karlsruhe, 1981), 39; v. anche G. Battelli, "I notai pubblici di nomina papale nel Duecento: Proposta di una ricerca d'interesse europeo," *Archivum historiae pontificiae* 36 (1998): 59-106.

[45] Cortese, *Il diritto*, 1:42-43.

> species eius sunt plures: nam publicum instrumentum est, quod scriptum est per manum publicam, id est per manum notarii publici, hoc est tabellionis, et in publica forma redactum...Item dicitur publicum, quod authentico sigillo sigillatum est...Tertio dicitur publicum, quod iudicis auctoritate est exemplatum et authenticatum...Quarto dicitur publicum, quod in iudicio scribitur apud acta publica...Quinto dicitur publicum, quod habet subscriptionem trium viventium testium...Sexto loco dicitur publicum, quod de archivo seu armario publico producitur.[46]

Tancredi è un canonista, nel 1226 arcidiacono e rettore dello *Studium* di Bologna e la sua opera conquista l'Europa. La sua posizione in tema di documento probatorio appare una sintesi straordinaria di antico e di moderno, di leggi e di consuetudini,[47] una sintesi che può comprendere documenti di diversa formazione ed anche variabili e tradizioni territoriali diverse. Questa sintesi sposta però l'accento circa la *fides* probatoria dal piano filologico della sequenza originale-copia al profilo di una autenticità legale che equivale in parole povere alla pubblicità del documento di prova.

Questa sintesi straordinaria è anche un esempio di quella teoria dell'accrocco (mix-up theory), che uso per spiegare la storia ai miei studenti, e rappresenta un grande traguardo. Ma, come sempre, non risolve tutti i problemi e ne apre di nuovi. Infatti continuerà la concorrenza tra *vox viva* dei testi e *vox mortua* dei documenti, ci si chiederà quale *sigillum* è *authenticum* e quale *archivum* è *publicum* e si discuterà, nella gerarchia bassomedievale delle prove, il valore dell'*instrumentum publicum* a fronte di testimoni (due o tre o quattro testi?). Aprirà quindi il problema del nesso fra originale, autentico e autentico legalmente, cioè pubblico in quanto riconosciuto dall'ordinamento pubblico; già Rolandino pone la questione:

> Exemplar dicitur ipsa originalis scriptura, genus videlicet ex quo generatur, et sumitur exemplum. Quod quidem exemplar appellatur etiam originale et auctenticum. Exemplum vero quod habetur inde vel sumptum est ex scriptura exemplata, generata vel sumpta ex priori sive

[46] Pillius, Tancredus, Gratia, *Libri de iudiciorum ordine*, ed. F. Ch. Bergmann (1842; rist. anast. Aalen, 1965), 220, 248-49.

[47] Secondo un antico atteggiamento della Chiesa, v. R. Grégoire, "Il diritto consuetudinario ecclesiastico e monastico: Riflessioni sul concetto agostiniano: 'Mos populi Dei vel instituta maiorum pro lege tenenda sunt,'" *Inter fratres* 47.2 (1997): 127-41.

originali scriptura. Unde versus: exemplar genus est, exemplum quod trahis inde. Vel sic exemplar generans, exemplum quod generatur;[48]

e in età moderna e fino ad oggi la gerarchia semantica del termine di autentico si rovescerà: dall'ordinamento giuridico saranno considerati originali i protocolli notarili, per esempio, e copie autentiche i documenti rilasciati alle parti committenti, mentre in un *Grande dizionario della lingua italiana* come quello del Battaglia (Torino, 1961–), s.v. *autentico*, il primo significato registrato sarà quello di «convalidato legalmente» e poi, per estensione, tutti gli altri—quello che «dimostratamente proviene dalla fonte alla quale è attribuito», «originale, vero, genuino...»—.

*

* *

Post scriptum. La soluzione di Tancredi si offre, mi sembra, alla riflessione di noi moderni. Mi dicono i colleghi archivisti che sono oppressi dal problema dell'autenticità del documento elettronico. Penso però che, reso onore agli archivisti delle loro preoccupazioni, questo sia innanzitutto problema per giuristi (costituzionalisti, processualisti, amministrativisti, civilisti ecc.) e che sia problema per diplomatisti. Penso anche che, rispetto ai significati sfuggenti del termine documento oggi e alla congerie di documenti raccolti dalle attuali banche dati, per affrontare questo problema sia necessario riproporre con chiarezza un concetto di documento diplomatico, e cioè di scritto giuridicamente rilevante, visto che la garanzia di testi e messaggi elettronici non diplomatici apre problemi di altro ordine. Peraltro, comunque si voglia impostare un problema relativo al documento diplomatico oggi, la differenza di supporto materiale non è influente in via di principio, lo è solo in quanto il testo da autenticare sia reso certo e fermo.

[48] Rolandini, *De iudiciis*, X, ed. in *Summa totius artis notariae* (Venetiis: apud Iuntas, 1546; rist. anast. Bologna, 1977), cc. 396vB-397rA.

Monastic Cartularies: Organizing Eternity

Constance B. Bouchard

To a medievalist at the dawn of the twenty-first century, French monastic cartularies may seem like a normal and unambiguous source. One goes to the library, to the DC 611 and DC 801 sections if one is in the land of Library of Congress classification, and there they are: edited by conscientious scholars, mostly between 50 and 125 years ago, printed on high-acid paper, dusty and a bit yellow but still perfectly serviceable. If one's library is smaller, one goes instead to Interlibrary Loan, and in a week or two the volumes arrive, ready to be used to verify that Count Geoffrey married a woman named Ava in the tenth century, or that the term *pignus* was used in the late twelfth century to mean the land pledged as security in a mortgage.

The familiarity these cartularies now have may obscure a crucial aspect of their composition: they were novel, even revolutionary when they were first put together in the eleventh through thirteenth centuries, and represented a new way of organizing and thinking about both a monastery's past and its possessions. In this paper I shall use the example of cartularies composed in the heartland of France during the high Middle Ages to suggest some of the ways that monastic scribes used them to create and to meditate upon a useful past for their houses.

There were essentially no French cartularies before the year 1000. In Burgundy, the monks of Saint-Pierre-le-Vif of Sens and of Flavigny seem to have created their initial cartularies during the opening decades of the eleventh century,[1] shortly to be joined by the multivolume productions of the scribes at Cluny.[2] But the first big wave of cartulary composition came only

[1] Only scraps still remain of Saint-Pierre-le-Vif's original cartulary, which its editors date to around 1000; Clarius of Sens, *Chronicon Sancti Petri Vivi Senonensis*, ed. Robert-Henri Bautier and Monique Gilles (Paris, 1979), 237-51. For Flavigny, see Constance Brittain Bouchard, ed., *The Cartulary of Flavigny, 717-1113,* Medieval Academy Books 99 (Cambridge, Mass., 1991), 5-6.

[2] Auguste Bernard and Alexander Bruel, eds., *Recueil des chartes de l'abbaye de Cluny,* 6 vols. (Paris, 1876-1903); Barbara H. Rosenwein, *To Be the Neighbor of*

a century later, during the 1120s, when a number of older monasteries organized the documents in their archives and copied them into a single codex. Burgundian examples include the cartularies of Saint-Marcel-lès-Chalon and Montier-en-Der.[3] The monks of Flavigny, who seem to have composed their first cartulary a century earlier, revised it and added to it during this same period, the 1120s. Those monasteries which were initially founded during the twelfth century waited longer still. Among the Cistercians of Burgundy, for example, Pontigny and Theuley put together their first cartularies only at the very end of the twelfth century, and many other houses, including Cîteaux and Clairvaux, did not compose their first cartularies until the 1220s.[4]

Once the first cartulary had been composed at a monastery, the monks might then make a second, but only after the passage of a number of decades, even a century or more. The monks of Cîteaux and Fontenay, for example, who had composed their first cartularies at the beginning of the thirteenth century, created their second cartularies only in the final years

---

Saint Peter: The Social Meaning of Cluny's Property, 909-1049 (Ithaca, N.Y., 1989), 15-16; Dominique Iogna-Prat, "La confection des cartulaires et l'historiographie à Cluny (XIe-XIIe siècles)," in *Les cartularies: Actes de la table ronde organisée par l'École nationale des chartes et le G.D.R. 121 du C.N.R.S. (Paris, 5-7 décembre 1991)*, ed. Olivier Guyotjeannin, Laurent Morelle, and Michel Parisse, Mémoires et documents de l'École des chartes 39 (Paris, 1993), 27-42.

[3] Constance Brittain Bouchard, ed., *The Cartulary of St.-Marcel-lès-Chalon, 779-1126*, Medieval Academy Books 102 (Cambridge, Mass., 1998). The cartulary of Montier-en-Der has never been printed, although I am currently preparing an edition; it is in Chaumont, AD de la Haute-Marne, 7 H 1. For a description of the cartulary, see Laurent Morelle, "Des moines face à leur chartrier: Étude sur le premier cartulaire de Montier-en-Der (vers 1127)," in *Les moines de Der, 673-1790*, ed. Patrick Corbet (Langres, 2000), 211-58.

[4] Martine Garrigues, ed., *Le premier cartulaire de l'abbaye cistercienne de Pontigny (XIIe-XIIIe siècles)* (Paris, 1981). The unedited cartulary of Theuley is in private hands, but a microfilm is on deposit in Vesoul, AD de la Haute-Saône, 1 Mi-3 (R1). Cîteaux's early-thirteenth-century cartulary is in Dijon, AD de la Côte-d'Or, 11 H 64; about half the documents have been edited in Jean Marilier, ed., *Chartes et documents concernant l'abbaye de Cîteaux, 1098-1182* (Rome, 1961). The two-volume cartulary of Clairvaux is in Troyes, AD de l'Aube, 3 H 9-10, and has been partially edited in Jean Waquet, ed., *Recueil des chartes de l'abbaye de Clairvaux, XIIe siècle*, 2 vols. (Troyes, 1950-82).

of that century.[5] The monks of Montier-en-Der, who had composed their first cartulary in the 1120s, similarly waited until the end of the thirteenth century to compose their second.[6]

Once the idea of a cartulary was established, however, monks of subsequent generations often took up the idea repeatedly. Some monasteries, such as those of Flavigny and Saint-Marcel, seem to have been satisfied with just one cartulary, for there is no evidence that these houses ever had a second. At Montier-en-Der, in contrast, there still exist some half dozen codices all entitled "Cartulary," composed between the twelfth century and the mid-seventeenth century.[7] The first two, from the twelfth and the thirteenth centuries, have essentially no overlap, and the second seems to have been composed at the end of the thirteenth century in order to collect the documents that the monastery had acquired since the first cartulary was put together. The third, fourth, and fifth so-called "cartularies," from the sixteenth and seventeenth centuries, do not contain any medieval documents. The "sixth cartulary," however, compiled in 1658, included a number of documents which were copied directly out of the first two cartularies and not from the originals, even when those still existed. Here the purpose seems to have been to organize the legal "titles" to the monastery's landholdings, and indeed Simon Berquin, the compiler of Montier-en-Der's "sixth cartulary," insisted that the very antiquity of the cartulary from which he copied a number of charters conveyed legal authority.

All of this, on how and when cartularies were composed, is straightforward. But the question still remains *why* medieval monks would create a cartulary, and what purpose they expected these volumes to serve. Most cartularies have no prologue, and those that do generally have a laconic statement such as, "In this volume are collected the privileges of our saint and the record of transfers of property in various locations," with at most some comment about the role of preserving memories against forgetfulness.[8] The cartulary of the cathedral chapter of Châlons-sur-Marne, compiled around 1110, composed almost entirely of privileges from kings and counts, states on the first folio, "Here are the *precepta* of the church of

[5] Cîteaux's late-thirteenth-century cartulary is in the AD de la Côte-d'Or, 11 H 63. Fontenay's two cartularies are bound together in the AD de la Côte-d'Or, 15 H 9.

[6] AD de la Haute-Marne, 7 H 2.

[7] AD de la Haute-Marne, 7 H 3-6.

[8] Pascale Bourgain and Marie-Clotilde Hubert, "Latin et rhétorique dans les préfaces de cartulaire," in *Les cartulaires,* 115-36.

Saint-Étienne of Châlons, which were scattered and nearly consumed with age, and which Warin the cantor collected and copied together with his own hand."[9]

Such comments have often been taken by modern scholars as an indication that cartularies were simply a transcription of everything in a monastery's archives. But most monastic archives, even now, contain at least a few documents that were not copied into the cartulary. In the case of the canons of Châlons, the cathedral chapter would certainly have preserved some more mundane charters at the beginning of the twelfth century, as well as the royal and papal charters which the cantor Warin selected for inclusion in his cartulary. Hence treating a cartulary as an unproblematic window into a monastery's archival holdings can, as Patrick Geary has warned, make the cartulary itself invisible.[10] Such invisibility has long prevented any sort of thorough appreciation of the intent of the monks who created this new kind of record.

The use of the cartulary as legal proof has been suggested, but these codices can only rarely have been used for this purpose. If the monks still had their original donation charters, the ones they copied into the cartulary, such a codex would have had *less* legal authority than the originals, not more. Even aside from the greater validity assigned to living witnesses in the twelfth and thirteenth centuries than to any written charters, the veracity of an old charter was considered to be found in its seals,[11] which of course could not be duplicated in a cartulary—although, interestingly enough, cartulary scribes sometimes drew a picture of an unusual seal, or at least wrote "sigillum" in the margin.[12]

Here it is also worth emphasizing something that should be obvious: even when, for the modern scholar, the cartulary records the text of charters whose originals are now long lost, at the time cartularies were composed, all the originals must have existed, or else copies could not have been made of them. This stands in contrast to what was done in cases

[9] Châlons-en-Champagne, AD de la Marne, G 462.

[10] Patrick Geary, "Entre gestion et *gesta*," in *Les cartulaires*, 13-24.

[11] Brigitte Bedos, "Signes et insignes du pouvoir royal et seigneurial au Moyen Âge: Le témoignage des sceaux," in Comité des travaux historiques et scientifiques, *Actes du 105ᵉ congrès national des sociétés savantes, Caen, 1980, Section de philologie et d'histoire jusqu'à 1610*, vol. 1, *Les pouvoirs de commandement jusqu'à 1610* (Paris, 1984), 47-62.

[12] Laurent Morelle, "De l'original à la copie: Remarques sur l'évaluation des transcriptions dans les cartulaires médiévaux," in *Les cartulaires*, 95-97.

where no original charter existed. If the monks felt the need to have a written record when a transaction had not been conveyed in writing originally, then the most common response in the twelfth century, especially for the monks of the Cistercian order, was to have the bishop draw up a *pancarte*.[13]

Such pancartes would typically be a listing, written and sealed at the bishop's direction, of a number of gifts that had been received in the last few years. The memory of such gifts would still be fresh, and in addition the monks had generally made brief notes at the time, which they could present to the episcopal chancery—such notes had little importance other than as an *aide-mémoire,* for once the pancarte was drawn up the notes seem frequently to have been sliced into thin strips, so they could be frugally recycled as the strips that attached a wax seal to a charter. The only exception I have seen in Burgundy is that of the Cistercian house of La Bussière, where the monks had composed so many lists of donated property—each entry being nothing more than a brief annotation of who had given what and where—that the bishop, rather than having his chancery rewrite the lists into a pancarte, merely sealed them all.[14]

Although at first glance a pancarte might thus be seen as a handy economy-sized version of a cartulary, the composition and function of pancartes and cartularies were quite different. A pancarte was drawn up in order to make the transition from the *living* memory of something done to the *written* memory. Gifts and privileges from the wealthy were generally recorded on parchment at the time they took place, either by the donor's own chancellor or by the local bishop, thus immediately becoming part of written memory. Pancartes created a similar written recollection for donations from the less powerful.

A cartulary, in contrast to a pancarte, copied together transactions which had *already* been preserved in writing and sealed. Thus the individual records copied into a cartulary had previously made the transition from living to written memory, even before the cartulary was composed. Indeed, at Cistercian houses the pancartes generally fill the first few dozen folios

[13] For such pancartes, see Constance Brittain Bouchard, *Holy Entrepreneurs: Cistercians, Knights, and Economic Exchange in Twelfth-Century Burgundy* (Ithaca, N.Y., 1991), 14-16.

[14] Bouchard, *Holy Entrepreneurs*, 16. The documents from La Bussière are in the series AD de la Côte-d'Or, 12 H.

of the cartulary.[15] Pancartes were thus not considered at the time as something that served the same purpose as a cartulary, but rather as something to be incorporated into one. And pancartes needed to be sealed by the bishop, even if, as in the case of La Bussière and its sealed notes, the hanging of the bishop's seal off the bottom of the parchment was the sum total of the episcopal chancery's involvement. Cartularies, in contrast, were never sealed, indeed not even presented to the bishop for confirmation or approval.

If then a cartulary would originally have had little to do with the relations between the monastery and the outside world, then its purpose must be seen as *internal*. Here the organization of material within cartularies becomes significant. This organization is generally lost in printed editions, where the editors have reorganized the charters into chronological order. Even the individual donations within a pancarte are sometimes separated in a modern edition into separate entries, thus giving each a distinction it never had, and was never intended to have, in the medieval cartulary. In addition, in modern French editions in particular, it is common to find references to "lost charters." Here, for example, if a document of Louis the Pious referred to a privilege from his grandfather Pippin, then the editor will insert an entry, with document number even if no actual text, into the mid-eighth-century section of his edition.

But no medieval scribe composed his cartulary strictly chronologically, nor did any insert references to "lost charters." For medievalists of the nineteenth and twentieth centuries, the past was to be organized as a series of events that all took place in order, and a privilege of Pippin needed to be correctly placed within that order—even if it is not altogether certain if such a written privilege ever existed. For cartulary scribes of the twelfth and thirteenth centuries, on the other hand, the past was arranged by theme or topic, so that privileges of popes all belonged together, even if issued over a period of centuries, as did privileges of emperors. Gifts from petty landowners of the region were organized geographically, so that a careful scribe would copy all of the donation charters that pertained to one area before moving on to the next. At most, he might arrange the charters

[15] For example, the pancarte that records Auberive's foundation, AD de la Haute-Marne, 1 H 7bis, begins both of the house's thirteenth-century cartularies: 1 H 3, fols. 3r-4r; and 1 H 4, fols. 1r-4r.

roughly chronologically within each geographically determined subsection.[16]

Thus, the past for a cartulary scribe was not a *chain* of events disappearing backwards into the distance. Rather, it was a *collection* of events, each with a very present and ongoing significance for the monastery: and that significance was far more important than the order of their occurrence. Many of the older Benedictine houses began their cartularies with privileges of popes and emperors, and for the monks such a privilege still had validity whether it had been issued a few years or a few centuries earlier. The foundation charters that began the cartularies at other houses, or were inserted immediately after great papal or imperial privileges at such houses as Saint-Marcel, similarly listed property which was still very much a present concern for the monks. In the same way, the organization of donation charters by geographic location indicates that the first gift of property in a certain *villa* would continue to be as important to the monks as the most recent. The property was theirs, given to them by benefactors for whom they prayed. Both the property itself and the long-dead benefactors continued as living presences, both part of a single body despite their separation in time.[17]

Here it should also be noted that while the cartulary scribes might be trying to regularize the record of their monasteries' possessions, they do not seem to have tried to improve this record. That is, although most cartularies ended up with at least a few forgeries in them, a close examination of these forgeries suggests that they were done well *before* the creation of the cartulary itself. (The only exceptions would be those cases where one is not speaking so much of a cartulary as of a small dossier of documents, put together specifically to argue a certain case.) At Montier-en-Der, for example, which has an unusually large number of forged papal bulls, these forgeries all date from the mid- and later eleventh century, a good fifty years before a cartulary scribe incorporated them as authentic.[18] Just as a

[16] The scribe of the late-thirteenth-century cartulary of Longué was more meticulous than most, adding an extra slip of parchment to record a transaction if he accidentally left it out of his chronological organization; AD de la Haute-Marne, 6 H 2. See also Bouchard, *Holy Entrepreneurs,* 17.

[17] For the incorporation of the lay donors to a monastery into the monks' undying community, see Stephen D. White, *Custom, Kinship, and Gifts to Saints: The "Laudatio Parentum" in Western France, 1050-1150* (Chapel Hill, 1988), 170-76.

[18] Constance B. Bouchard, "Forging Papal Authority: Charters from the Monastery of Montier-en-Der," *Church History* 69 (2000): 1-17.

charter had recorded an event that took place at a certain time, but the copying of that charter into a cartulary made it timeless, so the creation of a forgery addressed a particular challenge to the monastery's rights or possessions, but the cartulary scribe, in assuming the forgery's authenticity, made its contents part of the ongoing present reality of his house.

The creation of a cartulary then, for a strictly internal monastic audience, was an attempt to organize and rationalize what the monastery owned. It should not be surprising that the great age of cartularies was the twelfth and thirteenth centuries, the period of the Renaissance of the Twelfth Century and of Henry Adams's Greatest Century. The impulse that led to the systematic treatment of both canon law and theology also led to monks determining to work out exactly what their monastery owned and how they had obtained it. Even if a cartulary was not intended for anyone's eyes outside the cloister, it was certainly intended to be a continuing reference book for those within the monastery, as indicated by the well-thumbed nature of all cartularies and the many marginal notes, in handwritings that span six hundred years.

The rather timeless nature of the events that a monastery records was doubtless responsible for one aspect of cartularies which is extremely irritating to modern scholars: the scribes were notoriously careless about dating. Cartulary copies often *do* have dating formulae, but in many other cases the scribes simply did not bother with the date. Or in the case of an authentic papal privilege for Montier-en-Der for which the original still exists, the copy in the thirteenth-century cartulary gets the date wrong by two years.[19] The date had had a diplomatic significance at the time a charter was originally drawn up, but this ceased to be relevant once the charter was being copied into a cartulary intended for an internal, rather than external audience. In the same way, the lists of witnesses, those whose testimony could verify that a transaction had taken place, ceased to be relevant once the people were dead, and such lists were frequently abbreviated in cartulary copies.

But it would be wrong to see such changes as indications of sloppiness or of valuing speed over accuracy, for the actual body of a charter, both the detailing of donated property and the explanation of how the donor was related to the other people for whom he hoped the monks would also pray, would be copied very conscientiously and accurately. But the cartulary

[19] The original is in AD de la Haute-Marne, 7 H 15. The cartulary copy is 7 H 2, fols. 19v-20r.

scribe, organizing his monastery's archives and copying into his codex the charters that detailed how the monastery had acquired its now timeless possessions, might find irrelevant much of a charter's closing, the part that located it at a certain time and place.

It was certainly due to this perception of the past and present as both part of a seamless Now that the scribes would make their single biggest change in the body of a charter, altering the spelling of place names to correspond to the contemporary spelling. The orthography of proper names varied enormously anyway in the high Middle Ages, with someone called "Ulricus" at the beginning of a charter often becoming "Hulricus" by the end. But if the monks held property at a *villa* that was normally spelled one way in the twelfth century, and the scribe came across a Carolingian charter that spelled it differently, he would unhesitatingly give the place name in what he considered the correct form.

Documents from the ninth through eleventh centuries could be dealt with fairly easily by twelfth- and thirteenth-century scribes, requiring no more than a regularization of spelling and, in many cases, abbreviation or elimination of witnesses and dating formulae. But Merovingian charters were different. The protocols were foreign, the spellings strange, the handwriting, even the customary abbreviations, difficult to interpret. Documents from the time of Charlemagne on were copied into cartularies essentially unchanged, but the same cannot be said of documents from before his time. Although few enough Merovingian originals—or even close copies of Merovingian originals—survive to make generalizations hazardous, in the few cases where one can compare the original version of a Merovingian charter to the cartulary copy, it becomes clear that the scribe has not just transcribed but heavily reworked.

Such was the case, for example, at Flavigny, where the cartulary began with a reworked version of the early-eighth-century foundation charter—which original charter was then attached to the end of the cartulary.[20] The twelfth-century scribe regularized not just spelling but grammar, altered the invocation at the beginning, and pared down the subscriptions of the witnesses. Similarly, at Saint-Pierre-le-Vif, where the Merovingian versions of two early-eighth-century donation charters are preserved in a copy from around the year 1000, the twelfth-century cartulary copyist altered as he worked, sometimes with a minor emendation such as changing "donationem hanc" to "hanc donationem," but also with a fairly thorough overhaul

[20] Bouchard, ed., *The Cartulary of Flavigny,* 13-16.

of the preamble and of case endings throughout. A seventh-century privilege for Montier-en-Der, issued by the bishop of Châlons, was copied into both the cartulary of the cathedral of Châlons and also into the cartulary of Montier-en-Der. Although the two cartularies were composed within just a few years of each other, the two different scribes reached very different conclusions on a number of words as to what the seventh-century original actually said. For example, the scribe at Montier-en-Der easily recognized "Putiolos," the original name of the monastery, but Cantor Warin of Châlons, stumped, put "pociolus."[21]

For none of these churches, Flavigny, Saint-Pierre-le-Vif, Montier-en-Der, or Saint-Étienne of Châlons, do we have the original Merovingian papyrus, but such papyri do survive for a few documents of Saint-Denis, where they were used as backing for the reworked versions of their texts produced in the eleventh century. Although it has been suggested that a deliberate effort was made to "forget" the Merovingian past,[22] it makes more sense to speak of an effort to rationalize and make it comprehensible —indeed, useful and ultimately *present*. The impulse that made eleventh- and twelfth-century scribes improve the spelling and grammar of four-hundred-year-old charters was the same impulse that made them gather, organize, and copy all the charters they could find into a cartulary in the first place.

Thus the ordering of the material in a cartulary codex deliberately took the charters out of time. A community of donors would be created, whose names would be inscribed in the cartulary along with what they gave. A cartulary's purpose then should be seen as more commemorative than combative, less a legal brief than another form of a *liber memorialis*. Just as in high medieval art a donor, the monastery's patron saint, and the magi would all join together in adoration of the Christ child, an event that was considered to be happening *now* as well as in A.D. 1, so five centuries of gifts and privileges would bind together a monastery's friends in the eternal present.

But if a cartulary's original purpose was to create an orderly sense of what the monastery actually owned and how the monks had acquired it, supplementing rather than replacing their collection of original charters, then its purpose was modified once it existed. It quickly became in essence

[21] AD de la Haute-Marne, 7 H 1, fols. 4r-6v; AD de la Marne, G 462, fols. 30r-33r.

[22] Patrick J. Geary, *Phantoms of Remembrance: Memory and Oblivion at the End of the First Millennium* (Princeton, 1994).

a substitute for the archival documents from which it had been copied. Monks with a cartulary became much less concerned about their original charters. In times of trouble, a cartulary could be snatched up and carried to safety much more easily than could an armful of documents. A book that could be chained in place, as was the cartulary of the cathedral of Mâcon,[23] was more secure than an untidy pile of individual parchments. Although it is well known that enormous numbers of medieval charters were lost at the time of the French Revolution, for a number of monasteries the charters that had been copied into a cartulary were lost well before then. At Flavigny, for example, a late medieval scribe made a copy of the twelfth-century cartulary, but he made no effort to return to the originals.[24] At Saint-Marcel, all the monastery's original documents, except for one privilege from Charlemagne, were already long gone in the seventeenth century, when Mabillon went looking for them.[25]

Such carelessness with original documents was only possible when the cartulary itself had taken on an iconic quality that it never would have had for the scribe who put it together in the first place. The monks who created cartularies in the high Middle Ages had succeeded so thoroughly in organizing and regularizing the record of their monasteries' possessions that their productions were, in future generations, seen not as a guide to those possessions, but rather as a proof of their legitimacy. Monks carrying out future efforts to organize and regularize, frequently undertaken at monasteries in the early modern period, thus felt no need to look back any further than the high medieval cartulary.

[23] M.-C. Ragut, ed., *Cartulaire de Saint-Vincent de Mâcon* (Mâcon, 1864).
[24] Bouchard, ed., *The Cartulary of Flavigny*, 9.
[25] Bouchard, ed., *The Cartulary of St.-Marcel*, 3.

The Transmission of Lombard Documents (to 774)

Herbert Zielinski

"Lavoriamo su frammenti"—we are only working with fragments:[1] with these few but striking words, Luigi Schiaparelli, the renowned past master of Italian diplomatics, summarized his profound knowledge of the fragmentary tradition of Lombard documents, a few months before his death in 1933. His analysis of an eighth-century index written in Pisa listing one hundred Lombard documents, including seventeen royal *praecepta*, provoked this confession.[2] Half of the document collection, which we only know through this index, consists of documents addressed to an otherwise unknown layman named Alahis who lived in the days of King Liutprand (712-35).[3] Twenty documents concerning a smaller church in Pisa (S. Pietro ai Sette Pini) and about thirty documents that do not seem to fit in a specific category are also listed therein. It is believed that the bishop of Pisa requested that this register be made after a man named Teuspert gave the one hundred documents back to an *ancilla Dei* named Ghittia.[4] Under what circumstance Teuspert and Ghittia had received the documents and why their possession was controversial, we do not know.[5]

[1] For help with the translation of this article, I am very grateful to my wife Petra and to Ms. Anke Krug (Giessen).

[2] Luigi Schiaparelli, ed., *Codice diplomatico longobardo*, vol. 2, Fonti per la storia d'Italia 63 (Rome, 1933), no. 295, pp. 439-44, esp. 440. The index nearly always names the issuer and the recipient as well as the kind of the document. Vol. 2 contains charters from 757 to 774; the oldest Lombard charters (ca. 650-757) are edited in Luigi Schiaparelli, ed., *Codice diplomatico longobardo*, vol. 1, Fonti per la storia d'Italia 62 (Rome, 1929).

[3] See Pier Silverio Leicht, "L'archivio di Alahis," in Leicht, *Scritti vari di storia del diritto italiano* 2.1 (Milan, 1948), 233-39; Nicholas Everett, "Scribes and Charters in Lombard Italy," *Studi medievali*, 3d ser., 41 (2000): 39-81, esp. 39-40, 80-81.

[4] "Breve de moniminas quem reddidit Teuspert Ghittie Dei ancille et ad filie eius Aliperghe et Uuillerade" (Schiaparelli, ed., *Codice diplomatico longobardo*, vol. 2, no. 295, p. 440, lines 2-3).

[5] Teuspert and Ghittia are not named among the recipients.

If an unknown nun in the 770s owned these one hundred Lombard documents—among them seventeen royal documents—and an unknown *fidelis regis* received six royal diplomas of King Liutprand alone, thousands and thousands of Lombard documents must have been in existence, especially during the eighth century. Indeed, the fact that only around 450 Lombard documents (including royal, ducal, and private charters) have been passed on is very depressing.[6]

A particular catastrophe lies in the preservation of royal documents: only roughly two dozen genuine *praecepta* and at best one original thereof have been passed down through history.[7] Not much better is the situation in the case of the twenty-three documents of the dukes of Spoleto and the forty-nine documents of the dukes of Benevento, which almost exclusively survive in later cartularies, the Spoletan in the famous *Regestum Farfense* from the end of the eleventh century, the Beneventan in the so-called *Chronicon S. Sophiae* from the second decade of the twelfth century. Approximately seventy private charters of these two duchies have also survived in these cartularies.[8] Originals do not exist either in Spoleto or in Benevento.

Only in the Regnum Langobardorum proper—northern Italy and Tuscany—have a substantial number of original charters been preserved, 189 out of a total of 272.[9] But even in the Regnum the transmission is uneven and based on local circumstances: the Archivio Arcivescovile in Lucca, where many documents from other clerical town archives have come to-

[6] Carlrichard Brühl, "Die Urkunden der Langobarden. Überlieferung und Probleme," *Jahrbuch für internationale Germanistik* 11 (1980): 93-99, esp. 98 (repr. Brühl, *Aus Mittelalter und Diplomatik: Gesammelte Aufsätze*, 3 vols. [Hildesheim, 1979-97], 2:646-52, esp. 651) counts "ca. 540," a figure which includes documents issued in the duchies of Spoleto and Benevento between 774 and 787.

[7] The edition of the royal charters (Carlrichard Brühl, ed., *Codice diplomatico longobardo*, vol. 3.1, Fonti per la storia d'Italia 64 [Rome, 1973]) includes forty-six documents, but among these some fifteen are complete forgeries (Brühl, "Überlieferung und Probleme," 96 (repr. 2:649).

[8] Sixty-three Spoletan and eleven Beneventan charters (before 774) are edited in Herbert Zielinski, ed., *Codice diplomatico longobardo*, vol. 5, *Le chartae dei ducati di Spoleto e di Benevento*, Fonti per la storia d'Italia 66 (Rome, 1986).

[9] Schiaparelli, ed., *Codice diplomatico longobardo*, vols. 1-2 contain 295, but include 22 forgeries of Antonio Dragoni (d. 1860), the notorious forger from Cremona; see Brühl, "Überlieferung und Probleme," 96 (repr. 2:649).

gether, is in sole possession of 124 of these 189 originals.[10] The real tragedy is that this archive, which owns so many original Lombard documents, has not preserved any royal document: "Lavoriamo su frammenti."

Without doubt there are different reasons why the transmission of Lombard documents is rather poor, especially in comparison with the transmission of Frankish documents. The changing and complicated history of the Regnum Italiae after the Frankish conquest is certainly one factor. The rapid growth in the production of documents beginning in the eleventh century[11] may be a further reason why older documents were no longer handled with care, especially those that no longer had potential importance in a legal proceeding.

The subject of this paper is the situation in the Regnum Langobardorum itself. What was the contemporary perception of these documents? What were the conditions for and the circumstances of preservation and transmission in Lombard times? Were the documents in danger even then? What was done to ensure their preservation? Where were they preserved? On what kinds of occasions did they get lost?

The archive of Alahis is remarkable, especially since it was the archive of a layman.[12] Of course, the royal court at the *sacrum palatium* in Pavia had an archive of its own, as we know from several testimonies.[13] Likewise

[10] For the archives of Lucca, see Hansmartin Schwarzmaier, *Lucca und das Reich bis zum Ende des 11. Jahrhunderts*, Bibliothek des Deutschen Historischen Instituts in Rom 41 (Tübingen, 1972), 9-11. Ten original documents are preserved in the Archivio Arcivescovile of Pisa.

[11] See the remarkable numbers of documents in Schwarzmaier, *Lucca und das Reich*, 9-11, and in Cinzio Violante, "Lo studio dei documenti privati per la storia medievale fino al XII secolo," in *Fonti medioevali e problematica storiografica: Atti del Congresso internazionale tenuto in occasione del 90° anniversario della fondazione dell'Istituto storico italiano (1883-1973), Roma, ottobre 1973*, vol. 1, *Relazioni* (Rome, 1976), 69-129, esp. 80-81.

[12] See Everett, "Scribes and Charters in Lombard Italy," 80. An important but rather unknown "Besitzverzeichnis" of a Lombard layman in southern Italy is treated by Walter Pohl, *Werkstätte der Erinnerung: Montecassino und die Gestaltung der langobardischen Vergangenheit*, Mitteilungen des Instituts für österreichische Geschichtsforschung, Ergänzungsband 39 (Vienna, 2001), 53-55, 197-199 (edition). For lay archives in later times, see Harry Bresslau, *Handbuch der Urkundenlehre für Deutschland und Italien*, 4th ed., 2 vols. (Berlin, 1969), 1:182.

[13] See for example Zielinski, ed., *Codice diplomatico longobardo*, vol. 5, no. 8, pp. 32-41, at 41, lines 23-25: "Unum quidem brevem nobiscum (i.e., the royal *missus*

the ducal courts in Spoleto and Benevento had their own archives.[14] Even the numerous royal courts spread all over the peninsula, the *curtes domni regis*, seem to have preserved carefully important documents concerning their own matters, for example exchanges (*cartae commutationis*) with churches in the neighborhood.[15] We also find archives in towns, where the inhabitants, laymen of course, could preserve documents of concern to them.[16]

That bishoprics and grand abbeys also preserved their documents—often together with precious liturgical objects—either in the crypt, in the sacristy (*sacristarium*), or in the *domus* of the bishop or the abbot would be self-evident, even if we did not have any information about it.[17] A charter

---

Insarius) detulimus ad domni regis vestigia, qui in sacro palatio debeat esse"; see also Bresslau, *Handbuch der Urkundenlehre*, 1:165. Concerning the archive in the *palatium* of the Frankish emperor (the so-called "Pfalzarchiv"), see Heinrich Fichtenau, "Archive der Karolingerzeit," *Mitteilungen des Österreichischen Staatsarchivs* 25 (1972): 15-24, esp. 21-23, repr. in Fichtenau, *Beiträge zur Mediävistik: Ausgewählte Aufsätze*, vol. 2, *Zur Urkundenforschung* (Stuttgart, 1977), 115-25.

[14] For Spoleto, see Zielinski, ed., *Codice diplomatico longobardo*, vol. 5, no. 8, p. 41, lines 26-27: "tertium [brevem] dedimus Luponi duci, quod sit in Spoleto."

[15] Schiaparelli, ed., *Codice diplomatico longobardo*, vol. 1, no. 113, pp. 328-33; see below, pp. 38-39.

[16] Zielinski, ed., *Codice diplomatico longobardo*, vol. 5, no. 8, p. 41, lines 27-28: "quartum quidem [brevem] direximus ad suprascriptos homines in Reate." The second copy of the *notitia iudicati* was given to the monastery of Farfa: "alium consimilem reliquimus in ipso sancto monasterio." It seems to be rather unlikely that in the case of Rieti we are dealing with the remains of the Roman *gesta municipalia*. The situation in Ravenna (see Fichtenau, "Archive der Karolingerzeit," 23-24) cannot be compared with that of the old Lombard territories.

[17] See the previous note. For the early history of the archive of the monastery of Fulda, see Edmund E. Stengel and Oskar Semmelmann, "Fuldensia IV: Untersuchungen zur Frühgeschichte des Fuldaer Klosterarchivs," *AfD* 4 (1958): 120-82; for Sankt Gallen, see Albert Bruckner, "Die Anfänge des St. Galler Stiftsarchivs," in *Festschrift Gustav Binz* (Basel, 1935), 119-31, esp. 120-21, 128-31. The older archive of the monastery of Casauria, founded by emperor Louis II in 873 in the Abruzzese Appennines, is addressed in Alessandro Pratesi, "L'antico archivio di S. Clemente a Casauria," in *Storiografia e ricerca: Relazioni e comunicazioni del 10° congresso archivistico, L'Aquila 1978* (Rome, 1981), 207-20, and in Laurent Feller, "Le cartulaire-chronique de San Clemente à Casauria," in *Les cartularies: Actes de la Table ronde organisée par l'École nationale des chartes et le G.D.R. 121 du C.N.R.S. (Paris, 5-7 décembre 1991)*, ed. Olivier Guyotjeannin, Laurent Morelle, and Michel

from 764[18] tells us about the archive of the cathedral of Lucca in Tuscany, which was located at the residence of the bishops ("arcium ecclesiae S. Martini, ubi est domo episcoporum").[19] Of more interest is the fact that the small and unimportant church of S. Maria in that city, founded by the issuer of the charter just mentioned, also owned such an *arcium*: "alia cartola...emisi...in arcio eclesiae S. Marie." The church of S. Prospero di Antraccoli, situated near Lucca,[20] which Bishop Talesperianus of Lucca turned over to the presbyter Maurinus in 718,[21] preserved its documents as well within the church itself: when in 758 the successor of Talesperianus, Peredeo, wanted to have a look at the document of 718 (obviously there was no copy in the archive of the cathedral), he asked the priest of S. Prospero to bring it over. When the *autenticum* was read and copied (as an *exemplare*), Peredeo gave it back to the church: "ipsa autentica...qui in ipsa eglesia erat, quem Maurino presbitero miserat at nus."[22]

Parisse, Mémoires et documents de l'École des chartes 39 (Paris, 1993), 261-77, esp. 269-73. See also Luigi Schiaparelli, "Alcune osservazioni intorno al deposito archivistico della *confessio s. Petri*," in Schiaparelli, *Note di Diplomatica (1896-1934)*, ed. A. Pratesi (Turin, 1972), 43-62; Wilhelm Kurze, "Die langobardische Königsurkunde für S. Salvatore am Monte Amiata," *Quellen und Forschungen aus italienischen Archiven und Bibliotheken* 57 (1977): 315-31, esp. 321-22; Paolo Cherubini, "I notai di Salerno e la tradizione del documento," in *Scrittura e produzione documentaria nel Mezzogiorno longobardo: Atti del Convegno internazionale di studio (Badia di Cava, 3-5 ottobre 1990)*, ed. Giovanni Vitolo and Francesco Mottola (Badia di Cava, 1991), 333-74.

[18] Schiaparelli, ed., *Codice diplomatico longobardo*, vol. 2, no. 175, pp. 137-41. The *scrinium* of the church of Novara is mentioned in 729: Schiaparelli, ed., *Codice diplomatico longobardo*, vol. 1, no. 44, pp. 147-49, at 149, line 4; see Bresslau, *Handbuch der Urkundenlehre*, 1:179; Everett, "Scribes and Charters in Lombard Italy," 81. Around 840 we hear of the *armarium* of the bishop of Turin: Ernst Dümmler, ed., *Epistolae Karolini aevi*, vol. 3, MGH Epistolae 5 (Hanover, 1898-99), Epistolae variorum, no. 32, pp. 353-55, esp. 354, line 39.

[19] I do not consider here the question of changing terminology (*archivum, armarium, scrinium*, etc.) and the various locations of the archives (building, room, shrine, case, etc.); see Fichtenau, "Archive der Karolingerzeit," 15-18 (who does not, however, address the situation in Lombard Italy).

[20] Antroccoli (com. Borgo Mozzano, prov. Lucca). This place is mentioned several times in the documents of Lucca. See the map in Schwarzmaier, *Lucca und das Reich*, 219.

[21] Schiaparelli, ed., *Codice diplomatico longobardo*, vol. 1, no. 22, pp. 87-91.

[22] Schiaparelli, ed., *Codice diplomatico longobardo*, vol. 2, no. 128, pp. 11-12.

Such single copies, *exemplaria*, like the one Bishop Peredeo ordered in 758 of a charter of the year 718, often seemed to be needed. This is no surprise if we remember the great importance of written documents in the legal life of the Lombards. Thirty-three *exemplaria* were preserved in the cathedral archive of Lucca alone, seven of them together with the originals. These single copies do not owe their existence to an antiquarian interest—they were not written to "preserve history." They were obviously produced to play an important role in their own time: most of the *exemplaria* were written down only a few years after the issue of the original charter,[23] very often by the same notaries.[24]

Even charters documenting exchanges (*cartulae concambiationis* or *commutationis*) regularly produced as duplicate originals were copied once again whenever a further *exemplum* was needed.[25] Obviously the issuer as well as the receiver or an involved third party were interested in obtaining such a copy for information or security purposes when the circumstances required it. A *charta dotis* from 720 was copied not only about 760-70 but also in the 780s; around 800 the same charter was copied a third time in two more exemplars.[26] A *charta donationis* issued in 718 was copied three times within a few years: first in about 740, a second time in about 756-57, and finally in 758.[27]

The careful preservation of documents in the Regnum Langobardorum was of great importance because the possession of land was based on these documents. Their preservation was motivated by the constant danger that precious documents were exposed to. We often hear that originals were damaged or lost soon after their issue.

Very instructive in this regard is the disappearance of a document only a few months after its being issued by Bishop Walprand of Lucca in July 754. Walprand had taken the document concerning an exchange of land between his church and the *curtis regis* in Lucca with him as he followed

[23] Admittedly, this is often difficult to confirm.

[24] Nine of the thirty-three *exemplaria* from Lucca were written by the scribes of the original documents.

[25] See Schiaparelli, ed., *Codice diplomatico longobardo*, vol. 1, no. 113, pp. 328-33, and vol. 2, no. 164, pp. 113-115.

[26] Schiaparelli, ed., *Codice diplomatico longobardo*, vol. 1, no. 28, pp. 101-5.

[27] Schiaparelli, ed., *Codice diplomatico longobardo*, vol. 1, no. 22, pp. 87-89.

the royal army to the North against the Frankish army under King Pippin.[28] It was obviously due to this war that the document was lost: "in exercitus domno regi peruerat."[29] This was recognized only by Bishop Peredeo, the successor of Walprand, who some months later searched in vain for the document—"ipsa cartula minime invenire potuisset"—in order to have it confirmed by a royal *praeceptum*. When he was informed about the loss of the document, King Aistulf ordered a copy of the second original preserved in the *curtis regis* at Lucca.[30] The "reissue" was to be made by the same notary who had written the original: "alia tale cartula relevare per ipso notario qui ea antea scripserad." The order of the king was noted down in the reissue made in September 755: "Cartula ista relevata est per demandationem ipsius domno nostro Aistolf regi."

Even royal documents could be lost shortly after being issued. In the course of litigation from 762 about two contradictory charters issued at the time of King Aistulf (749-56), one of the two parties could not even present the confirmative document of the king, issued only a decade earlier.[31] (I will return to this trial below.)

Documents were not even safe from theft. A charter from about 758, by which the priest Deusdona invested a second priest called Deusdedit with a smaller church in Lucca (S. Angelo di Scragio), was removed a few years later under extraordinary circumstances.[32] It seems that Deusdona very soon regretted the investiture of Deusdedit, since he planned to depose Deusdedit and to invest a certain Alpert instead of him. In order to

[28] For the Frankish-Lombard war of the year 754, see Ludwig Oelsner, *Jahrbücher des fränkischen Reiches unter König Pippin* (Leipzig, 1871), 194-202.

[29] The bishop himself seems to have perished in this war; see Schwarzmaier, *Lucca und das Reich*, 160. The documents which Archbishop George of Ravenna took to the court of Emperor Lothar I in the year 840 were severely damaged in the battle of Fontenay; see Fichtenau, "Archive der Karolingerzeit," 18.

[30] Schiaparelli, ed., *Codice diplomatico longobardo*, vol. 1, no. 113, pp. 328-33, at 329, line 14, to 330, line 1: "alia tale cartula relevare per ipso notario qui ea antea scripserad, qualis ille erat, quem de parte eclesie ad curtis regia emissat fuerad."

[31] Schiaparelli, ed., *Codice diplomatico longobardo*, vol. 2, no. 163, pp. 110-12.

[32] See the *notitia iudicati* of the year 786, Schiaparelli, ed., *Codice diplomatico longobardo*, vol. 2, app., pp. 445-50; Chris Wickham, "Land Disputes and Their Social Framework in Lombard-Carolingian Italy, 700-900," in *The Settlement of Disputes in Early Medieval Europe*, ed. Wendy Davies and Paul Fouracre (Cambridge, 1986), 105-24, esp. 116-17 (repr. Wickham, *Land and Power: Studies in Italian and European Social History, 400-1200* [London, 1994], 229-56, esp. 242-43).

take such a step it was obviously necessary to destroy the charter, which was of course in the possession of Deusdedit. As he wanted to prevent being suspected himself, Deusdona persuaded his new favorite Alpert to steal the document. When Alpert, who was in possession of a key to the church or the archive ("ego claves eius haberem potestatem"),[33] handed the stolen document over to Deusdona, both caused an unconcerned third party, a pilgrim from Brittany, to put it into the fire: "ipse Alpertus clericus presenti ante me (i.e., Deusdona) dedit cartulam illam ad unum Brettonem peregrino, qui ibidem venerat; presenti ante nos ipse Britto misit ea in focum et ibi arsit." When Bishop John of Lucca initiated a trial in 786, Deusdona protested his innocence before the judges, asserting in accordance with the facts that he had neither stolen nor burned the document. Nevertheless his coup was detected and Deusdedit remained in possession of the church.[34]

Documents were not only lost, stolen, or removed; they were also manipulated. In 754 the duchess Scauniperga of Benevento could satisfy herself of the fact that "pravi homines" had deleted the names of two peasants from a *praeceptum* issued by Duke Romualdo II of Benevento (706-31): "delibata sunt...nomina de duas condomas...quem nostra gloria (i.e, Scauniperga) certam agnovimus veritatem." The duchess issued a confirmation with a complete list of all peasants to the affected monastery.[35]

Less spectacular than such losses and manipulations of documents are the surely more frequent cases when the simple ravages of time began to damage the documents, again often after only a few years. When Osprand,

[33] Schiaparelli, ed., *Codice diplomatico longobardo*, vol. 2, app., p. 447, lines 19-20: "Dum ego (i.e., Alpert) in obsequium ipsius Deusdedi presbiteri fuissem et ego claves eius haberem potestatem, tuli ei ipsam cartulam."

[34] The archive of the archbishop of Ravenna burned down around 700, before the Lombards took the city. Inhabitants who ran to the burning building used this opportunity to steal many documents not yet consumed by the flames. See Fichtenau, "Archive der Karolingerzeit," 17. Several examples of documents getting lost or being destroyed in Italy after the Frankish conquest are mentioned in Theo Kölzer, "*Codex libertatis*: Überlegungen zur Funktion des 'Regestum Farfense' und anderer Klosterchartulare," in *Atti del 9° Congresso internazionale di studi sull'alto medioevo, Spoleto 1982* (Spoleto, 1983), 609-53, esp. 638. See also Bresslau, *Handbuch der Urkundenlehre*, 1:181.

[35] Herbert Zielinski, ed., *Codice diplomatico longobardo*, vol. 4.2, *I Diplomi dei duchi di Benevento*, Fonti per la storia d'Italia 65* (Rome, 2002), no. 40, pp. 131-34.

a well-known notary of the cathedral of Lucca, copied in 755 a *charta donationis* from the year 730, two signatures were no longer legible, and Osprand made a number of smaller misreadings due to the bad condition of the charter.[36] In this particular case his subscription on the copy has to be taken literally: "Ego Osprand subdiaconus notarius s. Lucensis ecclesie, *quantum in autenticum inveni*, nec plus addedi, nec menime scripsi." Richiprand, who copied in about 770 several charters from Lucca, among them a *charta venditionis* from 738, also admitted frankly: "*in quantum cognuscere potui*, hec cartula fideliter exemplavi."[37] In particularly poor condition were three charters from 720, copied by Fluriprandus around 800 on one piece of parchment; he did so "ex autentico, *quantum cognoscere potui*," leaving nevertheless many gaps.[38]

It is obvious that Deusdedit, the priest whose document was stolen and burned, did not possess any *exemplum* of it. This is why in 780 the judges interrogated not only the accused culprits, but also the witnesses of the charter issued in 758, before they confirmed the investiture of Deusdedit. Would an *exemplum* have simplified the trial? Were *exemplaria* actually allowed in trials? Obviously they were. We know about the trial in 762, discussed above, through a document that was issued in the royal palace at Pavia before King Desiderius. It says that both parties could not present the original of the two charters issued a few years earlier, but only an *exemplum*. For two reasons the judges finally accepted only one of the two *exemplaria*. First, the charter of the party that won the case in the end had been confirmed by King Aistulf, and the new king, Desiderius, remembered this: "ipse princeps (i.e., Desiderius) dixit nobis, quod iudicatum ipsum vedisset et per eius rogum domnus Aistulf eum per suum preceptum firmassit." Second, the charter of the party that lost was without legal force because it was not confirmed "per garethinx" or "per launichild" as the law required.[39] The fact that the losing party was only in possession of an *exemplum* was not important at all; even if he could have presented his

36 Schiaparelli, ed., *Codice diplomatico longobardo*, vol. 1, no. 48, pp. 156-61.

37 Schiaparelli, ed., *Codice diplomatico longobardo*, vol. 1, no. 65, pp. 204-6, at 206, lines 7-8.

38 Schiaparelli, ed., *Codice diplomatico longobardo*, vol. 1, nos. 24-26, pp. 91-98, at 96, lines 15-16.

39 See Everett, "Scribes and Charters in Lombard Italy," 79; *Edictus Rothari*, esp. capp. 174-75 (ed. Franz Beyerle, *Leges Langobardorum 643-866*, 2d ed., Germanenrechte, n.F., Westgermanisches Recht, [9] [Witzenhausen, 1962], pp. 45-46).

autenticum, the charter would have been without legal force: "stare non potuisset, etiamsi autenticum exinde habuisses." The party that won did not have an *autenticum* either, and the confirmation they had received from King Aistulf had already perished completely.

Normally diplomatists are mainly interested in the transmission of documents because this knowledge is important for their work as editors, compiling the text and recognizing and commenting on forgeries. As this brief survey of Lombard documents makes clear, the transmission of documents has its own value and should be recognized as an important historical phenomenon in its own right. Knowledge of the transmission of documents, varying from age to age by types and forms, may not only provide us with valuable information about people's mentalities and attitudes towards written documents, but also with a better understanding of their legal culture. The transmission of documents not only reflects the changing needs and attitudes of medieval society; it also reveals to us when the past had become cut off from the present.[40] Naturally, more investigation is needed to see at what time the transmission of Lombard documents ceased to be part of the legal culture in Italy and what this meant for transmission itself.

[40] In a general context see Patrick J. Geary, *Phantoms of Remembrance: Memory and Oblivion at the End of the First Millennium* (Princeton, 1994), esp. 81-114 ("Archival Memory and the Destruction of the Past").

Towards an Archaeology of the Medieval Charter: Textual Production and Reproduction in Northern French *Chartriers*

Brigitte Bedos-Rezak

Quintilian observed that "it is often easier to achieve more than to achieve the same; producing an exact replica is very difficult."[1] Medieval scribes and, later, scholars of the French Ancien Régime have left us a legacy of texts known as copies which amply illustrate Quintilian's observation. The work of medieval copyists may perhaps be seen as modulating something already written, as working with, and between, the lines of antecedent texts which, although considered by us as originals, were, through the treatment they received when copied, evidently capable of becoming something more, or something less. It is as if there were no original documents but only texts, tacitly unfinished, never fully complete, ever available for a later hand to re-present their contents yet again. Such a strategy for reproduction may have been based upon a belief that all documentary texts were equally functional, whatever the material format or the specific textual version in which they appeared. Because strict duplication seems to have been eschewed in producing the various versions of a single deed, it may be that the so-called archetype was never an original document in our modern sense, but truly an "act" by which actions, transactions, or judgments were accomplished. In that sense, every surviving document reporting such events may best be understood as a copy.

This formulation is not, of course, the standard doctrine espoused by modern diplomatists who, since Mabillon (d. 1707), have tended, more or less systematically, to assume the existence of an original document perceived as unique, of an Ur-text from which later versions necessarily *had* to

---

In addition to hearing an earlier version of this paper at the meeting of the Commission internationale de diplomatique, Professor John Baldwin has also read the written version, which benefited very much from his insightful critique.

[1] Quoted by Gerald L. Bruns, "The Originality of Texts in a Manuscript Culture," *Comparative Literature* 32.2 (1980): 113-29, at 114.

originate, and against whose authenticity the adequateness of any other copy may and need be tested.[2] The normative definition of a medieval diplomatic original is a document extant as a single parchment and exhibiting signs of validation.[3] Thus the characteristics of an original reside mainly in its format and in its physical aspect. In seeking to identify those qualities which separate originals from copies, the discipline of diplomatics has promulgated a theoretical principle that situates and substantiates authenticity itself within the physical uniqueness of original documents. Medieval scribes, however, those who undertook the actual work of reproduction, seem not to have been so concerned with unique and authentic originals in the same sense that Mabillon was. Indeed, the very signs identified by Mabillon and retained by subsequent generations of diplomatists as undoubted markers of authenticity—e.g., seals, handwriting, dates, lists of witnesses—were actually de-emphasized by medieval copyists. It is possible that memory alone was the principal antecedent of deeds recorded in charters of confirmation, pancartes, or cartulary entries. Furthermore, in a certain sense, every diplomatic text, whatever its format, has a claim to originality since it is a unique, handcrafted artifact. Any preexisting text from which a copy was made might thus have served as an exemplar. There seems to have been no equivalent to our modern concept of an "original" in the medieval lexicon, where the word *authenticum*, when used to refer to a charter or diploma, simply invoked its authority, not its temporal primacy.[4] Originality can be a matter of authenticity, authority, or priority. How then are we to arrive at the medieval understanding of documentary originality which, I am suggesting, is possibly something other than the Urtext posited by Mabillon?

I propose here to examine the medieval concepts of "copy" and "original" by looking at the filiation of three groups of documents initially

[2] Dom Jean Mabillon's methodology is expounded in his *De re diplomatica libri VI* (Paris, 1681). For analyses of Mabillon's epistemological contributions to the discipline of history and of his role in the creation of the so-called "auxiliary sciences," see Blandine Barret-Kriegel's edition of Jean Mabillon, *Brèves réflexions sur quelques règles de l'histoire* (Paris, 1990).

[3] M. T. Clanchy, *From Memory to Written Record, England 1066-1307*, 2d ed. (Oxford, 1993), 84.

[4] Olivier Guyotjeannin, "Le vocabulaire de la diplomatique," in *Vocabulaire du livre et de l'écriture au Moyen Âge: Actes de la table ronde, Paris 24-26 septembre 1987*, ed. Olga Weijers, Études sur le vocabulaire intellectuel du Moyen Âge 2 (Turnhout, 1989), 128-29.

produced in northern France before 1200: first, all the *acta* given for and by the chapter of Saint-Fursy of Péronne; second, all the acta given for and by the abbey of Notre-Dame of Homblières; and third, all the acta given in the name of the counts of Ponthieu. The data of interest thus originate north of Paris, mainly in Picardy. In the case of the comital charters of Ponthieu, published by Clovis Brunel in 1930, we are dealing with a documentary corpus which, though articulated around the principle of authorship (the charters are all given in the name of the counts of Ponthieu), had no historical organic existence as such, since the charters were preserved in widely dispersed archives.[5] Most of the charters of Saint-Fursy, gathered by William Mendel Newman and published by John Benton and Mary Rouse, were, on the other hand, historically constituted as an archive by the chapter ever since their production and entered into a, now lost, thirteenth-century cartulary.[6] Similarly, a majority of the charters of Homblières, also gathered by William Mendel Newman and published by Theodore Evergates and Giles Constable, were organized as a medieval archive by the monks who produced a now lost cartulary around 1170.[7] Contrasting these two formats of charter grouping, the modern gathering and the historical archival formation, may help bring into focus those dynamics which underlay the production, reproduction, and preservation of medieval charters.

[5] Clovis Brunel, ed., *Recueil des actes des comtes de Pontieu, 1026-1279* (Paris, 1930).

[6] William Mendel Newman and Mary A. Rouse, eds., *Charters of St-Fursy of Péronne* (Cambridge, Mass., 1977). The thirteenth-century cartulary is discussed at 1-3, where the editors make it clear that they included in their edition texts not belonging to the archives of Saint-Fursy. Among the archives that contributed acta to this edition are those of the chapter of Noyon (no. 6), the abbey of Arrouaise (nos. 17, 22, 36, 37), Notre-Dame of Eaucourt (no. 2), the chapter of Arras (nos. 68, 69), Saint-Barthélemy of Noyon (no. 9), the abbey of Mont-Saint-Martin (no. 21), the Hôtel-Dieu of Péronne (no. 58), and the abbey of Saint-Thierry of Rheims (no. 30).

[7] William Mendel Newman, Theodore Evergates, and Giles Constable, eds., *The Cartulary and Charters of Notre-Dame of Homblières*, Medieval Academy Books 97 (Cambridge, Mass., 1990). The lost cartulary of ca. 1170 is discussed at 20-23; also included in the edition are acts issued by the abbots of Homblières or relevant to the abbey found in the archives of other monasteries: Ourscamps (no. 41), Mont-Saint-Martin (nos. 46A, 76), Vicoigne (nos. 70, 82, 85, 105), Prémontré (no. 75), Ribemont (nos. 91, 91A, 92, 92A, 92B, 93, 94, 99, 101), Saint-Quentin (nos. 100A, 104).

Even taking into account the destruction by fire, war, and other catastrophes, which obviously obscure the distinction between loss and simple absence, it is possible to detect significant patterns of charter preservation. There would seem to be three ways in which the diplomatic texts here under consideration might have existed before 1200. First, it is conceivable that they did *not* exist—here I refer to those texts whose only retrievable mention postdates the time of their alleged issue. Second, they may indeed once have existed, although evidence for their existence should not systematically be assumed merely from the presence of later copies. Medieval cartularies, for example, usually register texts without specifying their provenance, and I have not assumed that an "original" was copied unless this is specifically claimed. On the other hand, *vidimus* charters refer to particular documents purportedly being "renovated." The eighteenth-century Benedictines Dom P. N. Grenier and Dom Queinsert, who worked through Picardy's archival holdings, never failed to mention the fact when they transcribed from a so-called "original" those copies they made which later entered the Collection Moreau and the Collection Picardie at the Bibliothèque nationale in Paris. The third and last category are originals which, as earlier described, have come down to us in a direct material sense.

Saint-Fursy of Péronne, the burial site of the Irish monk and missionary Fursa (d. ca. 650), had housed a community of Irish monks since the seventh century. The monastery survived the Northmen's invasion of 880 and played an important role as a center from which the insular Irish culture spread to continental Europe. Sometime in the mid-eleventh century, Saint-Fursy was converted into a chapter of secular canons thus becoming a collegiate church. Its monastic past and subsequent secularization have left no documentary traces; there are neither extant nor copied charters for Saint-Fursy dated before the twelfth century. The fire that destroyed the church in 1130 may have claimed some charters, although the eighteenth-century Benedictine scholars still saw a fair number of originals pre-dating 1130. A cartulary, now lost, was composed in the thirteenth century, but the circumstances of its creation are unknown. A version of this cartulary is still extant but only in an abbreviated form produced in the seventeenth century.[8] I have analyzed the filiation of the seventy-six Saint-Fursy documents ranging from 1102 to 1200.

Only two originals are still extant, preserved in the archives of the

[8] Newman and Rouse, eds., *St-Fursy*, x, xiii-xviii.

beneficiaries of the dean of Saint-Fursy's deeds.[9] Twenty-three additional originals, though today no longer extant, were seen, transcribed, and described in the eighteenth century by Grenier or Queinsert, who give precious details about their physical appearance, including the state of their seals. Over half of the twenty-five originals still extant in early modern times predate 1150. All but three were entered in Saint-Fursy's thirteenth-century cartulary; of these three exceptions two were chirographs.[10]

Twenty of the now lost twenty-three originals came from the archives of Saint-Fursy. Fewer than half of these, which had been both preserved at Saint-Fursy and copied into its cartulary, were given in the names of authors other than the chapter of Saint-Fursy, and thus represented incoming documents which had been kept as both exemplars and copies; such authors included the pope, the archbishop of Rheims, the bishop of Arras, and two local abbots (of Saint-Pierre of Honnecourt and Vermand), but only two laymen, Ralph, count of Vermandois, and Peter, castellan of Péronne. Therefore, more than half of the documents preserved and copied at Saint-Fursy were acta given in the name of the local chapter and dean, that is, outgoing materials. The fact that Saint-Fursy was able to preserve and copy deeds given in its own name resulted from the relatively large number of chirographs issued by its chapter and dean. A chirograph recorded an agreement between two parties and was written out in duplicate on a single sheet which was then cut in half, with each party receiving an actual

[9] One, Newman and Rouse, eds., *St-Fursy*, no. 9, pp. 28-29, the charter given in 1122 by the treasurer of Saint-Fursy to the abbey of Saint-Barthélemy of Noyon, was kept by this abbey and never copied. The other, no. 38, pp. 55-57, was a chirograph given in 1177 by the dean of Saint-Fursy for the abbey of Vaucelles. The part of the chirograph which is still extant in the archives of Vaucelles was never copied, while the version retained by Saint-Fursy, and now lost, was entered in Saint-Fursy's thirteenth-century cartulary.

[10] First, Newman and Rouse, eds., *St-Fursy*, no. 9, pp. 28-29 (above, n. 9); second, no. 12, pp. 31-32, the version of a chirograph given in 1122 by the dean of Saint-Fursy to Notre-Dame of Eaucourt, in whose archive an eighteenth-century copy was made by Queinsert, thus implying that Saint-Fursy might have either lost its version by the thirteenth century or elected not to copy it within the thirteenth-century cartulary; and third, no. 19, pp. 37-38, a version of another chirograph given in 1126-35 by the dean of Saint-Fursy about Saint-Fursy's land at Aubregicourt. Although the eighteenth-century copy of this latter document was made in Saint-Fursy's archive, for reasons that are unclear the thirteenth-century cartulary had no copy of it.

half of the original document, usually authorized by the seal of the other party. As a matter of fact, twelve of these now lost originals, that is more than half, were chirographs. They must have initially existed in duplicate, in the archives and cartularies both of Saint-Fursy and of the other parties concerned. Although chirographs might serve as a record of outgoing documentary production, diplomatists tend to deny chirographs this explicit function, insisting that their duplicate format resulted from their role in settling property exchanges or agreements involving reciprocal obligations.[11]

Finally, forty-five out of the seventy-six charters (i.e., 59 percent) known to have been issued prior to 1200 have come down to us exclusively via medieval cartularies, with the bulk (forty charters) preserved within the lost thirteenth-century cartulary of Saint-Fursy.[12] Only four of these cartulary entries were completely transcribed by the eighteenth-century scholarly Benedictines, but in the absence of extant originals, Dom Grenier's transcriptions from the cartulary clearly demonstrate that the cartulary contained carefully copied texts, though without mention of the charters' physical aspects.[13]

The bulk of the cartulary entries without extant originals date from the last quarter of the twelfth century. One third of these, all charters but for one chirograph, are acta issued by the dean and chapter of Saint-Fursy. The remaining two-thirds are papal bulls and episcopal charters, though there are also two lay charters (issued by Ralph, count of Vermandois, and Philip, count of Flanders and Vermandois).

To recapitulate: Saint-Fursy's holdings of seventy-six texts dated prior

[11] Laurent Morelle, "Archives épiscopales et formulaire de chancellerie au XIIe siècle: Remarques sur les privilèges épiscopaux connus par le *Codex* de Lambert de Guînes, évêque d'Arras (1093/94-1115)," in *Die Diplomatik der Bischofsurkunde vor 1250: La diplomatique épiscopale avant 1250: Referate zum VIII. Internationalen Kongress für Diplomatik, Innsbruck, 1993*, ed. Christoph Haidacher and Werner Köfler (Innsbruck, 1995), 255-67, at 264 n. 8, where the author cites several corpuses of and studies on episcopal charters, all supporting the conclusion that the chirograph was not used by the bishop as a means of keeping exemplars of deeds expedited in his name. See below, pp. 49, 50, 55.

[12] The five charters not copied with the thirteenth-century cartulary of Saint-Fursy come from the twelfth-century cartulary of the abbey of Arrouaise (two), from the thirteenth-century cartulary of the chapter of Noyon (one), and from the thirteenth-century *Livre blanc* of the chapter of Arras (two).

[13] See for instance Newman and Rouse, eds., *St-Fursy*, no. 62, pp. 70-71.

to 1200 include twenty-five (one-third of the total) known from originals which span the eleventh and twelfth centuries, though with a concentration in the early part of the twelfth century. This suggests that the fire of 1130 cannot by itself explain the pattern of lost originals. Surviving originals, often in the form of chirographs, were for the most part issued by the dean and chapter of Saint-Fursy; they have also survived as cartulary entries. The forty-five texts that are known only from medieval cartularies, particularly Saint-Fursy's thirteenth-century cartulary, are primarily papal bulls and episcopal charters which date from the late twelfth century. This may have been the time when the now lost cartulary of Saint-Fursy was initiated, which may well suggest a tendency of discarding incoming materials after they had been copied. Significantly, those acta issued in the name of the dean and chapter of Saint-Fursy, and known only from the cartulary of Saint-Fursy, also tend to date from the second half of the twelfth century; furthermore, they are charters, and not chirographs as in the earlier period. This suggests, first, that once the cartulary was in operation the dean and chapter used it to enter their own outgoing deeds and, second, that chirographs may have, after all, also involved a concern for registering outgoing production.[14]

In examining the cartulary entries as a whole, by far the largest proportion was devoted to deeds issued in the name of Saint-Fursy which record the alienation of land by the chapter of Saint-Fursy, but do not refer to the chapter's rights and possessions. It is therefore not possible to trace how the chapter's patrimony was originally constituted since no reference is made to earlier donations or endowments. None of the charters from the Saint-Fursy corpus mentions the ritual manipulation of charters, such as their placement on altars, or their roles as symbolic objects in the conveyance of property. Interestingly, neither the original charters nor the cartulary assert the antiquity or the rights of the house. The pattern of archival holding, and of copying, emphasizes the documentary authorship and initiative of the dean and chapter; no lay protector emerges for the church of Saint-Fursy, and little reference is made, and then only rather late, to episcopal or papal authority. To the extent that an identity is projected, it is that of a collegiate and independent church, with strong ties to other religious institutions, but with virtually no evidence of lay patronage, and with no memory of either its own monastic past or of the constitution of its patrimony. The central message projected by both the cartulary and the

[14] See above, n. 11, and below, n. 16 and p. 55.

archival profile is that Saint-Fursy was engaged in a systematic documentary practice centered on administration rather than on proofs or assertion of property.

Homblières, a former nunnery which became a Benedictine abbey of monks at the end of the tenth century, produced a cartulary ca. 1170 specifically to resolve a dispute with the nearby abbey of Saint-Nicolas-des-Prés of Ribemont. Though now lost, the cartulary itself, together with some medieval charters, was transcribed in the seventeenth century.[15] Of the 107 known documents prior to 1200, 5 are still extant as originals, while 16 additional texts were transcribed directly from originals still extant in the seventeenth century. As with Saint-Fursy, these originals tend to belong to the earlier part of the period under consideration, with nine prior to 1100, another nine prior to 1150, and only three for 1150 to 1200. They all emanated from various donors and were copied into the cartulary of 1170, but for four charters issued by the abbots of Homblières which were preserved in the archives of their beneficiaries. Homblières also produced a substantial number of chirographs, most of which date from the middle of the twelfth century and which seem to be responsible in part for the registration within the cartulary of those *outgoing* charters issued in the name of the abbot of Homblières.[16] Only nine texts (including the four originals just mentioned) out of the twenty-eight given by the abbot of Homblières are found exclusively in the archives and cartularies of monasteries other than Homblières. These tend to involve concessions to the recipients of the acta, or settlements of disputes in which Homblières was either arbiter (rather than a party) or the losing party. Thus, the abbey seems to have maintained a comprehensive archive of its outgoing documents, with the preparation of a cartulary resulting at once in greater recording activity while rendering less necessary the retention of outgoing exemplars. Homblières's cartulary,

[15] Newman, Evergates, and Constable, eds., *Homblières*, 14, 20; see at 22 a table clearly rendering the filiation of all known copies of Homblières's thirteenth-century cartulary.

[16] In a chirograph of 1155-60 recording an exchange of land between the abbot of Homblières and the canons of Arrouaise living at Magières, the final clause reads: "In hunc modum inter se scriptum confecerunt et sigillorum impressione ita consignaverunt ut ecclesia de Humbleriis habeat ipsum scriptum consignatum sigillo ecclesiae de Arroisia, et canonici apud margellas commanentes idem scriptum habeant signatum sigillo ecclesiae de Humbleriis. Pactionis huius hi testes sunt..." (Newman, Evergates, and Constable, eds., *Homblières*, no. 78, pp. 154-55, at 155).

however, is more balanced than Saint-Fursy's, registering the protection and patronage of lay and ecclesiastical powers. Their incoming charters constitute more than half of the cartulary's content. Those incoming charters which preceded the redaction of the cartulary were preserved both as originals and as cartulary entries.

If the subsequent fate of Homblières's archives ultimately leaves open the question of a purposeful destruction of originals in connection with the drafting of the cartulary,[17] the very production of the cartulary seems to have been associated with two events. From an internal viewpoint, the cartulary displays a plethora of notices datable to the time of its production. In attempting to understand the origin of these many late cartulary entries, it is possible to suggest the hypothesis that Homblières might have maintained an inventory of minor oral transfers from the late eleventh century,[18] which may have been further elaborated at the time of their entry into the cartulary. It is also conceivable that such notices were formulated directly from the memory of the cartularist, who was contemporary with the transactions they record. In the cartulary title of one such notice, the knightly donor is called Rainerus "The Long," a nickname which does not appear within the text of the notice itself. This interpretive insertion by the cartularist testifies to his familiarity with the event recorded independently of the preserved text.[19] Whatever the antecedents of these notices were (memory, drafts, or inventories), it seems clear that the creation of the cartulary fostered an expanded textual format. The abbey seems to have remained economically viable until 1372, but there are very few documents to be found pertaining to Homblières after the completion of this cartulary. These later documents provide an extremely fragmentary picture of the

[17] Newman, Evergates, and Constable, eds., *Homblières*, 20-21, 30 n. 153: the abbey was abandoned in 1607, and its archives and cartulary were sent elsewhere for safekeeping. Both were seen and used in the first half of the sixteenth century. The cartulary had disappeared by the 1770s.

[18] Newman, Evergates, and Constable, eds., *Homblières*, 104.

[19] Newman, Evergates, and Constable, eds., *Homblières*, 163. For further discussions of the role of memory in cartulary redaction, see the studies in Olivier Guyotjeannin, Laurent Morelle, and Michel Parisse, eds., *Les cartulaires: Actes de la table ronde organisée par l'École nationale des chartes et le G.D.R. 121 du C.N.R.S. (Paris, 5-7 décembre 1991)*, Mémoires et documents de l'École des chartes 39 (Paris, 1993), particularly Laurent Morelle, "De l'original à la copie: Remarques sur l'évaluation des transcriptions dans les cartulaires médiévaux," 91-104, at 100, 104.

history of the abbey, of which virtually nothing is known after 1250.[20] Did the copying of charters into a cartulary somehow discourage donations by increasing their irreversibility? At the very least, the case of Homblières makes clear that the survival of outgoing acta was greatly jeopardized when dependent solely upon the archival policies of the charters' recipients.

The counts of Ponthieu were originally the *avoués*, the protectors, of the abbey of Saint-Riquier; they adopted the comital title sometime in the middle of the eleventh century, when a scion of the lineage married the widow of a count of Boulogne.[21] The 151 acta issued in the name of the counts of Ponthieu prior to 1200 have been collected. Only a very small number of such comital acts were preserved within the cartulary of Ponthieu. This was a lay project undertaken when Edward II, king of England, inherited the county of Ponthieu in 1290 and ordered the recording of all deeds implying rights of and upon the county.[22] It bears repetition here that this grouping of comital documents was not constituted as a medieval archive but is a modern corpus, a gathering of charters originally dispersed among the various recipients of comital acta. The extent to which the survival of these charters has chiefly depended upon these recipients' archival strategies is one of the issues that will be further considered here.

Of the 151 acta, 43 (roughly a third) remain extant as originals. All forty-three originals were kept in the archives of beneficiaries, mostly religious institutions, but also in a few lay archives, royal or urban. This is a much higher proportion of extant originals than at Saint-Fursy and Homblières. Since their survival corresponds not to a specific archive but to a specific author, one may wonder if perhaps the counts had some particular interest in the preservation of the acta produced and sealed in their names. Thus, ca. 1173-79, Jean, count of Ponthieu, in a charter for the abbey of Notre-Dame of Le Gard, which was never copied, specified that "ut hoc inconcussum atque durabile in eternum permaneat, cartam ecclesie Beate Marie de

[20] Newman, Evergates, and Constable, eds., *Homblières*, 15.

[21] Brunel, ed., *Pontieu*, ii-iii.

[22] Paris, BnF, lat. 10112; Ernest Prarond, ed., *Le cartulaire de Ponthieu* (Paris, 1897); Brunel, ed., *Pontieu*, xiv. Theodore Evergates, "The Chancery Archives of the Counts of Champagne: Codicology and History of the Cartulary Registers," *Viator* 16 (1985): 160-79, discusses briefly the chancery cartulary of Ponthieu at 161, and precedes his analysis of the cartulary registers of Champagne with a general review of secular cartularies at 159-61. More recently, Lucie Fossier and Olivier Guyotjeannin have established a list of extant secular cartularies: "Cartulaires français laïques: Seigneuries et particuliers," in *Les cartulaires*, 379-410.

Gardo dedi, testium subscriptione ac sigilli mei appositione premunitam."[23] How strong a comital injunction to retain the charter this really is cannot now be fully ascertained, but the rhetoric is slightly unusual and, accompanied by the actual preservation of the charter, supports the hypothesis that lay authors may have desired and ordered the conservation of their own sealed deeds of charity. At any rate, the majority of the Ponthieu originals were comital foundations or confirmations of donations. All were sealed. Those abbeys which did not draft cartularies, such as Perseigne, tended to have vidimus charters made of earlier comital grants in their favor.[24] Though the texts of all extant Ponthieu originals are also found in medieval cartularies of the thirteenth century onward, only the 1409 and sixteenth-century cartularies of the Templar house at Fieffes mention the seals.[25] Apart from these exceptions, descriptions of seals otherwise are noticed only in eighteenth-century scholarly copies.[26] Vernacular translations of Latin originals maintained in the archives of urban communities have survived from the fifteenth century onward.[27]

A further twenty-nine acta of Ponthieu, though now lost, were seen and copied from the originals, mostly by eighteenth-century scholars. However, in the medieval period vidimus charters were requested by those abbeys which apparently did not have a medieval cartulary at all (such as Saint-Pierre of Abbeville, whose *Livre noir* dates from 1487),[28] which had late car-

[23] "In order that this grant remain intact and be preserved for ever, I gave a charter to the church of Notre-Dame of Le Gard and provided it with witnesses' subscriptions and my appended seal"; Brunel, ed., *Pontieu*, no. 98, p. 141. A still extant original apparently not copied during the Middle Ages, this charter was nevertheless copied by seventeenth- and eighteenth-century scholars.

[24] Brunel, ed., *Pontieu*, no. 81, pp. 119-20.

[25] Brunel, ed., *Pontieu*, no. 49, pp. 74-75 (1154); no. 51, pp. 76-77 (1154); no. 65, p. 98 (1161); see below, n. 42.

[26] See a seventeenth-century seal description by Gaignières in Brunel, ed., *Pontieu*, no. 18, pp. 32-33 (1112), at 33; Gaignières also drew the seal. Most of Gaignière's seal drawings have been catalogued by Joseph Roman, "Les dessins de sceaux de la collection Gaignières à la Bibliothèque nationale," *Mémoires de la Société nationale des antiquaires de France* 9 (1909): 42-158.

[27] For instance: Brunel, ed., *Pontieu*, no. 60, pp. 89-91 (ca. 1159); no. 95, pp. 134-38 (1177); no. 109, pp. 157-66 (1184).

[28] Texts from the *Livre noir* of Saint-Pierre of Abbeville, now lost, were copied in the eighteenth century; see Brunel, ed., *Pontieu*, 41. See a 1482 vidimus of a 1136-37 comital donation to Saint-Pierre at no. 25, pp. 40-43.

tularies (such as the abbey of Ourscamps, whose cartulary dates from the fourteenth century),[29] or by towns which did not register their deed (like Crécy or Waben).[30] Surveying the use of vidimus charters in relationship to extant and lost originals, it appears that institutions without cartularies were more apt to have sought them. All twenty-nine of these now lost originals were sealed but for one, a mid-eleventh-century charter for Marmoutiers that predates the comital practice of sealing.[31]

Finally, seventy-six comital acts of Ponthieu prior to 1200 are known only through copies, constituting half of the corpus under consideration. Among these are the earliest known comital charters, given for the abbey of Saint-Riquier, whose archives perished in a fire in 1131. These charters are known both through their transcription by Hariulf in his *Chronicle* of that abbey written between 1088 and 1104, and through an inventory of Saint-Riquier's charters of 1098.[32]

Actually, comital charters of Ponthieu are not understandable according to a principle of filiation as were those of the chapter of Saint-Fursy and the abbey of Homblières. There is no clear-cut category of acta linked either to the originals or to copies as a class. However, even this observation may provide insight into the relationship between diplomatic discourse

[29] Brunel, ed., *Pontieu*, no. 123, pp. 185-86, where the fourteenth-century cartulary is mentioned; Ourscamps had a vidimus made in 1233 by Simon, count of Ponthieu, of its comital privileges (no. 291, pp. 424-45); the vidimus is referred to as a *carta transcripta*.

[30] Brunel, ed., *Pontieu*, no. 131, pp. 198-200, at 198, where is given the filiation of Crécy's charter of franchise (received from the count of Ponthieu in June 1194), and with it a survey of Crécy's archival arrangements. Crécy obtained a vidimus of its charter of franchise in 1484 from King Charles VIII. Waben received its communal charter from the count of Ponthieu in April 1199 (no. 148, p. 225) and a vidimus of this charter from Simon, count of Ponthieu, in May 1235 (no. 298, pp. 433-35).

[31] Brunel, ed., *Pontieu*, no. 14, p. 27.

[32] Hariulf, *Chronique de l'abbaye de Saint-Riquier (Ve siècle-1104)*, ed. Ferdinand Lot (Paris, 1894); the 1131 fire, provoked by the count of Saint-Pol, is discussed at xxxvii; the inventory is edited in app. IX, pp. 314-18. In his chronicle, Hariulf copied all charters given by the counts of Ponthieu and listed in the 1098 inventory but one, Brunel, ed., *Pontieu*, no. 2, p. 2 (1020-45). On Hariulf's relationship to the archival holdings of Saint-Riquier, which he selectively used as a source for his chronicle, and for specific reference to those documents which he did not include, see Laurent Morelle, "Histoire et archives vers l'an mil: Une nouvelle 'mutation,'" *Histoire et archives* 3 (1998): 119-41, at 130-31.

and medieval archival strategies. Both the chapter and the abbey archived and recorded their textual holdings, tapping memory and rough drafts, keeping track of the outgoing documents they had authored, and organizing the incoming charters in their favor which they had often originally scripted as well. Even when separated from their archival sequence, the comital charters of Ponthieu still share similar trends although manifestly emanating from, and recorded or archived in, different writing bureaus or scriptoria. On the basis of the empirical observations made thus far, I would now like to explore the possibility that the format of the charter prior to 1200 itself may have, at least in part, evolved in synchrony with particular ideas about the role of text in projecting permanence and in enabling preservation.

Ponthieu confirmations and notifications of land donations may be found in all three of the categories we have been considering: still extant originals, originals extant in the Middle Ages and now lost, and texts known to us exclusively in later versions. Cartulary entries record actions but not necessarily actions initially preserved in writing. These entries textualized without necessarily copying. Copying, however, was manifest in two different forms. First came the chirograph, which, as a duplicate text, enabled each party to keep a record. Perhaps chirographs, as has already been suggested here, should be seen as an antecedent of the copy for archival purposes.[33] An abbey's archival holding might thereby achieve a shift from passivity, that of mere recipient, to a more active posture, as an ongoing force in internal and local affairs. This conception emphasizes the role copying may have played in image-making: in the case of Saint-Fursy, and to a lesser extent of Homblières, the chirograph seems to have enabled such a shift in institutional profile. The other form of copying involved not straightforward duplication but the borrowing of pre-existing passages from diplomatic discourse: preambles, formulas, or geographic descriptions.[34]

[33] See above nn. 11, 16, and pp. 48-50.

[34] Both charters (of 1100) by Gui, count of Ponthieu, for the Cluniac priory of Saint-Pierre of Abbeville relate the same event in similar but slightly different terms: one may have been the draft for the other (Brunel, ed., *Pontieu*, nos. 8, 9, pp. 10-20). In no. 8, the invocation and preamble have been borrowed from a diploma given by Philip I in 1075-76 to the same priory: Maurice Prou, ed., *Recueil des actes de Philippe Ier* (Paris, 1908), no. 79, pp. 200-202. The charter (1145-71), extant as an original and confirming, in the name of William, count of Ponthieu, all donations made to the Cistercian abbey of Perseignes (Brunel, ed., *Pontieu*, no. 81, pp. 119-20), took for its model the founding charter of Perseignes, given by

Here the concept of conceptualizing an original document gave way to a need to appropriate authoritative textual formats. There is no evidence that a written formulary circulated in Ponthieu, but many comital charters share discursive arrangements which, apparently independent of their loci of production, reproduction, or preservation, testify to the importance of textual repetition in documentary authorization. Yet copying is intertextual, not from original sources to secondary texts, but between various texts invested with the same agency. The function of such copying was to produce an original, that is, in medieval terms, an authoritative text.

I mentioned earlier, in discussing Saint-Fursy's and Homblières's holdings, that earlier texts seemed to have a better chance of surviving in charter format. Might these charters particularly have been kept because of their symbolic value, the part they played in the *traditio* of the privilege or land transferred? I wish to suggest that another element of resonance and effectiveness may be found in the narrative format of these documents. The narratives focus on human presence and gesturing, referring to witnesses, to the presence of local elites, to the kisses exchanged, to the oaths

---

Count William in 1145 and also still extant as an original (no. 32, pp. 52-56). Three of Count Jean of Ponthieu's charters for the church of Saint-Josse-aux-Bois (Dommartin) show evidence of intertextual borrowings: no. 106, pp. 150-54 (extant original from 1183) was used in the comital charter no. 111, p. 167 (1183-85), which itself served as model for no. 112, pp. 167-72 (1185). Two comital charters granted for Valloires borrow various excerpts from each other (no. 72, pp. 107-9 [1170]; no. 103, pp. 146-47 [1183]). The preamble of another comital charter for Valloires (no. 144, pp. 216-20 [1198]) is also found in a charter of the bishop of Amiens, given in 1178 for Valloires. A grant of land to the leprosary of Val Buigny by Jean, count of Ponthieu, in 1186 (no. 114, pp. 174-75), simply repeats the invocation, preamble, *pro anima* formula, and corroborative clause from an earlier charter by the same count for the Val Buigny in 1177 (no. 95, pp. 134-38); both charters are extant as originals. The examples listed so far (which are discussed together with additional cases in Brunel, ed., *Pontieu*, xx, lxxxix-xc, xciii-xcviii) support the notion that beneficiaries of comital generosity drafted and preserved those deeds granted in their favor, which enabled them to use earlier charters as models. However, the circulation of models went beyond institutional boundaries. Two comital charters for the Val Buigny (no. 108, pp. 155-57 [1180-84]; no. 126, pp. 188-91 [1191]), both still extant in the original, have the same preamble found in a charter of Thibaut, bishop of Amiens, given in April 1156 to the Cistercian abbey of Valloires.

sworn.[35] Even when such documents were sealed, the seal typically remained unannounced within the final clauses.[36] The effect of such narratives located the act of initial recording within the medium, the single piece of parchment. After such a text was entered into a cartulary, however, there was no longer evidence of the document's independent existence. It may well be, therefore, that it was the developing practice of textual reproduction that fostered a particular need to distinguish between various versions of a deed, a distinction which came to be articulated around material considerations. It is striking to note the coterminous appearance within diplomatic discourse of literary preambles which assert the use of

[35] Newman, Evergates, and Constable, eds., *Homblières*, no. 66, pp. 137-38 (1152). The knights and their wives confirmed their gift of land to Homblières by oath and transferred the land by placing branch and turf with their own hands before the image of Saint Hunegund: "huius autem pactionis verba praefati milites cum uxoribus et liberis suis sacramento firmavere ipsamque terram ramo cespiteque sanctissimae virginis Hunegundis feretro propriis manibus in eleemosynam reliquentes posuerunt." In two extant originals (1173), Jean, count of Ponthieu confirms possessions respectively to the abbey of Cercamp and to the church of Notre-Dame of Le Gard (Brunel, ed., *Pontieu*, nos. 87, 88, pp. 124-26), ending each charter with the following clause: "et sciendum quod hanc elemosinam ego, Johannes comes, et Guido, frater meus, presentibus prefatis testibus in manu Hescelini, tunc abbatis Caricampi, reddidimus." In the charter (1159), still extant as an original, by which Jean, count of Ponthieu confirmed its possessions to the church of Saint-Josse-aux-Bois in the presence of the bishop of Amiens, the very final clause reads: "ego Teodericus, Dei gratia Ambianentium episcopus, presens scriptum Johannis, comitis de Pontivo, concessione ejusdem meo confirmo, et ne a quoquam ullo tempore unquam ausu temerario violetur, conturbetur, vel infringatur, pontificali auctoritate precipio, et pervasorem hujus rei a Patre, et Filio et Spiritu Sancto maledico, et donec resipuerit, ecclesiastica censura anathematizo. Amen. Amen" (Brunel, ed., *Pontieu*, no. 62, pp. 93-95, at 95). On the medieval use of kisses to seal contracts, see Yannick Carré, *Le baiser sur la bouche: Rites, symboles, mentalités, à travers les textes et les images, XIe-XVe siècles* (Paris, 1992).

[36] See for instance the charters given by Ralph, count of Vermandois, to Saint-Fursy in 1110 (Newman and Rouse, eds., *St-Fursy*, no. 7, pp. 26-27), and by Baldric, bishop of Noyon, in 1112 (no. 8, pp. 27-28); the charters of William and Gui, counts of Ponthieu, respectively for the priory of Saint-Pierre of Abbeville (Brunel, ed., *Pontieu*, no. 21, pp. 35-37 [1103-29]) and for the church of Anchin (no. 33, pp. 56-57 [1147]).

writing as necessary to keep peace and memory,[37] of narratives pointing to the material aspect of the charter,[38] to its drafting,[39] and to its various manipulations,[40] and of final clauses announcing in some detail the

[37] Preambles promoting the use of writing are numerous during the twelfth century. See for instance the charter of the abbot of Vermand for Saint-Fursy (Newman and Rouse, eds., *St-Fursy*, no. 42, pp. 59-60 [1182], at 59): "ego, Gillebertus, abbas Veromandi ecclesie,...propter labilis memorie fugam et nostri occasus instantiam vivacibus litteris notum esse volumus quod..." For preambles associating peace and writing, see the charter of Jean, count of Ponthieu (Brunel, ed., *Pontieu*, no. 52, pp. 78-79 [1154], at 78: "ut pax ecclesie conservetur, et res sibi deputate integre permaneant, grandi cum cautela providendum est. Inde est quod vir sanctus loquebatur: 'Propter fratres, inquit, meos et proximos qui in te habitant, loquebatur pacem de te, propter domum domini Dei nostri, que est in te, quesivi bona tibi.' Quod vero ad eandem rem pertinet litteris imprimendo ad posteros nostros mittimus..."), or the chirograph of Garin, abbot of Homblières (Newman, Evergates, and Constable, eds., *Homblières,* no. 71, pp. 144-46 [1155], at 145: "Quam quietissime viverent homines si duo verba e medio tollerentur, meum videlicet et tuum, sancta ecclesia ob concordiam filiorum chartularum reperit ingenium quatenus ipsarum lectione extinguantur litium flammae dato cuique suo jure").

[38] In this as in other charters, the count of Ponthieu draws attention to the materiality of the charter (Brunel, ed., *Pontieu*, no. 36, pp. 59-60 [1126-47], at 60): "predecessores nostri, sue paci ac nostre providentes utilitati, libertates et dona ecclesiarum scriptis publicis tradiderunt. Quorum exemplum ego Wido, gratia Dei comes Pontivensis, imitans, presentibus et futuris Ecclesie filiis hujus karte pagina volo notificari quod..."

[39] The bishop of Amiens ordered the document written and divided as a chirograph between the two parties (Newman, Evergates, and Constable, eds., *Homblières*, no. 47, pp. 106-8 [1142], at 107): "Quo praedicto modo factae commutationes ne aliqua in posterum oblivione aut occasione possint dissolvi, scripto eas mandari atque inter eos per chirographum dividi praecepimus, testiumque subscriptione et sigilli nostri impressione roborari curavimus."

[40] Charters deposited upon the altar: Brunel, ed., *Pontieu*, no. 73, pp. 109-10 (1119-70) ("Anno millesimo centesimo decimo octavo, Gaufridus de Ansnevilla firmavit cartam supradicte donationis, cum uxore sua Avitia, et filio suo Willelmo; ipsamque cartam posuerunt super altare Sanctae Trinitatis...Ego Willelmus, comes Pontivorum, concedo et confirmo sicut presens carta testatur..."); no. 81, pp. 119-20 (1145-71) ("Ego Vullelmus, Pontivorum comes et Alenconii...ad majorem confirmationem, ex propria manu mea super altare dicte abbatie posui presentem cartam sigilli mei munimine roboratam..."). For the reading of a comital charter by the count of Ponthieu's cleric, see no. 144, pp. 216-20 (1198), at 220: "Silvester, clericus meus, qui cartam ipsam relegit."

affixation of the seal.[41] Diplomatic discourse of the late twelfth century came to focus less on the transaction's human agency than on the steps taken for its recording and on the physical aspects of this recording. An important result of such narratives was that by describing the charter as an object within the text, the charter was freed from its former dependency upon a specific medium. Thereafter, whatever its material format, a kind of textual self-referentiality was achieved whereby the text-as-charter might continue to exist, whether in a cartulary or elsewhere. Two further conclusions may be essayed here. This newer "literate" narrative may account for the destruction of charters that sometimes followed the making of a cartulary, and for the preservation of earlier documents which had been couched in the earlier "human" narrative. The "literate" narrative may also account for the striking disinterest medieval cartularists evinced toward seals;[42] they saw no need to mention seals specifically, or to reproduce them, since the seals came to be textualized within the diplomatic discourse itself.

Textual retention of the sealed-charter format was thus important, though retention of the original charter itself may have become secondary. We must repeat here that the majority of deeds under scrutiny in this study have come down to us only in cartularized format. The phenomenon medieval diplomatists should be considering, in my opinion, is not so much the transformation of a putative original into a copy, but the medieval need for and process of repetition and re-enactment. Medieval documentary truths are in a sense the truths of action done double, of action re-produced. For it was when medieval society came to recognize itself through documents, that repetition—and I mean here registration, certification, cartularization —confirmed written records as testimonials. Whether in charters or in cartularies, a given diplomatic text belonged to an intertextual system, and

[41] Brunel, ed., *Pontieu*, no. 105, pp. 148-49 (1183), at 149: "Igitur ut elemosina ista rata permaneat, presentem cartam siggilli nostri appositione firmatam posteris nostris legendam atque tenendam transmittimus...Recognita est autem hec donatio in camera apud Cresci, coram Beatrice comitissa, ipsa concedente et testante, que etiam in testimonium presenti carte siggillum suum apposuit."

[42] For some rare mentions of seals by medieval cartularists, see above, n. 25, and Newman, Evergates, and Constable, eds., *Homblières*, no. 52, pp. 115-16 (1145). Homblières's medieval cartulary seems to have contained a drawing of the seal of Gerard, Lord of Ham, which the seventeenth-century cartularist copied (*circa scutum sigillum Gerardi Hamensis domini*), unless he was also able to see the original charter.

was probably not understood as a discrete instance of discourse in isolation from the archive which contained it. The very fact that medieval charters were transmitted in several medieval formats may indicate that they had to be thus transmitted in order to achieve institutional validation and to become an object of knowledge. The appearance of single-leaf charter-texts within cartulary codices may have been a primary sign that such texts were part of a canon of authorities, which in turn was to become the basis for yet other documentary formats such as subsequent confirmations from ruling elites. Thus the movement from charter, to cartulary, and back to charter is circular rather than linear, progressive, and hierarchical; such movement does not record a gradual loss of authority.[43]

The writing of a single diplomatic text could take several shapes in the Middle Ages, appearing as a charter, incorporated in a confirmation (*pancarte*), duplicated in a chirograph, entered into a cartulary, verified by a vidimus. Though all these formats contain evidence of duplication and may be seen as referring to a single transaction, they nevertheless do not simply involve replication. Even where a copy is textually identical, it typically is not, strictly speaking, a simple duplicate because it lacks autograph subscriptions and other signs of authorization such as the seal. In asking how medieval copies derived the means and meanings of their functions, and what these functions were, I would like to suggest, perhaps heretically in the bosom of the eminent Commission internationale de diplomatique, the possibility that, by eschewing precise replication while making "copies," medieval scribes and their literate superiors demonstrated that their goal was less to reproduce artifacts of the acts themselves than to maintain a process of textualization which would assure these acts' ongoing canonization as discursive practices. Perhaps for medieval literati, the text remained open, even as they increased their dependency upon writing for the management and evidence of business, even as they framed their charters in formulas and signs which finalized the act of writing and authorized its results.

[43] See for instance the acta of the counts of Ponthieu for the church of Saint-Josse-aux-Bois. In the case of Brunel, ed., *Pontieu*, no. 61, pp. 91-92 (1159), two copies were made in 1586, one by a member of the Parisian Parlement from a now lost cartulary and the other by the *greffier des francs-fiefs* from a copy said to have been collated from the original. No. 104, pp. 147-48 (1159), no. 107, pp. 154-55 (1183-84), no. 111, p. 167 (1183), and no. 112, pp. 167-69 (1185) were also copied in 1586 from the lost cartulary by the Parisian parlementaire.

The Contribution of Diplomatics to the Identification of an Early-Eleventh-Century Aquitanian Narrative

George T. Beech

This paper is about the use of diplomatics as an aid in the identification of a problematic medieval Latin text from early-eleventh-century Aquitaine. This text is a 341-line narrative occupying 15 manuscript pages which has until now eluded scholarly efforts to determine its precise identity. By identification I mean finding out just what kind of a text this is, to what genre it belongs, just as specialists in diplomatics classify medieval charters according to their form and the purposes they served into the categories of notices, treaties, acts of sale or donation, etc. But unlike most of these documentary texts the identity of this Aquitanian text is not obvious, and the scholars who have studied it disagree about just what it is.

What I propose here is to show how a close examination of the material appearance of this text in its manuscript setting may help to shed light on the question of its identity. I do not mean a paleographical analysis of the script but a study of the way the scribe presented it and laid it out on the page, punctuated it, and invested it with a number of so-called visual cues.[1] Medieval scribes had many means at their disposal for varying their presentation of written texts including (1) division into sections, (2) variations in letter size and spacing, (3) use of color highlighting, (4) capitalization, and (5) alternative forms of pointing or punctuation.[2] It is my contention that

[1] When describing the objectives and methods of diplomatics, Leonard Boyle (who defines diplomatics as the application of the principle of literary criticism to documentary sources: who wrote it, what does it say, how is it written, when, where, by whom?) wrote, "Like any form of literary criticism diplomatics...demands a thorough competence in the language of the document under scrutiny, of the handwriting, scribal practices of the period..." ("Diplomatics," in *Medieval Studies: An Introduction*, ed. James M. Powell, 2d ed. (Syracuse, 1992), 82-113, at 89.

[2] To my knowledge the most extensive and illuminating discussion of formatting (the layout of the writing on the page) and the use of graphic and spatial cues is by Katherine O'Brien O'Keeffe, *Visible Song: Transitional Literacy in Old English*

an analysis attentive to the specific choices made by the scribe in his copying of this text may reveal how he intended it to be read and understood, and this in turn may bring out what kind of a text he thought it to be. Let me add that previous examinations have held this to be a conventional, typical example of eleventh-century copying, but I am convinced that these earlier analyses did not look at it closely enough. It incorporates some unusual traits for which there is no provision in modern printing, and earlier editions, of which my own with two French colleagues in 1995 is the most recent, did not take account of these.[3] What follows is my attempt to do so.

First a brief description of the text in question with reference to its author, place and date of composition, subject matter, and manuscript tradition is in order.[4] The *Conventum*, as it has come to be known from the title given it by its first editor in his published edition in 1647,[5] is a narrative about a dispute between the Duke of Aquitaine/Count of Poitou, William IV (993-1030), and a castellan, Hugh, lord of Lusignan (d. ca. 1030), over lands and castles claimed by the latter. On good terms to begin with, their relations turn hostile when the lord/count uses deception and brute force to deny the claims of his vassal. The latter finally rebels bringing about a crisis prior to a final peaceful resolution.

Internal evidence suggests that an anonymous author, most likely a cleric, wrote this story somewhere in north-central Aquitaine, probably in Angoulême, around 1030. The steady intensification of the conflict occupies most of the narrative, which takes place in and around well-known castles in Poitou, La Marche, and the Angoumois, and involves altogether eighteen counts, viscounts, castellans, and prelates other than the two protagonists. Although all the characters and places are historically attested,

---

Verse (Cambridge, 1990), 204. The only limitation on the applicability of her findings for my study here is that she is analyzing vernacular verse as opposed to the Latin prose of my text.

[3] George Beech, Yves Chauvin, and Georges Pon, *Le Conventum (vers 1030): Un précurseur aquitain des premières épopées*, Publications romanes et françaises 212 (Geneva, 1995).

[4] The text survives in a manuscript from about 1060 (Paris, BnF, lat. 5927, pp. 265-80) and two later copies made from the same: Saint Petersburg, Public Library Saltykov-Schedrine, MS. Lat. E v. IVN3, fols. 89v-93 (ca. 1100), and Paris, BnF, lat. 9767, fols. 62v-66r (fifteenth century). On the manuscript record, see Beech, Chauvin, and Pon, *Le Conventum*, 8-11, 113-18.

[5] Jean Besly, *Histoire des comtes de Poictou et des ducs de Guyenne* (Paris, 1647), 288-94bis.

there are reasons for believing that the events narrated are to some degree fictional. There is no corroboration for any of these "events" from other writings of the time (see below, pp. 65-66), and in addition to this the author tells his story in ways more reminiscent of the early epics than of historical or documentary sources. He presents all the essential developments in the narrative through the words of the actors themselves in live speech in the present tense (41 percent of the whole). A second basic element is his own authorial commentary where he himself reveals the inner thoughts and motivations of his characters and interprets their actions. Finally he has organized his account in a series of episodes in which he develops his narrative through the modified repetition of themes and motifs, another trait of the early poetic epics. Modern scholars disagree as to the nature and identity of the *Conventum*. Most hold it to be a documentary text in the general category of charters—a *convenientia* or treaty, a *memorandum*, or even a complaint (*planctus*). A minority view is my own: that it is some kind of literary text and possibly a prose precursor of the earliest epics. The lack of any other comparable texts from the medieval period explains present uncertainty on this matter.[6]

THE MANUSCRIPT SETTING OF THE *CONVENTUM*

One question needs to be asked about the *Conventum* before proceeding to its analysis: is the text in the earliest manuscript, Paris, BnF, lat. 5927, the original composition from the pen of the author himself, or a later copy? Almost certainly the answer is that this is a later copy. As just mentioned, the anonymous author is thought to have written the *Conventum* just before 1030 when the two protagonists, the count and Hugh, were still alive, whereas manuscript 5927 has been dated to ca. 1060, some 30 years later. But the anonymous author could have written his narrative later, so this discrepancy need not rule out the possibility of the version in 5927 being the original. More decisive, however, is the fact the same scribe who entered the *Conventum* into 5927 was also the copyist of the texts which immediately precede and follow it. Thus after finishing the chronicle of Ademar of Chabannes and the royal act of Charles the Bald attached to it, he left two lines vacant (see Fig. 1) and began copying the *Conventum*.

[6] All of these issues are discussed at length in Beech, Chauvin, and Pon, *Le Conventum*, and in George Beech, "Narrative Structures and Techniques in the *Conventum* of Aquitaine ca. 1030," in *The Eleventh Century: Proceedings of the Third International Medieval Latin Congress, Cambridge, 9-12 Sept. 1998* (forthcoming).

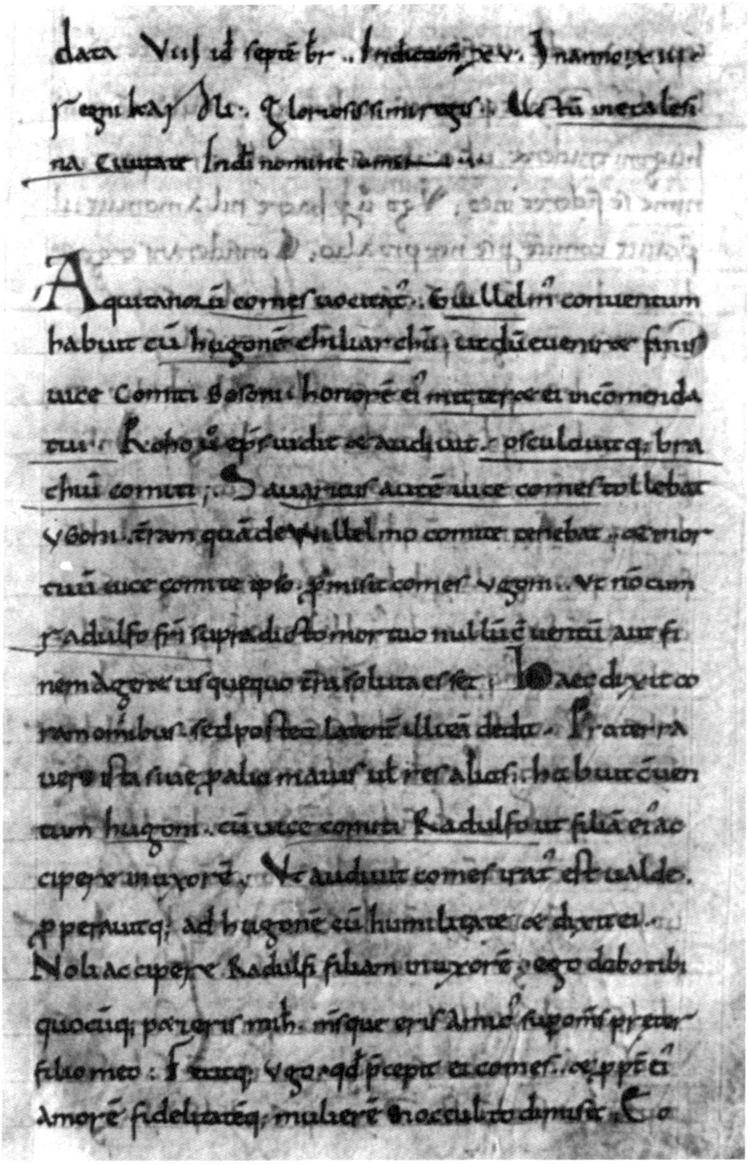

Figure 1. Paris, Bibliothèque nationale, lat. 5927 p. 265
Cliché Bibliothèque nationale de France, Paris

After finishing it, he again left two lines vacant and began his copy of Einhard's *Vita Karoli Magni*. In order for the version in 5927 to be the autograph original there would have to have been the following sequence. After finishing the chronicle of Ademar the scribe would have stopped his copying, and then as an autonomous author in his own right, he would have composed his own narrative into the manuscript. Then he would have reverted to his earlier role of copyist for entering the *Vita* of Einhard. This seems highly unlikely. Instead what presumably happened is that the scribe, working in the scriptorium of the abbey of Saint-Cybard of Angoulême,[7] drew on one, two, or three separate manuscripts from the monastic library for all three of the texts he copied into what became 5927. Thus he may have copied from the original composition of the *Conventum* which would have been only thirty years old at the time and may have been written by a monk from Saint-Cybard and then consigned to the abbey library; but this is all conjecture.

The juxtaposition of the *Conventum* with Ademar's chronicle may itself be of interest for the problem of its identity. The scribe gives no hint as to his reasons for inserting the *Conventum* after Ademar's chronicle, but the grouping of apparently unrelated texts is a commonplace in the history of medieval manuscripts. Thousands of those surviving bring together texts which have no obvious relationship with one another and are often unaccompanied by any clarification from the scribe. Nonetheless there is always the inclination to look for some kind of affinity between juxtaposed texts even when the scribe provides no illumination. In this instance there can be no doubt that Ademar's chronicle and the *Conventum* have much in common. The authors of both lived and wrote at precisely the same time —the late 1020s—in the same place—Angoulême—and with one important exception the same historical figures dominate the action in the same geographical region in their separate accounts of the recent past (the latter part of Book 3 in the case of the chronicle).[8]

The important exception is Hugh, one of the two leading characters in the *Conventum* narrative, who is never mentioned by Ademar, in sharp contrast to the count, who has an equally prominent role in both texts. A second notable difference is the "events" reported by the two authors, i.e.,

[7] The most likely place of origin of Paris, BnF, lat. 5927 according to the editor of the new edition of the *Chronicon* of Ademar of Chabannes (ed. Pascale Bourgain, Corpus christianorum, Continuatio mediaevalis 129 [Turnhout, 1999], xv).

[8] Ademar, *Chronicon*, 3.43-70 (ed. Bourgain, 164-89).

conflicts, parleys, campaigns, battles, treaties, etc. Ademar makes not the slightest reference to any of the "events" central to the *Conventum*, and vice versa. Though their common subject is the same prominent nobles (with the exception of Hugh's absence from the chronicle) in the same region at the same time period, it is as if the two authors were writing two different histories in their accounts of "events." Their respective portrayals of the central figure, the count, constitute the third striking difference between the two texts. Whereas Ademar presents him as a great figure of heroic dimensions, in the *Conventum* he emerges as a shifty, devious, indecisive, and finally treacherous lord.

When he decided to copy the *Conventum* directly after Ademar's chronicle in his manuscript, the scribe of 5927, who had probably come across the narrative in the library of Saint-Cybard and who perhaps knew the author, must have been aware of both the close similarities and the radical contrasts between the two. What did he think the *Conventum* was and why did he copy it there? One recent scholar thinks he may have put it there as additional documentation, just as modern historians insert appendices at the end of their works.[9] Another possibility might be that the scribe, struck more by the contrasts than the similarities between the two accounts, appended it here as an alternate view of the count. Or could it be that Ademar of Chabannes, who rewrote his work several times in the late 1020s and early 1030s, himself copied the *Conventum* as an addendum to his chronicle in an earlier now lost manuscript after coming across it and deciding to incorporate it into a later version of his history? If so, he did not in fact carry through with his project, but the scribe of 5927 some thirty years later may have decided to be faithful to his prototype and thus have copied both texts into his new manuscript.

The fact that one or the other decided to place the *Conventum* after the chronicle reveals that the person who made that choice saw these two texts in some way as comparable to one another. The *Conventum* owes its survival to having been copied into a manuscript containing two long narrative texts, not into a cartulary. Documentary texts such as charters, notices, treaties, and *convenientiae* (what most modern scholars consider the *Conventum* to be—above, p. 63) have usually survived as individual documents in original form or as copies in cartularies. I think it is significant that the contemporary to whom we owe the survival of the *Conventum*, whether Ademar or the scribe of 5927, copied it into a manuscript containing a

[9] Ademar, *Chronicon*, ed. Bourgain, xv.

chronicle and a biography. Whatever kind of text he thought it to be, he considered it to belong to the realm of narrative not documentary sources.

PUNCTUATION IN THE *CONVENTUM*

From this consideration of the manuscript context of the *Conventum* and the relation of the copy in 5927 to the original, the enquiry now turns now to an examination of what I earlier called unusual features or traits in the scribe's presentation of it. The first of these is one specialized use he makes of pointing or punctuation.[10] A good part of his pointing is grammatical. He closely follows ancient practices in using strong, intermediate, and weak punctuation (different combinations of and positions of points) to denote ends of sentences, and internally, to separate subordinate from independent clauses.[11] But in addition to this he frequently uses internal punctuation which cannot be explained grammatically but must serve some other function(s). These non-grammatical cases fall into three categories. In the first he frequently uses points with the personal names of the people figuring in the narrative, above all with the two main characters, Hugh and the count. In the opening line, for instance, he uses two points (strong punctuation) *before* the name "Guillelmus"—"Aquitanorum comes vocitatus ..Guillelmus conventum" (see Fig. 1), then in line six the same strong punctuation accompanies the name Hugh, but this time *after* instead of in front of the name—"tollebat Hugoni..terram quam" (Fig. 1, line 6).

In fact when the scribe points a name he nearly always does so in this way; rare are the examples where it precedes the name. It will be noticed furthermore that three words later in this same sentence (Fig. 1, line 6) he does not punctuate the name Guillelmus when he mentions him for a second time. Throughout the entire text he points Hugh's name eleven times and that of the count five times, even though he names both of them much more often (Hugh over one hundred times). This means either that he punctuates at random or that he is doing so selectively under specific circumstances. The scribe also pointed the names of seven of the other people who appear in his narrative, invariably when he first mentions them. Of

[10] I made a preliminary, incomplete, study of the scribe's punctuation of the text in Beech, Chauvin, and Pon, *Le Conventum* (pp. 80-82), as did my collaborators (pp. 120-21).

[11] M. B. Parkes, *Pause and Effect: An Introduction to the History of Punctuation in the West* (Berkeley, 1993), provides a background for the entire question of pointing by medieval scribes.

these seven, only one, Fulk (Count Fulk Nerra of Anjou), has his name pointed on some of his later appearances in the story, whereas the others are left without any punctuation when they reappear on the scene. In addition to these seven who are named or appear more than once, eleven other people enter into the narrative, but all have only minor roles during a single appearance and the scribe *does not point any* of their names.

The meaning of this pointing system cannot be in any doubt. By punctuating the names of nine of the twenty figures in the text when he names them as they first appear in the story, he is highlighting or calling attention to them and forecasting that they will be of importance in what is to come. As commas, colons, semi-colons, and periods in printed texts today denote to the silent reader a pause (or a dropping of the voice to one reading aloud), so the pointing of the name in this manuscript is the scribe's way of warning the reader to slow down and pay attention. By leaving the names of all the secondary characters unpointed in all subsequent appearances, the scribe is only alerting the reader to concentrate all his skill on the two major characters and not to be distracted by those who are only marginally relevant.

And the scribe's reason for only selectively pointing the names of Hugh and the count *after* their initial appearances was to reserve this visual cue for moments of special importance. One of these occurred when the count failed to make an agreement with Hugh as he had promised, and Hugh lost land as a result—"nihilque finem fecit..Hugone..et terra sua Ugo non habuit" (56-57).[12] The scribe underlines the count's failure to keep his promise, "in no way made an agreement with Hugh," by punctuating the latter's name and thereby calling attention to his losses.

The scribe also occasionally used non-grammatical pointing to highlight events he considered important in the unfolding of the story. One forty-line episode in the narrative (150-90) features the count secretly plotting with another baron against Hugh. The count demands that Hugh accompany him on a distant expedition, thereby leaving his lands, castles, and family exposed and unprotected. While on the expedition the count repeatedly dismisses the unknowing Hugh's growing anxiety that his enemy will take advantage of his absence. The denouement of the entire episode comes when the latter attacks as Hugh had feared, destroying, burning, and taking

[12] Henceforth numbers in parentheses following textual citations from the *Conventum* refer to the lines of the Latin edition of this narrative in Beech, Chauvin, and Pon, *Le Conventum*, pp. 123-38.

prisoners. The author spells out Hugh's losses in a four-line sentence which he pointed nine times: "Quando fuit ugo ad liziniaco.erat Bernardus ad confolensis castrum..et captum habebat burgum..et barrium..et habebat omnia incensa..accepta spolia.et viros captos..satisque alio malifacto..cucurrit nuntius ad ugonem.dixit ei" (178-82). In other comparable but less important passages in the narrative the author punctuated much less often and only when called for grammatically. Here he seems to be stressing the gravity of the count's treachery, and of Hugh's losses, by pauses after the enumeration of each new disaster.

Other instances where he punctuates for emphasis and not grammatical reasons are his accounts of Hugh's losses at Mouzeuil and Thouars (60-67) and at Gencay (276-80), Hugh's warning to the count (251-58), his demands of the count (279-80), his premonitions of being betrayed (270-71), and his proposal for a final settlement of their dispute (297-303).

Sometimes it is a single word or phrase which the author wants to bring out in relief: "In hunc vero conventum..mandavit comes pro vice comite radulfo" (27-28). In all the author makes use of *conventum*, a key word in his narrative, twenty-two times, but only six times does he point it in this way, each time because the context gives it a special significance. Another illustration of this special use of pointing comes at the beginning of the concluding episode when the author writes: "Antequam ugo vel sui homines..nullum malum fecissent..adprehenderunt homines comite" (280-82). The punctuation between *homines* and *nullum malum*, and again after *fecissent*, in no way justified grammatically, is intended to make the reader pause and thereby give extra weight to the assertion that neither Hugh nor his men were the aggressors in the violence about to be committed. Finally the scribe used pointing as a means of calling attention to the castles where the action of the narrative took place when he first mentions them by name.[13]

COLOR HIGHLIGHTING

The scribe of this text had another means at his disposal for calling special attention to specific words and letters and that was color highlighting. Throughout the entire narrative he regularly signaled the begin-

[13] *Vicvedoni.* (83); *Sivriaco..* (93); *Coacus.* (117); *mallavallis.* (122); *lemovicas..* (153); *liziniaco.* (179); *confolensis..* (180); *Gentiaco.* (191); *turrem metulo.* (226); *extra civitatem.* (233). One exception to this is Thouars castle, pointed only when named for the third time: *Toarcinse.* (74).

nings and ends of sentences by highlighting in red ink (which contrasted with the dark he used for other letters) the first letter (a capital) of the first word in each new sentence, and by using red for one of the two or three points after the last. These were his equivalents for the modern period at the end of a sentence. His highlighting consisted of his adding red either as a background to part of the capital letter or as an internal filler where appropriate as in the letters P and O.[14] His purpose was obviously to make each individual sentence stand out more clearly than it would have with black ink alone.

On four occasions he modified his practice slightly but significantly by writing initial capitals in solid red rather than using that color as a background highlighting to black majuscules (1, 25, 92, 191).[15] This is his way of calling attention to the beginning of a new section in the narrative, and this he makes unmistakably clear by creating a break in the continuity of his text in the line immediately preceding each of these red capitals.[16] He does this by leaving a vacant space after the end of the preceding sentence. He thus divides his 341-line narrative into four sections; I take it that he thereby intended to convey that each of these four parts somehow constituted a separate entity with a beginning and end, but that taken together they all contributed to the larger whole.[17]

That these are in fact structural divisions in his text is, I believe, confirmed by an analysis of the narrative as a whole. Each of these four sections begins with a change of characters, of place or location, and to a substantial degree, though not completely, of subject matter from what had gone before. On this I have elaborated at length elsewhere.[18] What is rele-

[14] Eleventh-century scribes from nearby Angers used color highlighting with initial capitals in a similar way; Jean Vezin, *Les scriptoria d'Angers au XIe siecle*, Bibliothèque de l'École des hautes études, 4e section, Sciences historiques et philologiques, fasc. 322 (Paris, 1974), 149.

[15] The initial capitals in biblical lessons in an eleventh-century Angevin liturgical book were written in solid vermillion; Vezin, *Les scriptoria*, 150.

[16] This was also a customary practice of eleventh-century Angevin scribes; Vezin, *Les scriptoria*, 154.

[17] Tenth-century Anglo-Saxon and eleventh-century Angevin scribes marked out sectional divisions in their texts through similar use of spacing and capitalization, though not apparently through the use of solid red coloring; Vezin, *Les scriptoria*, 154; O'Keeffe, *Visible Song*, 157.

[18] Not having noticed this use of solid red lettering at the beginnings of new sections I did not take account of it in my earlier discussions of the structure of the

vant to the present context is that the scribe has combined two techniques to achieve his graphic equivalent to the paragraph in modern printing. Where he differs from the latter is in using solid red capitals instead of indentation of the first line to indicate the beginning of a new paragraph (section).

In addition to using red (either highlighting or solid color) for capitals at the beginnings of sentences, and pointing at the end, the scribe also highlighted capitals and punctuation within sentences (on personal names) but did this so rarely that no coherent pattern may be detected and the practice does not seem significant.

CAPITALIZATION

Capitalization afforded still another opportunity for the scribe to modify the presentation of his text. Although his usage on the whole resembles that of modern printing, particularly in the capitalization of the first letter of words beginning new sentences, he differed significantly in other contexts, both using capitals in unexpected situations, and failing to use them where they might have seemed to be called for. Sometimes his practices seem to have been random, perhaps for decoration, but in others he was obviously guiding his reader. To give an idea of the range of different uses he makes of capitals, I will list all his variants but will only comment on those intended in my judgment to guide his reader/narrator. With regard to color he normally wrote his capitals in solid black ink, though as just described he highlighted in red at the beginnings of sentences and in solid red to mark new sections. He made his capitals in two different sizes, what I would call *large*—that is as tall as the upper strokes in his b's and l's, or approximately twice as large as his minuscules or lowercase letters—and *extra large*—three times the size, both vertically and horizontally, of his lowercase letters.[19] He reserved these latter, i.e., the extra-large capitals, to mark the beginnings of new sentences, clearly for better visibility (see Fig. 1: *Aquitanorum*, line 1; *Roho*, line 4; *Savaricus*, line 5; *Frater*, line 10). He used capitalization *within* sentences only for personal names (never place names) but by no means invariably, and his variants deserve attention. Finally, twenty times he began new sentences well out to the left of

---

Conventum; Beech, Chauvin, and Pon, *Le Conventum*, 29-36.

[19] The late-tenth-century scribe of the *Exeter Book* of Old English verse also made use of two different sizes of initial capitals; O'Keeffe, *Visible Song*, 156.

the left margin of his text which he otherwise scrupulously observed, and this practice is noteworthy.

I turn first to his use of capitals for personal names *within* sentences. The contrast between the scribe's treatment of the names of his two principal characters, Hugh and the count, is interesting. When he calls the count by his personal name *Guillelmus* (six times; 6, 39, 43, 45, 47, 95) he always capitalizes. Most of the time, however, he refers to him as the count, *comes*, and the *c* he never capitalizes (except at the beginning of one sentence [25]). Why he makes this distinction is problematic; differences in context do not account for it. Could it be that pronouncing the personal name of a dignitary as opposed to his title of office was to assume a familiarity normally reserved for his intimates and that capitalization was a way of showing deference or respect, whereas referring to the same person by his title of office was more impersonal and less in need of such deference?

When the author spoke of Hugh—who bore no title and hence is always addressed by his personal name—he almost never capitalized the first letter (three times out of over one hundred references; 50, 63, 113). The contrast is thus striking. Regardless of the count's behavior in the story (which the author presents as despicable), his superior aristocratic status elevates him above all others including his counterpart Hugh, who, even though noble in thought and action, still belongs to a lower social category. Through his use of, and withholding of, capitalization for these two men's names the author explicitly acknowledges this distinction, as does Hugh through his deferential manner in addressing the count as "meus senior."[20]

But when dealing with the secondary characters in the story the author is less consistent. He tends to capitalize their names on their first appearances as if to introduce them, and then to revert to lowercase for subsequent mentions. Four characters, however, never have their names capitalized. For three of them this is not surprising since they enter the scene only once each and then briefly, but the case of Fulk, count of Anjou (the famous Fulk Nerra) is puzzling. He figures prominently in the action in two different contexts, having a central role and speaking lines of his own in direct discourse, but the author never capitalizes his name, and after identifying him as count in his first appearance, thereafter refers to him simply as Fulk. Quite different is his treatment of Ralph, viscount of Thouars, who plays an important secondary role and also speaks for himself in direct

[20] George Beech, "The Lord/Dependant (Vassal) Relationship: A Case Study from Aquitaine c. 1030," *Journal of Medieval History* 24 (1998): 1-30, at 8-11.

speech. In his first naming of Ralph, whom he also initially identifies as viscount, the author leaves the *r* in lowercase (8) but then capitalizes it in all the later references (12, 15, 28, 33, 41, 46, 47, 48, 49, 50, 52). Obviously it would be unwise to attach too much significance to these cases. At the same time the overall utility of name capitalization in the text cannot be overlooked: the initial capital made the name stand out from the rest of the written text and was a practical guide for the reader.[21]

The final distinctive usage of capitalization in this text comes at the end when the author concludes with the statement: FINIUNT CONVENTI INTER COMITEM ET UGONEM. By capitalizing every letter as well as highlighting them all in red, he sets this sentence off from the rest of his text and thus brings his narrative to an end with a flourish.

LETTER SPACING

In addition to varying the sizes of letters (capitals), this author also conveyed meaning through letter *spacing*. A close look at his script (see Fig. 1) shows that he has broadened certain words by spreading out the letters (leaving more space between them). For instance: line 1, *Guillelmus*; line 5, *Savaricus*; line 9, *Haec*; etc. Quite clearly he did this intentionally for purposes of emphasis, to draw attention. The words so treated are usually personal names at the beginnings of sentences but not invariably. By spreading out *Haec* (line 9, "these things") when he comments that the count had made a commitment to Hugh publicly which he then secretly broke—"*These things* he said in the presence of everyone"—he is using letter spacing to stress the promises made by the count. Similar examples are scattered throughout the entire narrative.

EXTRA-MARGINAL CAPITALS

The last category of this author's visual or graphic cues concerns variations in what might be called his layout of his text on the manuscript page. He planned his copying to give himself space for twenty-three lines, separated by equal intervals, on each page and rigorously observed margins on both sides, particularly on the left. An occasional slight unevenness on

[21] The mid-tenth-century scribe of the *Salomon and Saturn* poems similarly capitalized the initial letters of the two principal characters (O'Keeffe, *Visible Song*, 73), whereas an eleventh-century scribe from Angers capitalized important personal names (but all the letters, not just the first one) in his copy of lives of the bishops of that town (Vezin, *Les scriptoria*, 155).

the right margin resulted from his failure to anticipate correctly the amount of space he would need for the last words in the line. A small number of times he deliberately chose not to respect his margins in two different ways, and both are significant. I have already dealt with the first of these (above, p. 70—his leaving the last part of a line vacant on the right margin after the end of sentence (on three occasions; 25, 91, 191) to signify the end of a section in his narrative. His other modification of his standard page came when twenty times he began new sentences well out to the left of his left margin (47, 51, 68, 92, 129, 143, 152, 161, 167, 174, 175, 186, 189, 191, 195, 201, 229, 258, 317, 323). This is yet another technique for calling attention to the sentence just beginning.[22] If he had done this every time a new sentence began at the left margin, the previous one having ended at the right margin, one would be tempted to believe that this move had no meaning other than his desire to take advantage of the fact that pure chance will always dictate that on any page with controlled margins, a certain number of new sentences will begin on a new line on the left. In such a case he might merely have been trying to break the monotony of the uniform left margin in favor of some variation, perhaps for decorative purposes only. But this is not the case here; a third of the time (nine out of twenty-nine times) he does not begin new sentences extra-marginally but instead observes his margin. This inevitably leads to the question: what motivated him to violate his margin two-thirds of the time but not the other third?

Given the fact that this narrative not only consists of four major episodes or sections, but also that these in turn break down into sub-sections or phases, it is conceivable that the author used extra-marginal beginnings to highlight these latter. Further, as noted earlier (above, p. 63), the author uses three different types of statements to tell the story: (1) impersonal narrative in the third person in the present perfect tense; "the count did this" (this includes indirect discourse; "the count ordered Hugh"); (2) direct discourse or live speech in the present tense, where the story develops through the words of the actors themselves; and (3) authorial commentary in the present perfect tense, where he himself reveals the inner thoughts

[22] On extra-marginal capitals see J. P. Gumbert, "La page intelligible: Quelques remarques," in *Vocabulaire du livre et de l'écriture au Moyen Âge: Actes de la table ronde, Paris 24-26 septembre 1987*, ed. Olga Weijers, Études sur le vocabulaire intellectuel du Moyen Âge 2 (Turnhout, 1989), 111-19.

and motivations of his characters and interprets their actions.[23] Thus a further question could be posed: did he use extra-marginal beginnings to single out any one particular kind of statement as opposed to the others: direct speech, for instance, which he clearly favors for the decisive moments in his plot?

An analysis of the twenty extra-marginal sentences and the nine marginal ones from these two perspectives yields the following results. Seven of the twenty extra-marginal sentences are the beginnings of new phases within the four episodes, involving changes in characters or type or scene of action. At the same time none of the nine new sentences which respect the left margin coincide with the beginnings of new phases: all are continuations of phases already underway. Thus more than half the time (sixteen of twenty-nine instances) the author's decision to avail himself of extra-marginal space *may* have been motivated by his desire to point out new phases in the narrative when the opportunity arose—i.e., when a new sentence happened to begin at the left margin (seven times)—and to conform to the margin when a sentence of this kind did not signal a change in character, scene, or action (nine times).

But thirteen of the twenty extra-marginal sentences do not denote new phases, so other considerations must have moved the author to call attention to them in this way. Classifying these thirteen sentences into the three different categories of (1) third person narrative, (2) direct speech, and (3) authorial commentary does *not* lead to the conclusion that he reserved extra-marginal beginnings for any one of those to the exclusion of the others. Instead, those thirteen sentences include all three types of statement, live speech accounting for six or nearly half the instances.

Thus this author did not make use of extra-marginal beginnings for one single overriding purpose. When the opportunity offered itself he took advantage of it to call attention to the beginnings of new phases in his narrative, but in those cases where there was no change in action he used extra-marginal beginnings to highlight speeches, to narrate in the third person, and to make his own commentaries. And his choosing not to underline the same kinds of statements about a third of the time leads me to believe that he was attributing greater significance to those sentences which he began out in the left margin than to those left in their customary place.

[23] For an analysis of these elements in the *Conventum*, see Beech, Chauvin, and Pon, *Le Conventum*, 41-46, 47-61.

So far, I have described and discussed the different usages of the scribe in copying the text of the *Conventum* into manuscript 5927: (1) punctuation; (2) color highlighting; (3) capitalization; (4) variations in letter spacing; and (5) division into sections. I have tried to show that he varied the ways in which he applied each of these graphic practices to accomplish specific ends; the extra-large capitals and color highlighting serve the purpose of making individual sentences, and especially those in live speech—the core of his narrative—stand out more clearly than otherwise; solid red capitals denote the beginnings of new sections; extra-marginal capitals point to shifts or new phases in the action, to the speeches of his actors, and to his own commentaries. Capitalization of personal names and non-grammatical punctuation *within* sentences highlight the appearances, words, actions, and sufferings of individual characters. As noted above (p. 62) modern editions of the *Conventum*, including my own, have not taken account of most of these variant usages, and in any case the conventions of modern printing do not provide for them.

I am well aware there is a danger in exaggerating the importance of these usages, namely of seeing a system in the scribe's use of them where he may have had none. To resist that temptation I have concentrated on those practices such as non-grammatical pointing within sentences which are too systematic and consistent to have been the whim of a copyist indulging in flights of fancy, perhaps to ease his boredom. I am more reserved about his use of extra-marginal sentences because they could have served several purposes.

There is evidence, furthermore, that in copying this text the scribe went to greater lengths in giving graphic and visual emphasis to individual characters, words, speeches, sequences, etc. than he did normally. For other examples of his copying exist in the same manuscript 5927; for instance he has been identified as the scribe of part of the chronicle of Ademar of Chabannes and for the following *Vita* of Einhard.[24] A comparison of his writing practices in those two texts shows beyond any doubt that he made greater use of all the techniques in question, and especially internal non-grammatical punctuation, in his copy of the *Conventum* than he did in the other two.[25] Why would he have done this?

[24] Ademar of Chabannes, *Chronicon* (ed. Bourgain, xviii).

[25] In Paris, BnF, lat. 5927 he copied pages 5-50 and 243-65 of the *Chronicon* of Ademar and pages 280-302 of the *Vita Karoli Magni* in addition to pages 265-80 of the *Conventum*. I compared his copying practices in these three texts to see how fre-

Before proceeding further it must be noted that the scribe may have had no responsibility at all for laying out and marking his copy of the *Conventum* in 5927. The scribe of his master text, perhaps the author of the story, may have done all of this himself, with the result that the copyist of 5927 simply reproduced the manuscript as he found it in the library where he worked. Or, the other possibility, if the author (or an intermediate scribe) had written the narrative without any markings, then the scribe of 5927 will have formatted it and added visual and spatial cues of his own initiative. Whatever may be the correct explanation is of little importance for the interpretation of the punctuation and layout of the text. If it was the author who pointed it, he did so in such a way as to convey to his readers what kind of a narrative it was and how he intended it to be read. If it was the scribe, and he had no instructions from the author, he did so in accordance with what he thought the *Conventum* to be and how it ought to be read.[26] In either case the layout and punctuation of this otherwise enigmatic text may well contain clues as to its identity—and the search for that identity was what led to this inquiry to begin with: "It is my contention that an analysis attentive to the specific choices made by the scribe in his copying of this text can reveal how he intended it to be read and understood, and this in turn may bring out what kind of a text he thought it to be" (above, pp. 61-62).

The combination of internal non-grammatical punctuation, the capitalization of personal names, red highlighting, and better sentence visibility would obviously have benefited a silent reader of this text. But I suspect that the scribe intended these markings principally for a narrator or jongleur reading the narrative aloud to an audience. I suspect that the text of the *Conventum* in 5927 is the written version of an oral story. The author, or the scribe (if they are of his making), intended these various visual cues

---

quently he made use of pointing, capitalization, rubrication, intrusion into the left margin, etc., in each of them. In Einhard's *Vita* he made almost no use of any of these techniques, in sharp contrast to his marking of the *Conventum*, and the same holds true for his pages 5-50 of Ademar. For the pages at the end of Ademar immediately preceeding the *Conventum* (i.e., 243-65) he had recourse to all of these techniques but much less frequently than in the latter text.

[26] In this case one would have to inquire about the origin of the system he used —and I would contend that the evidence presented in this paper demonstrates that the scribe of 5927 did not punctuate at random but took a systematic approach to his text. Presumably he did not invent it himself but borrowed it from usages encountered in his readings or earlier work as a copyist.

as warnings to the narrator that he should not only pause and modify his voice, but also convey emotion through gestures, movements, and facial expressions at the indicated places. Seeing these scribal devices as visual cues for a narrator making a live presentation would be fully consistent with other internal evidence favoring the view that the *Conventum* is an oral text. The predominance of live speech, the importance of authorial commentary, the use of tense switching, and the reference to manual gestures all argue for the same belief.[27] The analysis of the 5927 text of the *Conventum* from the diplomatic perspective presented in this paper will, then, if I am correct, serve to strengthen the hypothesis that this is a written version of an oral prose narrative.

One way of testing the validity of this hypothesis would be to compare the layout and marking of the *Conventum* in 5927 with that of other contemporary texts thought or known to be oral narratives. Unfortunately this does not appear to be possible at the present time: as noted in the introduction to this paper, one of the principal obstacles to the identification of the *Conventum* has been the apparent lack of other stories which it resembles in structure, language, narrative techniques, subject matter, etc. And any comparison of the punctuation system of the *Conventum* with those of the scattering of eleventh-century texts with which it has certain affinities—e.g., the *Passion of Clermont*, the lives of Saint Leger and Saint Alexis, the Gospels, and the earliest epics such as the *Chanson de Roland*—is complicated by the fact that none of the published editions of these works reproduce that information in precise detail. Only direct consultation of their manuscripts would make that possible.

The punctuation systems of a number of medieval texts have been subjected to close analysis in recent years but without exception they differ so markedly from the *Conventum* in language, form, structure, and sometimes date of composition that they bear little resemblance to it in formatting and graphic and spatial cues. The Old English poems studied by Katherine O'Keeffe invite comparison with the *Conventum* by reason of their dates, tenth and eleventh centuries, but a major concern of the scribes who copied them, pointing the ends of lines of verse, has no parallel in the Latin prose text from Aquitaine. A distinctive feature of the latter, selectively singling out important characters through capitalization and pointing of names even within sentences, is non-existent in the Anglo-Saxon verse rid-

[27] See Beech, Chauvin, and Pon, *Le Conventum*, 78-86 for discussion of these points.

dles from the late tenth century, due to their lack of personal names.[28] Nor does a comparison with literary texts from a later period prove more fruitful. For instance the punctuation and layout of the late medieval manuscripts of the romances of Chrétien de Troyes appear to be much less concentrated and systematic than that of the *Conventum*.[29]

The failure of these preliminary attempts to find parallel texts which might shed light on the question as to whether the *Conventum* is punctuated for oral performance does not invalidate the hypothesis that such is the case, but simply leaves the question open. Further comparisons with manuscripts of Latin prose texts closer to the date of 5927 offer the best hope for answering it.

If the *Conventum* is, as argued in this essay, a Latin prose narrative intended for oral performance, then several questions immediately arise. For whom was it intended and under what circumstances, in what kind of setting? The silence of the author and the text itself on these matters means that one can only speculate about them. Yet the types of people involved in the story and the nature of the dispute presented hardly leave room for doubt: it was above all an aristocratic audience which would have appreciated a narrative of this kind. Historical sources are full of accounts of interminable struggles over land and castles between members of this class at this time. One can easily imagine that the author wrote this account of the troubles of Hugh and the count, fictionalizing them to some extent to enhance the drama, for nobles of the Angoulême region. They would have listened with particular interest to the story both because they may have known the two protagonists but also because disputes of this kind were central to their daily lives. The length of the *Conventum* (341 lines), moreover, encourages the belief that the author had in mind just such a presentation when he wrote it, for other studies have suggested that oral storytelling in the early eleventh century typically involved narratives having 200-400 lines.[30] During the amount of time necessary to present (not per-

[28] Craig Williamson, ed., *The Old English Riddles of the Exeter Book* (Chapel Hill, 1977).

[29] G. Hasenohr, "De l'écriture à la lecture: Reflections sur les manuscrits d'Érec et Énide," in *Les manuscrits de Chrétien de Troyes*, ed. Keith Busby et al., 2 vols. (Amsterdam, 1995), 1:97-130.

[30] Jean Rychner, *La chanson de geste: Essai sur l'art épique des jongleurs* (Geneva, 1955), 48-54; Beech, Chauvin, and Pon, *Le Conventum*, 101.

form) a story of this length a narrator could capture and hold the attention of his audience.

Finally there is the question of the language of the *Conventum* which has always been viewed as a Latin narrative. In fact there is a good possibility that despite the Latin orthography, declensions, and conjugations, the version in Paris 5927 is a written form of the local vernacular, possibly Romance but more likely Occitan. If the latter had not yet become a written language, and this development took place in the eleventh century, the scribe would have had no choice but to use Latin orthography, etc., for his text, and the narrator, recognizing it for what it was, would automatically have presented it in the vernacular. Thus the story would have been accessible to an aristocratic audience which could hardly have understood it if the jongleur had given it the Latin pronunciation.[31]

But once again it must be recognized that this is pure speculation. Only the uncovering of another narrative of a similar type or new evidence of some other kind about the *Conventum* will lead to a better understanding of what it is.

[31] Roger Wright, "On Editing Latin Texts Written by Romance Speakers," in *Linguistic Studies in Medieval Spanish*, ed. Ray Harris-Northall and Thomas D. Cravens (Madison, 1991), 191-208.

La tradition de l'ombre: Les actes sous le regard des archivistes médiévaux (Saint-Denis, XIIe-XVe siècle)

Olivier Guyotjeannin

Depuis un siècle et demi, la diplomatique médiévale n'a cessé de perfectionner et d'enrichir son questionnaire sur la «tradition» des actes: d'abord dominée par une approche utilitaire, critique philologique des témoins ou quête élargie des *deperdita*, elle commence à regarder du côté de la réception des actes. Que les recherches sur les cartulaires aient ici joué le rôle de catalyseur ne saurait étonner, puisque ces monuments emblématiques de l'érudition médiévale sont aussi des formes de compilation, qui appellent le plus évidemment, et le plus facilement, l'importation des curiosités de l'histoire littéraire comme de l'histoire de l'histoire.[1] Déterminant, l'engouement sans cesse renouvelé pour les cartulaires a peut-être eu pourtant le défaut de focaliser l'attention sur un genre et de rejeter dans l'ombre d'autres supports de la mémoire écrite, et surtout un autre secteur d'enquête: l'histoire spécifique des modes de gestion archivistiques aux temps médiévaux.

[1] Pour se limiter à des travaux français, voir, outre les contributions au volume Olivier Guyotjeannin, Laurent Morelle, and Michel Parisse, éd., *Les cartulaires: Actes de la table ronde organisée par l'École nationale des chartes et le G.D.R. 121 du C.N.R.S. (Paris, 5-7 décembre 1991)*, Mémoires et documents de l'École des chartes 39 (Paris, 1993), l'étude pionnière de Jean-Philippe Genet, "Cartulaires, registres et histoire: L'exemple anglais," dans *Le métier d'historien au Moyen Âge: Études sur l'historiographie médiévale*, éd. Bernard Guenée (Paris, 1977), 95-138, et l'enquête ibérique d'Adeline Rucquoi, "La invención de una memoria: Los cabildos peninsulares del siglo XII," *Temas medievales* 2 (1992): 67-80. On dispose désormais, à partir des cartulaires du Bas-Languedoc, de la superbe étude de Pierre Chastang, *Lire, écrire, transcrire: Le travail des rédacteurs de cartulaires en Bas-Languedoc*, CTHS Histoire, 2 (Paris, 2001). Et l'on commence à peine à prendre en considération un genre intermédiaire de compilation, dont l'appellation générique de "pancarte" cache les multiples avatars: Michel Parisse, Pierre Pégeot et Benoît-Michel Tock, éd., *Pancartes monastiques des XIe et XIIe siècles*, ARTEM (Turnhout, 1998).

1. COTES, NOTES DORSALES ET INVENTAIRES

Quand bien même le cartulaire est une pièce intégrante du chartrier, voire celle autour de laquelle il peut tout entier s'ordonner, il n'en épuise pas toutes les facettes, et pas seulement parce que la période privilégiée de sa confection et de son usage est très loin de recouvrir les dix siècles médiévaux. Or, dans la prise en compte des outils archivistiques, l'approche utilitariste de la «tradition» prime encore largement: parmi les notes constellant le dos des originaux, l'un ne recherchera au mieux que les formes plus récentes facilitant les identifications toponymiques, l'autre ne reprendra que par acquis de conscience les «cotes» anciennes pour les imprimer dans les notes d'une édition «soignée»; dans l'«inventaire» d'archives, le plus méticuleux des éditeurs tentera de débusquer, maigre trophée, la mention, souvent ambiguë, d'un acte autrement inconnu....

Mis en rapport avec l'ardeur que déploient les codicologues à inventorier, peser et éditer «catalogues» de livres, ex libris et mentions de lecture, ce constat ne peut manquer d'interpeler le diplomatiste, encore qu'il en trouvera sans peine des explications, à défaut de justifications: rareté relative des inventaires d'archives conservés avant le quatorzième siècle; reconnaissons-le aussi d'entrée, manque évident de séduction de ces entreprises aussi souvent besogneuses que rarement systématiques. En sorte, on le sait, qu'il a fallu tout le génie diplomatique de quelques grands chercheurs, Heinrich Fichtenau ou Peter Rück, pour aborder frontalement le sujet et transformer ces maigres jalons de la tradition en autant de dépôts laissés, en strates fines et enchevêtrées, par des lecteurs médiévaux.[2]

Il est vrai, aussi, que les difficultés de méthode sont immenses. Pour aller vite, on en relèvera trois. Le fait tout pratique, d'abord, que, faute de recensement, l'enquête doit se constituer un corpus au gré de recherches monographiques approfondies,[3] de trouvailles ponctuelles, d'éditions raris-

[2] Heinrich Fichtenau, "Archive der Karolingerzeit," *Mitteilungen des Österreichischen Staatsarchiv* 25 (1972): 15-24, réimp. dans Fichtenau, *Beiträge zur Mediävistik: Ausgewählte Aufsätze*, t. 2, *Zur Urkundenforschung* (Stuttgart, 1977), 115-25 (surtout sur les bâtiments); fondamentales pour une approche renouvelée des méthodes de cotation et d'inventaire, les contributions de Peter Rück, dont la synthèse "Die Anfänge des Archivwesens in der Schweiz, 800-1400," *Mitteilungen der Vereinigung schweizerischer Archivare* 26 (1975): 5-40, et la version italienne élargie d'un article de 1971, *L'ordinamento degli archivi ducali di Savoia sotto Amadeo VIII, 1398-1451*, Quaderni della rassegna degli Archivi di stato 48 (Rome, 1977).

[3] Par exemple, toujours pour se limiter à des cas français, Martin Schoebel, *Archiv und Besitz der Abtei Sankt Viktor in Paris*, Pariser historische Studien 31 (Bonn,

simes et plus volontiers limitées aux archives royales et princières de la fin du Moyen Âge. Le fait, ensuite, que à l'éclatement et au disparate des sources conservées correspond aussi un très fort particularisme des pratiques médiévales de classement, de cotation, de regeste: à peine devine-t-on ici, comme dans les cartulaires, la diffusion lente et incertaine, comme par capillarité, de recettes et d'habitudes de présentation. Particularisme qui se montre jusque dans la variété, quand ce n'est l'inexistence, du lexique «technique», celui des contenants (layettes, coffres...), celui des actions archivistiques, qui rendent parfois l'interprétation des plus délicates: que recouvre ainsi, à Saint-Antoine-des-Champs, au quatorzième siècle, un emboîtement de *raustra*, d'*ergastula* et de *bacula*? Et comment décider, ailleurs, si *intitulari* est écrire (ou coudre) un regeste sur le parchemin, le composer, le mettre en volume ou en rouleau? Le fait, enfin, que nous tendions à manier, par commodité, des catégories largement anachroniques: parler de «cote» masque le passage, lent et essentiel, d'un vieux système de repérage-marquage (le *signum*), qui exprime l'altérité d'un document par rapport à un autre,[4] au système de la *quota/cota*, quote-part qui dit aussi la place du document dans un ensemble, le plus souvent dans une structure arborescente: d'abord dérivée de l'organisation des livres-cartulaires (subdivisions par chapitres et chartes: «Toury I», «Toury II»), elle devient plus

---

1990) ou, plus spécialement dédiés aux techniques archivistiques, Liliane Delaume-Boutet, "Le chartrier de l'évêché de Limoges, cotation et inventaires," *BEC* 152 (1994): 159-203, et Agnès Bos, "Les archives des fabriques parisiennes à la fin du Moyen Âge et à l'époque moderne," *BEC* 156 (1998): 369-405. Premières tentatives de revue générale par Emmanuel Poulle, "Classement et cotation des chartriers au Moyen Âge," *Scriptorium* 50 (1996): 345-55, et Georges Declercq, "Le classement des chartriers ecclésiastiques en Flandre au Moyen Âge," *Scriptorium* 50 (1996): 331-44.

[4] Sur la longue permanence du *signum*, jusque sous sa forme la plus extrême du dessin (longtemps promue en Angleterre), voir les deux exemples reproduits ci-après: (1) inventaire du quinzième siècle des archives du chapitre cathédral de Rouen (Fig. 1: Rouen, AD de la Seine-Maritime, G 2081, p. 9), où le contenu de chaque "coffre" fait l'objet d'une description globale, indexée en marge (localités concernées) et suivie d'une double "cote": un numéro d'ordre progressif, mais aussi, la plupart du temps, une marque visuelle distinctive (sur la page reproduite: "unum caput horribile" [!], "signatum ad papegaudum," "unum florem lilii"); (2) inventaire du trésor des chartes comtal de Lille en 1399 (Fig. 2: Lille, AD du Nord, B 113, fol. LXXIIII), où la description cède la place au dessin, tantôt pour des coffres, tantôt même, comme ici, pour des actes.

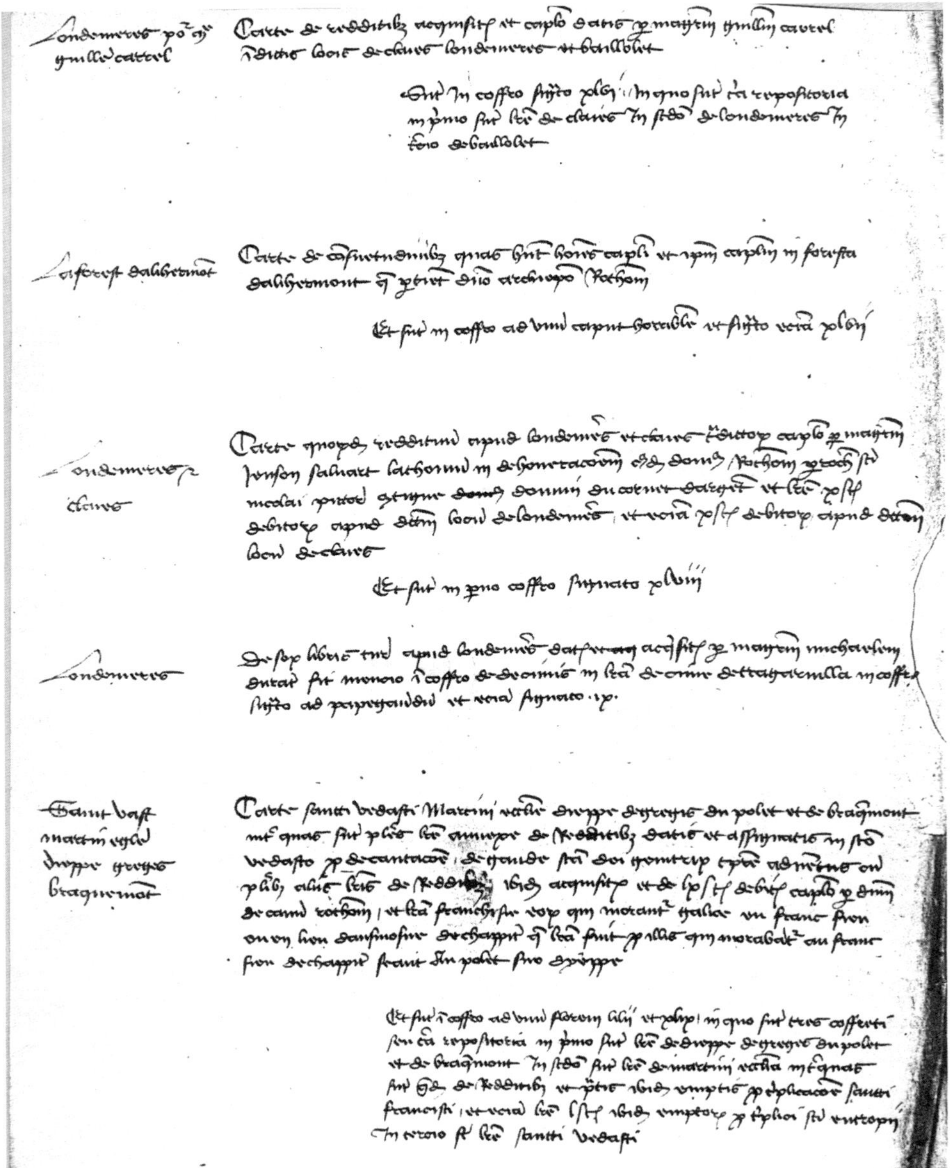

Figure 1. Inventaire des archives du chapitre cathédral de Rouen, XVe siècle (Rouen, AD de la Seine-Maritime, G 2081, p. 9). Reproduit avec l'aimable authorisation des AD.

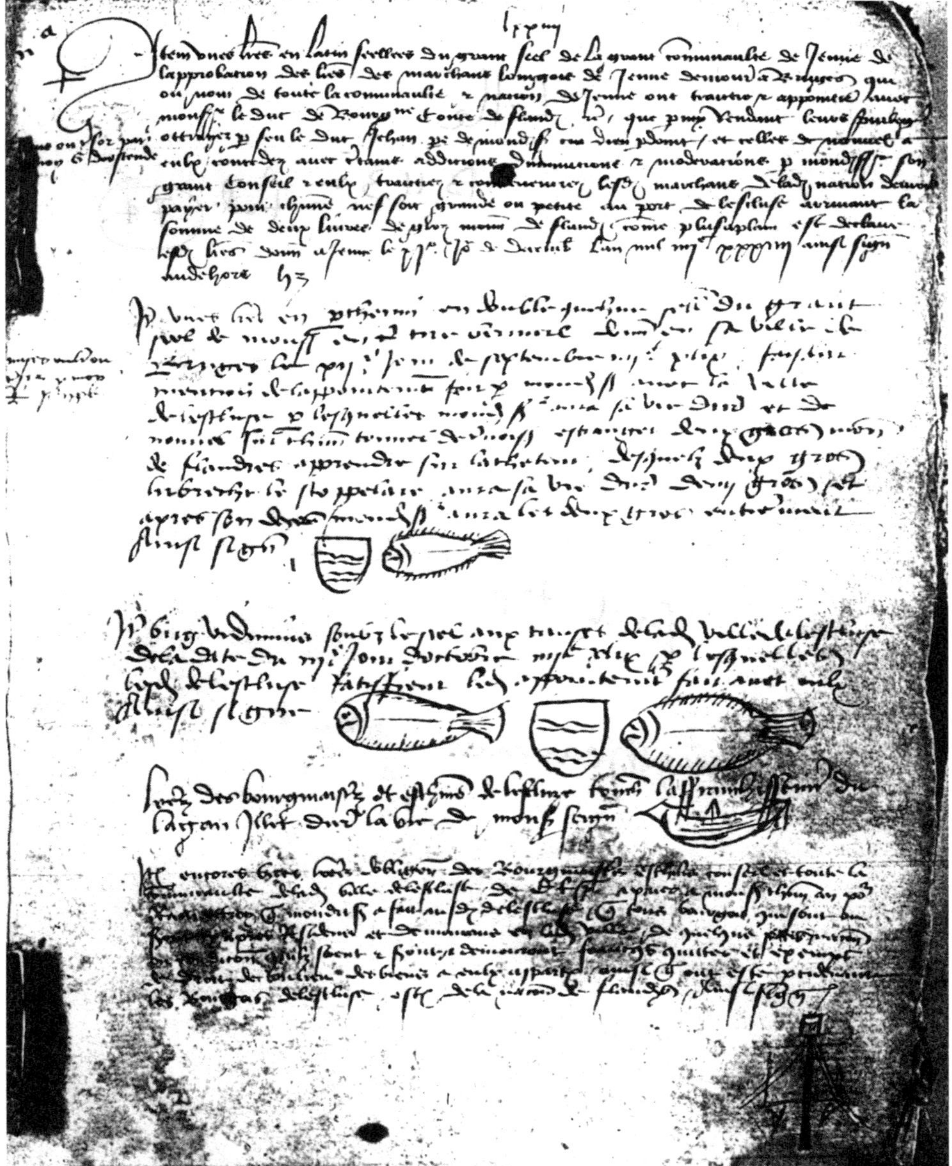

Figure 2. Inventaire du trésor des chartes des comtes de Flandre, 1399 (Lille, AD du Nord, B 113, fol. LXXIIII). Reproduit avec l'aimable authorisation des AD.

abstraite et complexe («Valois A I», «Valois A II»...), puis totalement symbolique, renvoyant au mieux à des séries de coffres et layettes («XXII A 8»), empruntant aussi bien aux innovations de la cotation des bibliothèques qu'à la progression scolastique du raisonnement.[5]

Pourtant, difficulté majeure, en l'absence fréquente des inventaires correspondants, ces mentions ne se laissent ni bien dater ni bien comprendre, quand bien même elles ne figurent pas qu'au dos des actes retirés d'un coffre, pour faciliter ensuite leur réintégration («de primo coffro»). Des «cotes» fort complexes en apparence, comme celles que l'on pratique à Saint-Denis au début du quatorzième siècle («A + E»), peuvent fort bien ne prendre aux classements méthodiques du savoir et des livres que leur enveloppe formelle, sans aucune signification intrinsèque: elles relèvent encore du marquage par *signum*, plus que de la cote proprement dite. Et parler tout uniment d'«inventaire» recouvre du même voile, par assimilation à nos modernes instruments de recherche, des listes aussi diverses dans leur but que dans leur rédaction: de la sèche énumération d'actes dont on ignore et l'exhaustivité et la fonction,[6] aussi délicate à manier que la liste de reliques et l'«inventaire» de trésor—ce que les archives sont bien après tout—, au regeste raisonné, aussi expert au plan juridico-diplomatique qu'attentif à indiquer la date et le scellement des actes, où notaires publics et serviteurs du prince commencent à exceller au quatorzième siècle, et encore aux premières adaptations de la technique de l'indexation-matière.[7]

[5] Un rapide sondage dans le recueil des actes du roi Louis VI par Jean Dufour (cf. n. 20) montre ainsi l'absence totale de "cotes" médiévales au dos des diplômes conservés à Sainte-Geneviève comme à Saint-Victor, et ailleurs des solutions des plus variées: *LIIII^a de 2 ° coffro* à Notre-Dame de Paris au quinzième siècle (no. 97); *VII. T* à Saint-Remi de Reims au treizième siècle (no. 52); *Regum XX* à Saint-Corneille de Compiègne au quinzième siècle (no. 54); *XXII A 8* à Sainte-Croix d'Orléans, s.d. (no. 67); *III prima T* à Saint-Martin-des-Champs au treizième ou quatorzième siècle (no. 103)....

[6] C'est le cas d'une liste composée à Saint-Riquier à la fin du onzième siècle et dont Laurent Morelle vient de reprendre l'examen, en livrant les premiers éléments dans "Les chartes dans la gestion des conflits, France du nord, XIe-début XIIe siècle," *BEC* 155 (1997): 267-98, spéc. 268-76.

[7] Sur ces derniers points, et pour les seuls chartriers princiers, je me permets de renvoyer aux références données dans Olivier Guyotjeannin, "Les méthodes de travail des archivistes du roi de France (XIIIe-début XVIe siècle)," *AfD* 42 (1996): 295-373, à compléter par Archivo de la Corona de Aragón, *Catálogo de memoriales e inventarios, siglos XIV-XIX* (Barcelona, 1999), qui montre bien la rapide diffusion

Croit-on les autres notes dorsales plus simples à manier au motif qu'elles visent à fournir un commode résumé du recto? Leur raison d'être principale est bien là, comme leur intérêt—montrer comment l'on parvient, plus ou moins bien, à extraire la «substance» d'un acte plutôt qu'à indiquer les noms des protagonistes ou des lieux concernés, ce qui implique d'avoir assimilé les conquêtes du droit comme les débats sur le statut des mots et de la langue. Mais c'est oublier que ces «analyses» peuvent donner bien autre chose, à l'occasion: des indications de valeur à l'attention du cartulariste, plus largement de l'utilisateur (comme ces «magnum est» ou «dampnosum» que mettent les clercs du roi de France au dos de chartes remontées de Toulouse quand ils les inspectent à toute hâte); parfois aussi, des informations complémentaires sur le sort des biens concernés, la vie juridique du recto étant prolongée au verso d'une étape gestionnaire, à pure valeur interne, comme dans l'attente d'un recensement domanial.

Il reste encore, pour en finir avec cet avant-propos, programmatique par la force des choses, que l'intérêt pour ce petit secteur encore bien mal balisé ne saurait se muer en enthousiasme aveugle. D'abord parce que l'activité, intermittente, des «archivistes» médiévaux est souvent dominée par la pression de la conjoncture et encline, par économie, à reproduire l'existant: urgence, lassitude,[8] respect des classements antérieurs, reprise des «inventaires» anciens dès qu'il se peut (les choses ont-elles d'ailleurs tant changé?) interdisent de passer de la cartographie des solutions au simple bilan des «innovations», voire des conquêtes de l'esprit. Ensuite parce que les genres sont tout sauf étanches: il suffit d'avoir édité un chartrier médiéval pour savoir quelle circulation, et dans les deux sens, s'établit entre analyses dorsales et rubriques du cartulaire, entre «inventaire» et table des matières du même cartulaire.

Il est donc sage d'attendre que les matériaux soient un peu plus systématiquement réunis en ce qui concerne les systèmes de «cotation», le taux

---

de pratiques entre France et Aragon d'un bout à l'autre du quatorzième siècle.

[8] Et découragement symétrique chez l'historien. Voir Ekkehard IV, *Casus Sancti Galli* (éd. Georg Heinrich Pertz, MGH Scriptores 2 [Hanovre, 1829], p. 90) à propos de l'acquisition de l'abbaye de Pfeffers par l'abbé de Saint-Gall Salomon: "Longum dictu qualibus per illum sancto Gallo quaesita et stabilita sit artibus; cujus quidem fere omnium locorum cartae quae tunc ad illam pertinebant in sancti Galli adhuc hodie servantur armario....Sunt et alia multa quae sancto Gallo conquisierat loca quae, quia senes interrogati in armario quaeri oportere tam plurima dicerent, intacta relinquimus, hoc verissime asserentes quia prae omnibus quae rexit monasteriis, Gallo suo semper conquisivit."

de couverture et le rythme de confection des «inventaires». Mais il me semble (tant la variété est de mise...) que dès aujourd'hui l'on pourrait, sans trop pâtir d'une approche purement monographique, tirer quelques leçons de l'examen de la façon dont les «archivistes» médiévaux pratiquaient l'art du regeste. N'est-ce pas aussi, après tout, le domaine qui promet, le plus vite, d'apporter sa contribution, modeste certes, à l'histoire de l'expertise juridico-diplomatique, de la maîtrise historique, voire de l'outillage intellectuel?

2. Les trésors archivistiques de Saint-Denis

Pour compenser les défauts d'une approche limitée, j'ai choisi un exemple entre tous riche de beaux actes, d'une bibliothèque magnifiquement étudiée,[9] et de têtes bien faites: l'abbaye de Saint-Denis, où un travail collectif d'édition, mené avec les étudiants de l'École des chartes, m'a mis sur la piste d'une série d'«inventaires» d'archives médiévaux qui me semble assez exceptionnelle par sa densité et son intérêt. Ce sera, pourquoi le taire, pour constater que ces compilations, formidables créations intellectuelles, prennent bien lentement le chemin de l'inventaire d'archives...

Ayant tenté ailleurs de dégager l'orientation générale des activités archivistiques à Saint-Denis,[10] je prendrai ici un autre angle d'approche: l'étude de détail du traitement réservé à quelques diplômes obtenus par l'abbaye du roi Louis VI, assez prestigieux pour n'être jamais négligés par nos héros, depuis l'impétrant en personne, l'abbé Suger, jusqu'aux savants moines qui traitent le chartrier, de la fin du treizième au début du seizième siècle. Mais il faut auparavant brièvement faire le tour du trésor archivistique de Saint-Denis.

La chronologie des entreprises de compilation de cartulaires à l'abbaye est aujourd'hui bien débrouillée dans ses grandes lignes:[11] pour autant que l'on en puisse juger, on voit succéder à un modeste cartulaire-dossier des

[9] Donatella Nebbiai-Dalla Guarda, *La bibliothèque de l'abbaye de Saint-Denis en France, du IXe au XVIIIe siècle* (Paris, 1985), qui a eu aussi le souci, assez rare, de mettre en regard les systèmes de cotation des livres et des actes, mais sans trouver, pour ceux-ci, la clef que fournissent les "inventaires" que l'on va ici examiner.

[10] Olivier Guyotjeannin, "La science des archives à Saint-Denis, fin du XIIIe-début du XVIe siècle," dans *Saint-Denis et la royauté: Études offertes à Bernard Guenée*, éd. Françoise Autrand, Claude Gauvard et Jean-Marie Moeglin, Histoire ancienne et médiévale 59 (Paris, 1999), 339-53.

[11] Rolf Grosse, "Remarques sur les cartulaires de Saint-Denis aux XIIIe et XIVe siècles," dans *Les cartulaires*, 279-88.

années 1060 un «Livre des privilèges» (avant 1278) et un cartulaire du convent, dit «de l'Aumônerie» (jusqu'en 1277, mais avec un noyau initial des années 1220); puis le grand monument de mémoire que constituent les deux volumes du Cartulaire blanc (premier noyau achevé en 1278, mis à jour jusqu'en 1300, totalisant quelque deux mille six cent transcriptions) et un cartulaire parallèle du convent, ensuite dit «de la Pitancerie» et plus tard encore considéré comme le tome III du Cartulaire blanc;[12] la compilation enfin, dans la première moitié du quatorzième siècle, de cartulaires spécialisés par offices ou domaines, entreprise un peu hâtive, manifestement abandonnée en chemin. Saint-Denis n'est pas des plus précoces en matière de cartulaire, mais après tout n'a guère à rougir face à d'autres établissements parisiens, sans compter que l'agencement même du Cartulaire blanc n'exclut pas l'existence d'une compilation antérieure, qui serait aujourd'hui perdue.

Les constatations que l'on peut faire sur ces montages ne sont pas des plus originales: les cartulaires, même massifs, sont fort sélectifs.[13] Surtout, ils font largement écran devant les archives, et c'est d'ailleurs le motif premier de leur compilation. La répartition et la numérotation des actes dans le Cartulaire blanc suivent bien l'ordre qui a été donné au chartrier dans les décennies précédant sa compilation, mais l'on ne soucie ni d'y corriger les écarts de numérotation simplement introduits par le rubricateur, ni de le mettre à jour des remaniements postérieurs des contenants. C'est en principe la table du cartulaire qui accueille ces remarques, c'est elle qui tient lieu de clef d'accès au chartrier. Pour le reste, le cartulaire est un chartrier mis en codex, avec ses livres et ses chapitres («titres» et «chartes»), qui le rapprochent singulièrement d'une Bible.

Les dos des originaux encore conservés, de leur côté, sont constellés de

[12] Paris, Archives nationales, respectivement LL 1157-58 et LL 1159.

[13] Tant d'actes mérovingiens et carolingiens ont ainsi tranquillement pourri dans les coffres des *antique commutationes*, des *litterarum vetustissimarum*, au témoignage des notes dorsales de ceux qui subsistent encore… Sur les dix-sept actes originaux sincères que le chartrier de Saint-Denis nous a transmis de Charles le Chauve, six seulement, à peine plus d'un tiers, sont copiés au Cartulaire blanc et/ou au cartulaire dit "de Thou" (XIVe siècle). Le phénomène a déjà été souligné, pour les papyri, par Patrick J. Geary, *Phantoms of Remembrance: Memory and Oblivion at the End of the First Millennium* (Princeton, 1994), traduit sous le titre *La mémoire et l'oubli à la fin du premier millénaire*, trad. Jean-Pierre Ricard (Paris, 1996), 161 sqq.

notes dorsales: mentions de «cotes», sur lesquelles je ne reviens pas;[14] «analyses», dont l'originalité, au moins relative, est sans doute moins dans la présence, et dans le nombre, que dans leur caractère (quasi) systématique dès le haut Moyen Âge et, peut-être, dès l'entrée du document au chartrier.[15]

[14] Guyotjeannin, "La science des archives." Pour faire bref, les "cotes" du treizième siècle n'indiquent la plupart du temps qu'un numéro d'ordre (suite progressive de chiffres romains) à l'intérieur d'un contenant pas mieux précisé, et dont la désignation (qui correspond la plupart du temps au titre de chapitre du Cartulaire blanc) ne figure que par exception: d'où de multiples méprises dans le reclassement des actes et dans leur copie à un mauvais chapitre du Cartulaire. Les "cotes" du quatorzième siècle (maintenant systématiquement reportées sur les cartulaires spécialisés) reprennent les mêmes errements, sauf que leur apparence se complexifie: en fait, elles sont, plus encore que les précédentes, de simples marquages, *signa*, lettres de l'alphabet isolées ou combinaisons complexes de lettres et de signes diacritiques, qui, à la différence des "cotes" du siècle précédent, ne donnent même plus la possibilité de définir un classement progressif à l'intérieur du contenant (lui-même réaménagé à l'occasion). C'est seulement dans le cours (à la fin?) du quinzième siècle qu'apparaissent de véritables cotes, en structure arborescente, qui indiquent d'abord le coffre (chiffre, ou groupes de lettres qui sont souvent les initiales du domaine concerné: "To" par exemple pour Toury), puis (en chiffres romains) le numéro d'ordre du document à l'intérieur du coffre.

[15] Hartmut Atsma, "Le fonds des chartes mérovingiennes de Saint-Denis, rapport sur une recherche en cours," *Paris et Île-de-France: Mémoires publiés par la Fédération des sociétés historiques et archéologiques de Paris et de l'Île-de-France* 32 (1981): 259-72, a attiré l'attention sur la question, qu'Alain Stoclet (Université Lyon II) se propose de reprendre. Saint-Denis étant notre seul pourvoyeur en originaux mérovingiens, il est évidemment difficile de décider si l'originalité est si grande. Il me semble, à titre d'hypothèse, que les pratiques antiques (*scriptura exterior* donnant des renseignements sur le contenu de l'acte écrit sur un dyptique ensuite clos) ont fourni un modèle tout trouvé aux gestionnaires de chartriers haut-médiévaux, quand bien même la fonction des annotations se modifie—si ce n'est qu'elle vise toujours à faciliter une première prise de contact avec le contenu. Ces analyses du haut Moyen Âge sont aussi brèves qu'expertes: catégorie juridico-diplomatique, assez raffinée pour les actes royaux (*iudicium*, *tracturia*, *emunitas*...), et nom de l'auteur de l'acte (voire de l'abbé cité) l'emportent en fréquence sur les mentions précises des lieux concernés (voir par exemple Albert Bruckner et Robert Marichal, éd, *Chartae latinae antiquiores: Facsimile-Edition of the Latin Charters Prior to the Ninth Century* (Olten, 1954-), t. 13, no. 567, "Hic sunt chartas Amalgero de Belvacinse," pour un acte royal de 679 reconnaissant à un particulier des droit sur la *villa* de Bailleval en Beauvaisis). Ces "analyses" peuvent ensuite servir

Où l'affaire devient nettement plus intéressante, c'est par les fils qui se tissent entre les entreprises archivistiques et les travaux historiographiques: c'est dans les années ou décennies postérieures à 1274, date de remise officielle par Primat du premier noyau de ce qui va devenir les *Grandes chroniques* (on gardera ce nom par commodité, même s'il s'agit pour l'heure d'un *Roman aux rois*), qu'une opération de grande envergure amène à la confection du Cartulaire blanc, puis à sa mise à jour et, parallèlement, à la réalisation d'une entreprise beaucoup plus orginale et dont l'initiative ne peut guère être attribuée qu'à l'un des protagonistes majeurs de l'atelier historiographique, Guillaume de Nangis: le premier d'une série de trois «inventaires» médiévaux, compilé d'une traite entre 1287 et 1289.[16] Un obscur destin lui a valu le nom d'«ancien inventaire noir», mais rien n'est plus ambigu que cette appellation: le volume est, fondamentalement, un «digest» du Cartulaire blanc, dont il résume le contenu, titre par titre, acte par acte. La récolte est providentielle non seulement parce que cartulaire et inventaire seront bientôt rangés dans la bibliothèque abbatiale, à la section des livres d'histoire, mais encore parce que, par vagues successives, se détachant péniblement du «modèle Nangis», d'autres archivistes éprouveront le besoin de réaliser de nouveaux inventaires, dont l'appellation sera progressivement moins usurpée.

Le deuxième en date des inventaires conservés accompagne, d'un peu loin, la compilation des cartulaires spécialisés, autour de 1320-30, chrono-

---

de simple marquage: une immunité délivrée par Charlemagne (Bruckner et Marichal, éd., *Chartae latinae antiquiores*, t. 15, no. 617) porte la mention, du début du quatorzième siècle: "Ista carta quasi et prope similis est illi carte Karoli magni quae sic intitulatur 'Immunitates K. per diversis provinciis de omnibus rebus.'" Or cette *intitulatio* se retrouve bien, sous cette forme, d'une main du douzième siècle, au dos du premier acte d'immunité (Bruckner et Marichal, éd., *Chartae latinae antiquiores*, t. 15, no. 616). Autre piste de recherche: une rapide enquête sur les originaux de Charles le Chauve semble suggérer que les analyses dorsales, apparemment contemporaines des actes, se font, au milieu du neuvième siècle, nettement plus précises et systématiques dans leur expression qu'elles ne l'étaient encore sous Charlemagne: l'indication de la *villa* concernée, par exemple, devient de règle.

[16] Paris, Archives nationales, LL 1184. Le volume compte 524 pages mais quelques lacunes (voir Fig. 3: reproduction des pp. 79b-80a). La datation est facilitée par la comparaison avec le Cartulaire blanc, dont les transcriptions donnent naturellement les dates des actes. Le volume dit "inventaire jaune" (Paris, Archives nationales, LL 1186) n'est qu'une copie un peu aérée de l'ancien inventaire noir.

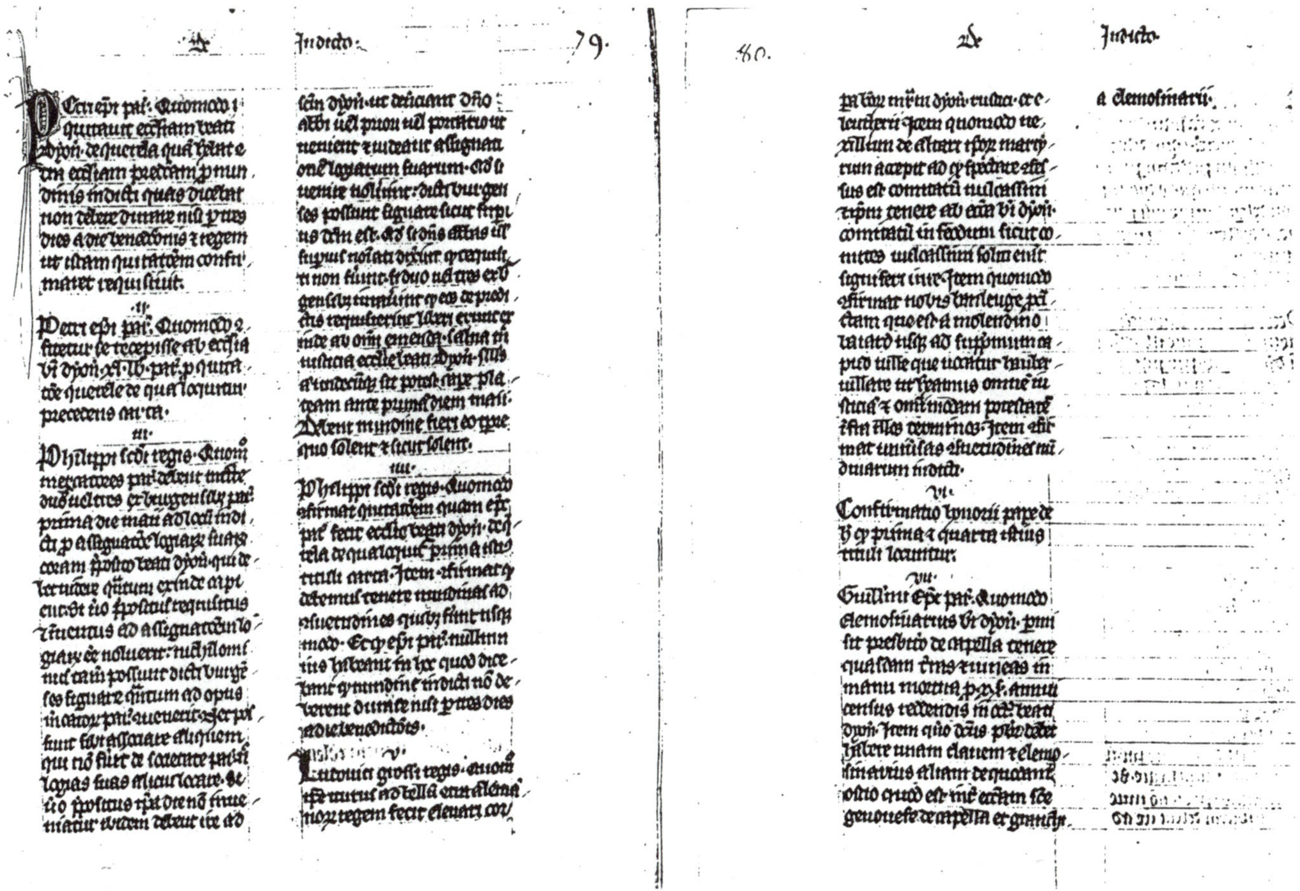

Figure 3. "Ancien inventaire noir" de Saint-Denis [1287-89] (Paris, Archives nationales, LL 1184, pp. 79-80). Document conservé au Centre historique des Archives nationales. Reproduit avec l'aimable autorisation des Archives nationales.

logie lâche; on le dit «ancien inventaire jaune».[17] Les innovations sont apparemment modestes: s'il emploie le papier et non plus le parchemin, il conserve le petit format d'un livre maniable; s'il mentionne de nouvelles «cotes», c'est qu'elles ont changé entre-temps. Mais, s'il emprunte largement les méthodes de regeste de son prédécesseur, il est maintenant en partie dissocié de la fabrication des cartulaires—compilations partielles, éclatées, pas moins éloignées que l'inventaire de la suite raisonnée des nouvelles cotes: la fin du cartulaire approche. On sent donc poindre un début de modification radicale: là où l'ancien inventaire noir permettait de prendre rapidement connaissance du contenu des deux énormes volumes du Cartulaire blanc, l'ancien inventaire jaune commence à être le Baedecker du chartrier, autorisant un accès direct, (un peu mieux) dégagé de l'écran du cartulaire.

L'évolution ainsi esquissée s'achève avec le dernier inventaire médiéval, connu par une transcription de 1520 mais apparemment engagé à la fin du quinzième siècle, et livrant aussi une troisième série de cotes, entièrement revues.[18] Il est rédigé indépendamment de tout cartulaire et permet maintenant un accès direct aux chartes—celles du moins que l'on juge utiles: il

[17] Paris, Archives nationales, LL 1185. Le volume ne mentionne pas plus les dates que le précédent, et il faudra ici une recherche longue pour tenter de resserrer la fourchette chronologique de la compilation, les étapes (assez limitées) de mise à jour, les rapports avec les cartulaires spécialisés entrepris vers la même époque. Des sondages préliminaires montrent que, même si les formats, les intentions (on cite partout les cotes, et les mêmes cotes) et les méthodes (on travaille toujours, sur nouveaux frais, sur les originaux) rapprochent les deux entreprises, l'inventaire, d'une part, les cartulaires spécialisés, de l'autre, ne prennent pas en compte strictement le même matériau, et ne suivent pas le même plan. L'inventaire, qui peut signaler une particularité externe non déductible du texte, mais du seul original (par exemple Paris, Archives nationales, LL 1185, p. 288, acte "+ A," signalé *per cyrographum*), ne peut, à la différence de son prédécesseur, avoir été compilé sur la base des cartulaires; et, surtout, il semble procéder, coffre après coffre, sans autre ordre apparent que celui de l'extraction d'actes passablement déclassés, alors que les cartulaires, qui donnent tantôt plus tantôt moins d'actes, tentent d'esquisser un plan de classement, plutôt combiné par type d'auteurs et dates. Dans la mesure où l'on voit mal de tels déclassements effectifs se produire en si peu de temps, il est *a priori* plus logique de penser que l'inventaire aura aussi servi de récolement, pour donner une première mesure de l'existant, avant le lancement de cartulaires tentant de remettre un peu d'ordre, au moins intellectuel, et procédant parfois à de nouveaux choix.

[18] Paris, Archives nationales, LL 1187.

faudra attendre le «Grand inventaire» du dix-huitième siècle pour voir pris en compte l'ensemble des monuments archivistiques, généreusement analysés, copieusement référencés, reclassés chronologiquement.

Le matériau n'est pas encore épuisé, puisqu'il nous reste par chance à voir le traitement que les historiens monastiques ont réservé à tel acte dans leur production. Enquête qui à vrai dire sera à peine esquissée et réservée aux best-sellers déjà édités, œuvres de Suger et *Grandes chroniques.*[19]

3. Le traitement des actes de Louis VI

Pour entrer vraiment dans le vif du sujet, il m'a semblé que le plus expédient, quitte à élargir les remarques de constatations faites sur quelques autres diplômes, serait de partir d'un corpus modeste en nombre, celui des actes de Louis VI pour l'abbaye[20] et, tout spécialement, du groupe des trois actes les plus prestigieux, obtenus à l'insistante pression de Suger et tous trois rédigés à l'abbaye, mais aussi les plus complexes dans leurs dispositions et les plus riches dans leur tradition.

[19] Suger, *Vie de Louis VI le Gros*, éd. et trad. Henri Waquet, Les classiques de l'histoire de France au Moyen Âge 11 (Paris, 1929); Suger, *Gesta*, dans Suger, *Œuvres*, t. 1, éd. et trad. Françoise Gasparri, Les classiques de l'histoire de France au Moyen Âge 37 (Paris, 1996), 54-155, sous le titre *L'œuvre administrative*; Jules Viard, éd., *Les Grandes chroniques de France*, Société de l'histoire de France, t. 4 (Paris, 1927), t. 5 (Paris, 1928). L'étude de Laurent Morelle, "La mise en 'œuvre' des actes diplomatiques: L'*auctoritas* des chartes chez quelques historiographes monastiques, IXe-XIe s.," dans *Auctor et auctoritas: Invention et conformisme dans l'écriture médiévale*, éd. Michel Zimmermann, Mémoires et documents de l'École des chartes 59 (Paris, 2001), 73-96, scrute la façon dont plusieurs rédacteurs monastiques du neuvième au milieu du onzième siècle (*Gesta* de Fontenelle, Vie de Bouchard, *Gesta Dagoberti*, Hariulf de Saint-Riquier, Richer de Reims...) ont pu traité des actes de leur chartrier, pour conclure que le large spectre des interventions possibles semble tenir à des goûts et à des mobiles des plus variés, plutôt qu'à un radicale différence de conception, de l'histoire ou de la mémoire. Pour un autre volet de ce genre d'enquête (traitement par des historiens plus tardifs, imprégnés de l'art documentaire du notariat public), voir les très importantes remarques de Bernard Guenée, "Documents insérés et documents abrégés dans la Chronique du Religieux de Saint-Denis," *BEC* 152 (1994): 375-428, et celles d'Anne-Marie Lamarrigue, *Bernard Gui (1261-1331): Un historien et sa méthode*, Études d'histoire médiévale 5 (Paris, 2000), 69-71, 137-57.

[20] Sur la base, ici encore des plus commodes, offerte par Jean Dufour, éd., *Recueil des actes de Louis VI, roi de France, 1108-1137*, 4 t. (Paris, 1992-94).

Acte de 1120 (Dufour, éd., *Recueil...Louis VI*, no. 163): Louis VI restitue la couronne de son père Philippe à l'abbaye de Saint-Denis et lui offre l'église de Cergy.

Original: K 21^{C}, no. 16 (= AE II 1706). —Copie au Cartulaire blanc, t. I, p. 625 [«De Cergiaca» (*sic*), II.] —Ancien inventaire noir, p. 189a [«De Cergiaco et Boissiaco», II]. —Ancien inventaire jaune, p. 310 [«De Cergiaco et Cormeliis in Vulcassino, primum scrinium», cote + A]. —Inventaire de 1520, p. 53 [cote II CXIII].

Acte de 1124 (Dufour, éd., *Recueil...Louis VI*, no. 220): Louis VI, après l'annonce de l'invasion du royaume par l'empereur Henri, se rend à la basilique de Saint-Denis, fait élever les reliques de ses patrons sur l'autel et lève l'étendard à la manière des comtes de Vexin, fief qu'il tient de l'abbaye; il abandonne la voirie qu'il détenait sur le territoire, délimité par des bornes, entre Saint-Denis et Paris, et toute coutume sur le Lendit; l'abbaye est qualifiée de *caput regni*.

Original: K 22^{A}, no. 4. —Épisode annexe de la tradition du document, les clercs du roi Philippe Auguste se font remettre un moment l'acte pour le transcrire au registre «E» du roi, vers 1220 (JJ 26, fol. VII^{xx}V verso, chapitre *Abbacie*). —Copie au Cartulaire blanc, t. I, pp. 348-49 [«De Indicto», V]. —Ancien inventaire noir, pp. 79b-80a [«De Indicto», V]. —Ancien inventaire jaune, pp. 106-7 [«De Indicto et Haubertovillari et Capella Sancte Genovefe», cote A + E]. —Inventaire de 1520, p. 8 [cote I XX].

Acte de 1129 (Dufour, éd., *Recueil...Louis VI*, no. 281): Louis VI et son fils Philippe reconnaissent les droits de Saint-Denis sur l'abbaye d'Argenteuil; ils mentionnent au passage leur souhait d'être ensevelis dans la basilique des saints (*apud quos sepeliri optamus et devovimus*)—souhait, on le sait, réalisé dès 1131 pour Philippe après sa mort accidentelle.

Original: perdu. —Copie au Cartulaire blanc, t. II, p. 279 [«De Argentolio», V]. —Ancien inventaire noir, p. 433a [«De Argentolio», V]. —Ancien inventaire jaune: partie perdue. —Inventaire de 1520: regeste non retrouvé.

L'analyse de la lecture dionysienne de l'acte de 1129 est entravée par la perte de l'original et de la partie correspondante de l'inventaire du quatorzième siècle, mais les deux premiers diplômes permettent de saisir sur le vif sept siècles de tradition interne presque continue, jusqu'au retraitement érudit du dix-huitième siècle, qui ne me retiendra pas ici. Je m'appuierai essentiellement sur celui de 1124, le plus riche dans sa tradition, convoquant au passage les deux autres.

a. De l'art d'interpréter au XIIe siècle

Outre qu'ils sont de magnifiques créations stylistiques et qu'ils offrent des cas d'école sur la façon dont des actes royaux composés par le destinataire dans les années 1120 peuvent encore livrer un récit des plus narratifs et une version des plus tendancieuses, «maximaliste», des droits ecclésiastiques—toutes constatations qui relèvent de la genèse des actes[21]—, les trois diplômes examinés contiennent à la fois des dispositions sur le temporel de l'abbaye (des droits, des dépendances...) et des affirmations beaucoup plus générales, sur les «honneurs» de l'abbaye, sur son rôle dans le royaume, sur ses relations privilégiées avec le pouvoir royal. Ceux qui analysent, classent, cotent les actes sont du coup placés devant un dilemme: quel aspect souligner le plus?

Du point de vue du classement, puis de la cotation, l'évolution est claire: quelque capitales que soient les dispositions directes ou les remarques incidentes faites, au fil des actes, sur le statut éminent de l'abbaye, c'est dans des coffres, dans des chapitres de cartulaire relatifs à des lieux bien précis qu'ils seront bientôt rangés, Cergy, Lendit, Argenteuil. Le propos, tout gestionnaire, n'est renversé, et radicalement, qu'avec le reclassement de la fin du quinzième siècle, qui obéit à une logique défensive et replace les deux premiers actes dans les coffres initiaux, ceux qui concernent les privilèges généraux de l'abbaye.

Il existait pourtant d'autres façons, comme alternatives, de tirer parti des magnifiques affirmations des chartes: et très tôt (voire immédiatement) les notes dorsales du douzième siècle le montrent, qui n'hésitent pas même à amplifier encore le contenu des documents. Le plus extraordinaire, ici, est fourni par l'analyse inscrite au dos de l'acte de 1124: «De libertate et munificentia ecclesie beati Dyonisii a molendino *Baiard* usque ad Halbervillare». L'*intitulatio* monastique ne craint pas de fusionner deux expressions tirées de leur contexte. Le diplôme de Louis VI en effet évoquait, d'une part la *liberalitas et munificentia* des anciens rois, généreux bienfaiteurs de l'abbaye (l. 12-13 de l'original), d'autre part la *justicia plenariaque libertas* cédée sur le territoire au sud de Saint-Denis (l. 16). Foin du Vexin et de

[21] Je renvoie sur ce point aux données définitives qu'a accumulées Jean Dufour dans les dissertations introductives à l'édition de chacun de ces textes.

l'oriflamme, foin du Lendit! On a les yeux tout entier tournés sur la dernière étape de la construction d'une seigneurie monastique, délimitée dans l'espace, totale dans son pouvoir: une *libertas* bien grégorienne, qui se conjugue à une séculaire *munificentia*.

Pour l'acte de 1120, par contre, l'analyse dorsale contemporaine (ou presque) confirme son ancrage gestionnaire. L'enjeu est moins grand, l'analyse est terne. Les analyses plutôt, puisque l'inscription se fait en deux temps, avant d'être amalgamée et reproduite presque à l'identique dans la rubrique du Cartulaire blanc: l'une sur l'objet, *De ecclesia de Cergiaco et de rebus pertinentibus ad eam*, l'autre sur l'auteur, *Ludovici senioris regis* (le compilateur du Cartulaire y ajoutera simplement *Francorum*, en fort bon diplomatiste, là où un historien eût dit *Francie*).

Suger a évidemment plus de champ pour reprendre, dans ses écrits «historiques», *Vie de Louis VI* ou auto-*Gesta*, la matière des actes qu'il avait fort vraisemblablement dictés. Qu'il sélectionne et amplifie ne saurait étonner. Mais, plus remarquable, il amalgame les données tirées de deux actes, ou fractionne le contenu d'un seul diplôme, et parfois même sans respect de la chronologie: le diplôme royal est d'un métal noble, mais fort malléable entre les mains de cet orfèvre.

C'est ainsi que, dans la *Vie de Louis VI*, le contenu de l'acte de 1124 se retrouve morcelé, dissocié dans le temps, sans rappel de l'un à l'autre, entre deux passages, consacrés l'un à la levée de l'étendard et au comté de Vexin (naturellement raccrochés au récit de l'invasion allemande), l'autre à la délimitation du territoire haut-justicier de l'abbaye.

Le premier thème est traité comme une amplification rhétorique de l'acte, avec pourtant de nombreux mots communs, qui montre que ce connaisseur de longue date du chartrier avait bien le diplôme ou sa copie sous les yeux:

ACTE DE 1124	*VIE DE LOUIS VI* (éd. Waquet, p. 220)
cognovimus...nobili monasterio ter beati Dionysii sociorumque ejus...ad ipsam sanctissimorum martyrum basilicam **more** antecessorum **festinavimus**...pro **regni defensione** eosdem **patronos** nostros **super altare** eorundem elevari pio affectu et amore effecimus.	Et quoniam beatum Dionisium specialem **patronum** et singularem post Deum regni protectorem et multorum relatione et crebro **cognoverat** experimento, ad eum **festinans**, tam precibus quam benefitiis precordialiter pulut **regnum defendat**, personam conservet, hostibus **more** solito resistat et, quoniam hanc ab eo habent

prerogativam ut, si regnum aliud regnum Francorum invadere audeat, ipse beatus et admirabilis defensor cum sociis suis tanquam ad defendendum **altari** suo **superponatur**, eo presente fit tam gloriose quam devote.

...**vexillum de altario** beatorum martyrum, ad quod **comitatus Vilcassini**, quem nos ab ipsis in feodum habemus, **spectare** dinoscitur, morem antiquorum antecessorum nostrorum servantes et imitantes, signiferi jure, sicut comites Vilcassini soliti erant, **suscepimus**...

Rex autem **vexillum ab altari suscipiens**, quod de **comitatu Vilcassini**, quod ad ecclesiam **feodatus** est, **spectat**, votive a domino suo suscipiens, pauca manu contra hostes...

Dans les *Gesta*, la rédaction se fait nettement plus juridique, et c'est là que l'abbé développe le thème féodal et ajoute celui de l'hommage (que l'on a eu peut-être tort d'interpréter à outrance comme une belle théorie concoctée pour venir au secours idéologique de la royauté):

> Rex Francorum Ludovici...accelerans contra imperatorem Romanum insurgentem in regnum Francorum, in pleno capitulo beati Dyonisii professus est se ab eo habere et jure signiferi, si rex non esset, hominium ei debere...[22]

[22] Éd. Gasparri, p. 66. *Jure signiferi* est repris à l'acte de 1124, mais pas *accelerare* (on y lisait *festinans*), qui se trouve dans l'acte de 1120: et il ne s'applique plus dans les *Gesta* au marathon Paris–Saint-Denis que Suger adorait faire courir au souverain, au moins dans ses actes, mais à l'expédition armée. Henri Waquet (*Vie de Louis VI*, p. 221 n. 2) n'a pas vu que c'est aux *Gesta* qu'a puisé le compilateur anonyme du manuscrit *F* de la *Vie de Louis VI* pour l'une de ses additions. Les *Grandes chroniques*, mais le point dépasse mon propos, tant l'étude fine de leur art de la traduction/trahison mériterait une longue étude, enfoncent le clou: "la contee de Vouquesim que li rois tient en fié de saint Denys come de son lige segnor" (éd. Viard, 5:238), comme elles confirment sur ce petit passage leur propension aux menues inflexions, très révélatrices (la prière du roi ne s'appuie plus que sur les intentions du cœur: le *tam precibus quam benefitiis precordialiter pulsat* de la Vie de Louis VI y devient "commença a prier de tot son cuer"), comme à la glose pédagogique ("cil gloriex martyrs...sont mis hors de la fort voute ou gisent et sont mis

Suger orchestre ensuite un thème qui torture la chronologie, puisque les libéralités royales énumérées dans la seconde partie de l'acte de 1124 sont présentées après la victoire sur l'empereur, comme une action de grâce, et non comme une concession arrachée au roi avant son départ en campagne… Et la fusion continue, puisque la concession à double ressort de l'acte de 1124 (territoire haut-justicier, puis confirmation des coutumes de la foire du Lendit) est maintenant unifiée dans une construction territoriale unique, celle du «Lendit extérieur», marquée par une métamorphose des modestes bornes mentionnées dans l'acte (*sicut certa metarum distintione terminavimus*, a-t-on fait dire au roi, l. 17-18):

> Indictum exterius in platea (interius enim sanctorum erat) libentissime reddidit, viaturam omnimodam, quibus spatiis cruces et columne statuuntur marmoree, quasi Gades Herculis omnibus obsistentes hostibus, precepti regii confirmatione sanctivit.[23]

Il y a mieux encore, puisque le passage embrigade aussi, en la mentionnant juste avant, la restitution de la couronne du roi Philippe Ier, qui avait été notifiée en fait en 1120, alors que le don de Cergy viendra fort logiquement s'enchâsser dans les *Gesta*, assez rapides du reste pour en oublier les dîmes:

ensemble sus l'autel, ou l'ansegne saint Denys que il appellent l'oriflambe"; éd. Viard, 5:237).

[23] Éd. Waquet, p. 228. Les bornes sont célèbres dans la tradition locale, et feront l'objet au dix-septième siècle d'une belle enquête sur le terrain: Jacques Doublet, *Histoire de l'abbaye de Saint-Denys en France* (Paris, 1625), 421: "La banlieuë de la ville de Sainct-Denys commence à une borne de marbre qui est sur la rivière de Seine vers la porte de Pontoise (anciennement Compoise) entre les villages de Sainct-Oüen et Clipchy, en venant de droit à un grand coulombier…et là mesme proche de ce lieu y a aussi une autre borne de marbre de l'autre costé…sur la chaussée du village de Haubervilleirs, où sont assises deux autres bornes de marbre par-delà la Croix du Lendit (dite la Croix aux fiens d'ancienneté, et depuis la Croix qui panche)…et sont icelles bornes plantées à l'endroit de la pointe Liziart…" Tous éléments utiles sur les croix et le bornage de la "banlieue" dans le magnifique volume réuni sous la direction de Michaël Wyss, *Atlas historique de Saint-Denis, des origines au XVIIIe siècle*, Documents d'archéologie française 59 (Paris, 1996), 348-50 et 367-72.

ACTE DE 1120	*VIE DE LOUIS VI* (éd. Waquet, pp. 226-8)
Communicato cum palatinis nostris concilio, ad ipsam sanctissimorum martirum basilicam...acceleravimus et ..., quoniam **jure** et consuetudine regum Francorum demigrantium insignia regni ipsi sancto martiro, tanquam duci et protectori suo, referuntur, **coronam patris** nostri ei reddidimus,	Ad protectores suos sanctissimos martires humillime devenit eique post Deum gratias magnas referens, **coronam patris** sui quam injuste retinuerat (**jure** enim ad eos omnes pertinent) devotissime **restituit**
	GESTA (éd. Gasparri, p. 68)
pro dilatione redditionis satisfecimus et...**ecclesiam de Cirgiaco**, sicut libere possidebamus, cum decimis ...ecclesie **restituendo**...contulimus; **curie** etiam et propriis domibus...in eadem curia perennem indulgemus **libertatem**, vicariam omnimodam in curia ipsa et curie domibus conferimus...	**Ecclesiam de Cergiaco** et **curiae libertatem** ab eodem rege Ludovico obtinuimus.

Ici encore Suger travaille au mot près: l'omission du rappel de la «coutume» vise sans doute à renforcer la seule invocation du «droit», une invocation renforcée encore par l'introduction du couple *injuste/juste* et d'un *restituere* pris à la suite de l'acte, plus marquant que *reddere*: Grégoire VII et le pseudo-Constantin (on sait que la Donation est utilisée, peu avant, par un faussaire dionysien) eussent-ils souhaité mieux?

Retenons surtout que, par contraste, du modeste annotateur au grand abbé, toutes les entreprises se rejoignent, dans leurs motifs et leurs mobiles.

b. L'art du résumé pédagogique au XIIIe siècle

Les historiens-archivistes de la seconde moitié du treizième siècle trouvent l'acte de 1124 dans le «coffre» Lendit; celui de 1120 dans le coffre Cergy; celui de 1129 dans le coffre Argenteuil. Cette radicalisation de l'aspect le plus utilitaire de l'acte ne tient bien évidemment pas à un dédain des données plus prestigieuses, sur les *regalia*, les sépultures royales, l'étendard—toute l'historiographie et la liturgie dionysiennes sont là pour le montrer. Mais, sans doute avec moins d'état d'âme que leurs prédécesseurs, les «archivistes» du milieu du treizième au début du quatorzième siècle peuvent traiter les actes sous l'influence accentuée du droit: peut-être parce que (surtout pour la couronne) les actes de Louis VI ne sont plus sur ces chapitres des preuves assez fortes; surtout parce que toute cette symbolique est précisément reprise en compte par un atelier d'écriture qui associe hagiographie, chroniques, cartulaires et même «inventaires» d'archives. L'histoire ne se murmure plus à coup de notes dorsales.

Confirmant l'approche de Suger, l'analyse dorsale qui est mise à l'acte de 1124 vers le milieu du treizième siècle (ici encore, elle sera largement reprise par la rubrique du Cartulaire blanc) insiste sur le lien avec le coffre où se trouve le document: *Ludovici senioris de Indicto et libertate ecclesie beati Dyonisii*, deux ajouts très proches dans le temps précisant successivement: *et bannleuga* (un terme qui n'était pas dans l'acte, mais qui est le terme officiel à Saint-Denis pour définir le territoire immuniste, *bannleuga, banleuge procinctum*), puis *de molendino de* Baart *usque ad alias metas*. C'est, avant le retour en force des «analystes» du dix-huitième siècle, la dernière entreprise à peu près systématique d'*intitulatio*. De la même façon, et toujours dans l'esprit du temps, le Cartulaire blanc procède à des transcriptions des plus méticuleuses des actes.[24]

Par chance, et c'est vraiment ce qui fait la différence en faveur de Saint-Denis, la même époque nous transmet, avec l'ancien inventaire noir, le moyen de suivre de très près une entreprise, plus historiographique encore qu'archivistique, et qui consiste à résumer, à transposer, au besoin à retraduire en latin les actes du Cartulaire blanc.[25] Les actes y subissent une

[24] Ainsi, la collation avec l'original de 1124 ne révèle-t-elle que de rares variantes, purement graphiques. Mais aussi une terrible bévue: à la différence des cinq autres monogrammes de Louis VI ailleurs reproduits dans le cartulaire, celui qui figure sous la transcription de l'acte de 1124...n'est pas celui de l'original, ni même de ceux que l'on connaît à Louis VI. Ses particularités (le O coupant la barre centrale du H et surmontant un V) le rapprochent des monogrammes de Louis VII et saint Louis: permutation accidentelle des modèles remis à un illustrateur?

[25] Que la compilation vise à faciliter l'accès au cartulaire plutôt qu'aux originaux ne ressort pas seulement de son plan, qui suit aveuglement l'ordre de celui-ci (en répétant et parfois en agravant ses erreurs de numérotation des actes), mais encore de remarques qui expliquent pourquoi l'analyse d'un texte, répétitif, a été négligée: par exemple, "XXXII/Eadem est ista carta que et vicesima quarta istius tituli" (p. 7b). Le compilateur ne se meut pas de coffres en layettes, mais de copies en chapitres.

relecture experte, mais subtilement infléchie dans certains cas, par exemple pour le diplôme de 1124:

> Ludovici Grossi regis quomodo ipse, iturus ad bellum contra Alemannorum regem, fecit elevari corpora beatorum martyrum Dyonisii, Rustici et Eleutherii. Item quomodo vexillum de altari ipsorum martyrum accepit ad quod spectare confessus est comitatum Vulcassini et ipsum tenere ab ecclesia beati Dyonisii comitatum in feodum sicut comites Vulcassini soliti erant signiferi jure. Item quomodo confirmat nobis banleuge procinctam que est a molendino *Baiard* usque ad suppremum capud ville que vocatur Haubervillare, ut habeamus omnem justiciam et omnimodam potestatem infra illos terminos. Item confirmat universas consuetudines nundinarum Indicti.

Même s'il néglige le passage final sur les reliques de la Passion, le rédacteur de l'«inventaire» (Guillaume de Nangis ou un proche collaborateur) a beaucoup plus de champ qu'un classeur d'archives ou qu'un abbé dédié à l'autopromotion pour ne négliger aucune des facettes du texte. Il a en tête les listes royales élaborées à l'abbaye pour distinguer les homonymes (*Ludovicus Grossus* et non plus *senior*). Comme les autres «inventaires» (à tout le moins monastiques) de son temps, il est parfaitement insensible aux dates des documents. Mais le plus intéressant pour notre propos est dans les retouches lexicographiques et stylistiques apportées à l'acte:

ACTE DE 1124	ANCIEN INVENTAIRE NOIR
Alemannorum regem...exercitum preparare	[Ludovicus] iturus ad bellum <u>centrage sur la France: annonce l'oriflamme</u>
Dyonisii sociorumque ejus...patronos nostros	Dyonisii, Rustici et Eleutherii. <u>glose pédagogique, mais centrage sur Saint-Denis dont les moines accaparent la première personne</u>
antiquorum regum liberalitate et munificentia	≠ <u>centrage sur Saint-Denis</u>

quem nos...comites...signiferi jure	**confessus est** ... comites ... signiferi jure avec ce mot typique de la juridiction gracieuse, c'est tout l'acte qui est subverti au plan juridique: à un récit qui narrait, l'analyse substitue une *confessio in jure*, créatrice d'obligations, ce que Suger déjà insinuait, avec un vocabulaire plus monastique, «in pleno capitulo...professus est»
juxta villam	banleuge procinctam condense et explique; *banleuga* était au dos de l'acte; *procincta* dans le grand faux de Robert II
vicariam quoque et omnimodam justiciam plenariamque libertatem quam ...regum...et nostra occupaverat potestas (*libertas* ecclésiastique vs. *potestas* laïque oppressive)	omnem justiciam et omnimodam potestatem condense outrageusement: reprend la *potestas* aux rois; évacue la *vicaria* qui, maintenant confondue avec la «voirie», tirerait vers le bas la construction d'une seigneurie de haute justice et de plein exercice
universas consuetudines nundinarum Indicti	universas consuetudines nundinarum Indicti

Ces menus gauchissements, qui montrent non seulement un art éblouissant du résumé et une maîtrise linguistique parfaite, mais encore un recentrage systématique du discours sur l'abbaye, faisant d'un modeste résumé de cartulaire le matériau brut de *Gesta* monastiques, transparaît encore dans l'analyse de l'acte de 1120, sur la couronne et Cergy:

> Ludovici grossi regis quomodo ipse reddidit nobis coronam patris sui et quomodo ipse satisfecit nobis pro dilatione *quia in morte regis, sicut dicitur in carta ista, debent apud Sanctum Dyonisium afferri insignia regia et corona*. Item quomodo ipse dedit nobis ecclesiam de Cergiaco, sicut ipse libere eam possidebat cum ominibus ad ecclesiam pertinentibus; curie etiam nostre cum domibus in eadem curia perhennem li-

bertatem indulxit et omnimodam vicariam in ipsa curia et curie domibus contulit.

Le plus évident est l'insistance mise ici sur la sépulture des rois, en un passage qui constitue une véritable interpolation, plus d'ailleurs sur le mode de la constatation (toujours la «pédagogie»). Mais notons aussi que, plus proche de l'acte que Suger, le rédacteur de l'inventaire reprend bien le «rendre» la couronne, et transmue même le très grégorien «restituer» Cergy en «donner», pour insister sur le pleine possession dont jouissait le roi avant le don (et ici, il ne répugne pas à remployer le mot *vicaria*; est-ce parce que la possession est plus modeste?).

Tempérons une louange méritée. Le troisième regeste qui nous retiendra dans l'ancien inventaire noir, celui de l'acte de 1129, montre que la vigilance peut se relâcher. Le passage sur l'élection de sépulture du roi et de son fils était sans doute été trop bien caché dans l'acte; du coup, le compilateur se laisse prendre à un double piège: il saute le passage pour ne parler que d'Argenteuil; et, pis, il attribue l'acte (co-intitulé au nom de Louis VI et de son premier fils Philippe) à Louis VII et Philippe Auguste...: «Ludovici junioris et Philippi filii ejus regum, quomodo ipsi restituerunt prioratum Argentolii ecclesie Beati Dyonisii, conferentes nobis quicquid ibidem habebant...» (le Cartulaire blanc s'était prudemment tenu à «Louis et Philippe», tout en donnant une graphie *Hludowicus* archaïsante, qui dans l'acte ne s'appliquait pas à l'auteur, mais au rappel de Louis le Pieux...).

Une approche classique—et toujours pertinente—de l'ancien inventaire noir au regard des problèmes de la tradition donnerait des sueurs froides à qui tenterait le jeu de la diplomatique-fiction, imaginant un instant que l'inventaire soit notre seule source de connaissances de *deperdita*.[26] Pas de dates; des attributions laissant hésiter entre plusieurs rois; une sélection, un gauchissement, voire une interpolation, même «honnête». Rassurons-nous vite et redisons l'exceptionnel intérêt de ce monument monastique... qui est finalement tout sauf un inventaire d'archives!

c. Vers une archivistique gestionnaire: Les travaux des XIVe et XVe siècles

Pas plus d'un demi-siècle après, le paysage commence à se modifier avec les analyses de l'ancien inventaire jaune. Pourtant, si quelques indices montrent que le compilateur travaille sur nouveaux frais, les originaux sous

[26] C'est le seul aspect qui a été présenté dans Olivier Guyotjeannin, Jacques Pycke et Benoît-Michel Tock, *Diplomatique médiévale*, L'atelier du médiéviste 2 (Turnhout, 1993), 303-4.

les yeux, d'autres manifestent qu'il ne peut se déprendre de la tradition «maison» créée par l'ancien inventaire noir, ce qui incite à quelque prudence dans l'interprétation. Des trois actes de Louis VI sous examen, deux seulement sont mentionnés dans la partie conservée du volume. Et d'abord l'acte de 1124, dont la nouvelle analyse, à tout seigneur tout honneur, ne le cède en rien, en longueur et en complexité, à l'ancienne:

> Ludovici senioris regis, quomodo dedit ecclesie Sancti Dyonisii libertatem et omnem justiciam et potestatem de fluvio Secane, videlicet a molendino qui vocatur Molendinum de *Bajard* usque ad summum caput ville que vocatur Hauberviller, sicut metes se comportant, nominate in privilegiis antiquorum regum. Item voluit et concessit dicte ecclesie quod omnes antiquas consuetudines Indicti servarentur et tenerentur prout consuetum est ab antiquis regibus Francorum. Recognovit etiam se tenere comitatum Vulcassini de ecclesia Sancti Dyonisii, et ista omnia confirmavit ecclesie supradicte. Cum isto signo: A + E.

Le regeste, à peine moins long (soixante-dix-neuf mots contre quatre-vingt-sept), s'ouvre à quelques variantes—le retour à *Ludovicus senior*, la référence au bornage (*mete*)—mais confirme la sélection des termes désignant la seigneurie haut-justicière (*libertas, justicia, potestas*), comme l'abandon de la *vicaria*. Même tic, surtout, dans l'insertion de remarques extérieures au texte du document, qui font de l'inventaire un guide du bon usage des archives: mais c'est maintenant pour renvoyer à d'autres actes (*nominate in privilegiis antiquorum regum*). Tout cela ne doit pas cacher l'essentiel: plus «juriste» encore, le rédacteur omet le matériau proprement historique qui attirait son prédécesseur: plus de place ici pour l'histoire du règne de Louis VI, pour l'invasion allemande...ni même pour la levée de l'étendard. Le regeste néglige l'exposé, va droit au dispositif, quitte à pervertir l'ordre du document (la vassalité du Vexin passe en dernière position). Non que son prédécesseur fût moins sensible au fond de la chose (le roi «confesse» ou «reconnaît», c'est tout un), mais il la situait dans la coulée du récit de l'acte et de l'histoire.

Ces constatations se renforcent avec le regeste de l'acte de 1120, ici encore légèrement plus court (soixante-cinq mots contre soixante-quatorze):

> Ludovici regis quomodo reddidit ecclesie Sancti Dyonisii coronam patris sui quam abstulerat et recognoscit quod de jure et consuetudine insignia regum Francorum demigrantium sint et debent deferri ad ecclesiam sancti Dyonisii tamquam ducis et protectoris regni. Item quod pro dilacione reddicionis satisfecit dicte ecclesie et dedit ecclesiam de

> Cergiaco cum decimis et omnibus ad ecclesiam pertinentibus cum omni vicaria et curia, sicut eam libere possidebat.

Le rédacteur de l'ancien inventaire jaune suit de beaucoup plus près le texte de l'acte; il l'abrège aussi davantage en ce qui concerne Cergy. Il revient, du coup, au caractère proclamatoire de l'acte. Mais celui-ci, à nouveau, est pris dans une stricte acception juridique: l'incise de l'acte de Louis VI («j'ai rendu la couronne de mon père») est devenue une «action juridique» de plein exercice (*recognoscit*). Emporté (ou déterminé à le comprendre ainsi?) par le *rediddit* de l'acte (décidemment, quel souci de traquer le «dispositif»...), l'archiviste glose, et à contretemps: Louis VI n'est plus présenté comme ayant tardé à remettre la couronne, mais comme l'ayant arrachée (*abstulerat*)... Autre moyen (délibéré ou non) de manifester que le dépôt des *regalia* est la situation normale, indice aussi que les rapports de droit sont restitués dans leur inéluctable déroulement causal. Là où l'acte disait dans une séquence largement chronologique, spatiale, «émotive» («Je suis allé à Saint-Denis [aspect de déplacement qui est totalement gommé, comme plus haut]; et puisque les insignes..., j'ai rendu...,»), l'inventaire déroule la séquence logique au plan du droit: restitution du bien naguère arraché, reconnaissance impliquant obligation, dédommagement, bref des rapports de droit, saisis comme dans l'acte privé contemporain, plus simples au premier regard qu'au douzième siècle...

Les analyses de l'inventaire sont donc en apparence seulement plus détachées (l'abbaye est désignée de façon objective, alors que l'ancien inventaire noir glissait partout le «nous» monastique). Elles savent aussi, quand il le faut, se faire beaucoup plus laconiques, dans leur parti pris d'élaguer tout ce qui n'est pas créateur de droit.[27]

La dernière entreprise d'analyse médiévale, connue par la copie de 1520, consacre l'évolution, finalement un peu contrariée à Saint-Denis par le poids des modèles du treizième siècle. Les regestes, plus brefs, ne sont plus là que pour guider vers les originaux, des originaux qui, bien éloignés maintenant dans le temps, peuvent être transmués en monuments univoques de la gloire de l'abbaye. Ainsi pour l'acte de 1124:

[27] Ainsi, pour le faux, examiné ci-dessous, de Charles le Chauve, l'analyse (p. 166) donne-t-elle: "Karoli Calvi imperatoris quomodo dedit ecclesie Sancti Dyonisii villam que vocatur Ruolium cum omnibus apendiciis tam in aquis quam aliis et quomodo in quolibet mense debet fieri commemoratio de ipso et aliis regibus Francie et propter hoc fratres debent habere pitanciam; et est ista carta sigillata de auro puro, cum isto signo: A."

> Une aultre chartre de Loys le Gros de l'immunité de l'eglise de la foire du Lendit et comme il tient en foy et homaige de l'eglise le Vexin comme les comtes dudit Vexin le souloit tenir.

Belle entreprise de réécriture, qui va plus loin que Suger (pour qui le roi eût fait hommage s'il n'avait été roi!), mais glisse un peu vite sur la seigneurie territoriale... Mais aussi belle maîtrise de la traduction française, qui finalement rend mieux qu'aucun de ses prédécesseurs la lettre de l'acte de 1120:

> Chartre du roy Loys ⟨le Gros⟩ par laquelle il confesse les couronnes et aultres ornemens royaulx des roys de France aprés leur decés appartenir a l'eglise Sainct Denis et restitue celle de son pere qu'il avoit par aucun temps detenu, pour la dilation de laquelle il a satisffaict et donna l'eglise de Cergy...

4. Des archives à l'histoire

Quelque remarquable qu'ait été le savoir historique des moines-archivistes, quelque grandiose même qu'ait été le projet proprement historique qui a animé Nangis (ou son adjoint, peu importe), il reste que le bilan de ces deux grands siècles est mélangé: sans y introduire le péril du jugement de valeur, il faut constater d'une part que les méthodes archivistiques dionysiennes ont presque été entravées par les solutions adoptées sur la fin du treizième siècle (mais le grand laboratoire des innovations archivistiques se trouve surtout dès lors dans les chartriers princiers); d'autre part que l'intense activité de mise en regeste n'a pas eu d'autres débouchés. C'est bien sûr que l'écriture de l'histoire à Saint-Denis a été, finalement très tôt, conditionnée par une volonté de dépassement, qui a mis la chronique monastique à l'arrière-plan et relégué les actes dans l'atmosphère feutrée du chartrier.[28]

C'est un fait bien connu que l'œuvre de Primat n'est pas retournée, pour le règne de Louis VI, aux actes. Et, plus largement, que l'historien n'est allé prendre aux archives de sa maison qu'une poignée de diplômes, les plus prestigieux tout de même, qui étayent de façon ambivalente et la gloire de l'abbaye et la piété des rois, et qui en outre permettent d'étoffer un peu une documentation décidément trop pauvre: diplômes de Dagobert et de Clo-

[28] Cette volonté de détachement, de surpassement de l'histoire de l'établissement, condition de la réussite du projet, a été déjà fortement soulignée, pour les travaux antérieurs, par Pascale Bourgain, "La protohistoire des *Chroniques latines de Saint-Denis* (BNF, lat. 5925)," dans *Saint-Denis et la royauté*, 375-94.

taire III, et encore, en un traitement si révélateur qu'il mérite un rapide détour, actes (archi-faux et archi-lus) de Charles le Chauve et de Robert le Pieux, qui nous permettront de mieux remettre en situation l'ancien inventaire noir.

Pour faire bref, disons que Primat et son atelier manifestent un savoir de la traduction/résumé qui ne le cède guère à l'art qui se déploie, une quinzaine d'années plus tard, dans l'ancien inventaire noir. À les comparer, on découvrira, entre les deux entreprises, une forte communauté de connaissances, mais aussi de pratiques, et une nette dissemblance de regards, laissant de côté pour l'heure un problème connexe: la possibilité que Primat n'ait pas directement travaillé sur les chartes originales, pas plus que sur des copies, mais sur des sortes de fiches qu'il a pu, à l'occasion, mélanger.[29]

Dissemblance des regards, d'abord, que manifeste de façon éclatante le traitement réservé à un diplôme de Robert le Pieux, fameux (et précisément falsifié) pour sa longue interpolation relative à la destruction du château de Bouchard le Barbu, comme à la construction de la seigneurie entourant l'abbaye. Le traitement des deux abréviateurs, en dehors même de l'incroyable détail où tous deux entrent sur l'affaire Bouchard, illustre au mieux leur propos inversé sur le seul passage du diplôme qui nous retiendra ici: du don que le roi avait fait de la *curtis* qu'il possédait dans le bourg abbatial fortifié, assorti de la promesse de ne plus y tenir de cour solennelle,[30] est sélectionné, chez l'un ce qui apporte une source à l'histoire des rois, chez l'autre ce qui fonde les droits du monastère, taisant même une résidence rayée de la topographie.

[29] En dépit de l'annotation un peu embrouillée de J. Viard, éd. cit., 5:32-35, qui tente manifestement de sauver l'honneur de Primat, je ne vois pas à quoi rapporter, sinon à une méprise, la présentation qu'il fait de deux, ou plutôt trois, dispositions du même acte de Robert le Pieux (sur lequel on revient ci-après), comme étant le contenu de deux actes différents: "Mainte bele chartre dona a l'eglise. Si fu la premiere...Aprés ceste chartre, conferma la chartre du roi Dagobert..."

[30] Pseudo-original: Paris, Archives nationales, K 18, no. 2 (= William Mendel Newman, *Catalogue des actes de Robert II, roi de France* [Paris, 1937], no. † 120), ici l. 8-10; Viard, éd., *Grandes chroniques*, 5:33; Ancien inventaire noir, p. 8a.

ACTE DE ROBERT LE PIEUX	*GRANDES CHRONIQUES* (éd. Viard)	ANCIEN INVENTAIRE NOIR
Curtem itaque nostram cum in ipso castello haberemus, ut nos ab inquietudine ipsius aecclesie et fratrum...longe faceremus...placuit... remittere, ut sollempnem **curiam**, hoc est in Natali Domini, in Teophania, in Pascha, in Pentecoste, neque nos neque successores nostri in ipso castello ulterius ullo modo presumamus celebrare...	Et si dona **sa cort et son palais** que il et li autre roi avoeint touz jors eue laienz et i venoient tenir leur **coorz** aus festes sollempniex come a Noel, a la Thiphene, a Pasques, a Penthecoste.	Concessit ecclesie Beati Dyonisii ne reges Francie teneant **curiam** sollempnem in villa Sancti Dyonisii in Natali Domini, Theophania, Pascha et Penthecoste et hoc concessit ne ecclesia gravaretur expensis.

Communauté de pratiques et, plus loin encore, identique arrière-plan de la tradition orale qui vient enrichir la tradition écrite, avec le grand faux de Charles le Chauve. Quand il traite du Carolingien, Primat est à nouveau confronté à une pénurie de sources; à nouveau donc, il se fait abréviateur d'un acte «maison» et intègre, au chapitre des largesses du roi, entre un merveilleux passage sur la fondation de Saint-Corneille de Compiègne et un long catalogue de reliques, le résumé du plus beau diplôme disponible du souverain, le plus falsifié (l'acte authentique, négligé par toute la tradition dionysienne, s'est pourtant conservé en original jusqu'à nous), le plus célèbre aussi à l'abbaye.[31] L'atelier de Primat et l'atelier de Nangis ont,

[31] Viard, éd., *Grandes chroniques*, 4:254-55 (= Georges Tessier, éd., *Recueil des actes de Charles II le Chauve, roi de France* [Paris, 1943-55], no. † 496), ici comparées avec l'analyse de l'acte dans l'ancien inventaire noir (p. 145a). La double donation de Charles (droits sur une portion de la Seine, objet principal du remaniement, et don de Rueil) était aussi rappelée de façon insistante (c'est la seule donation explicitée, *Sequanii fluvii Ruoliique dator*, avec celle de reliques de la Passion) sur le tombeau du Carolingien: Anne Lombard-Jourdan, "L'invention du 'roi fondateur' à Paris au XIIe siècle, de l'obligation morale au thème sculptural," *BEC* 155 (1997): 485-542, à la p. 495 (qui date l'inscription des alentours de

ici encore, des points de vue opposés: le traitement, d'une part, de la description du bien, de l'autre, des personnages historiques cités est parfaitement symétrique dans le mélange de précision et d'omission. Mais, pour le reste, ils concordent de près dans leur art, et surtout dans leur identique besoin d'insérer une glose qui n'est pas dans l'acte et qui reporte aux temps présents de la discipline monastique[32] (en gras dans les extraits qui suivent, limités à la donation de Rueil):

Grandes chroniques (éd. Viard)	Ancien inventaire noir
La vile de Rueil dona a l'eglise de Saint Denise a toutes les apartenances	Karoli Calvi regis quomodo ipse dedit nobis Ruolium cum omni integritate suarum rerum et mancipiorum, cum terris arabilibus, cultis et incultis, vineis, campis, silvis, pascuis, aquis aquarumve decursibus, piscatoriis, molendinis, exitibus et regressibus...

1200). Plus largement, Andrea Decker-Heuer, *Studien zur Memorialüberlieferung im frühmittelalterlichen Paris*, Beihefte der Francia 40 (Sigmaringen, 1998), 167-76, a montré combien l'acte (le faux) bullé d'or de Charles, *tertius imperator*, avait une place essentielle dans la mise en place de la commémoration des morts à l'abbaye, amplifiée encore sous Suger.

[32] Il s'agit moins d'ajout que d'explication: l'acte de Charles disait simplement que les quinze luminaires mis au réfectoire, par groupe de cinq en trois endroits, seraient allumés "tempore congruo (l'acte disait avant remaniement 'tempore necessario') quia omni tempore (au sens de 'saison') non plena et sufficienti luce causa sollempnitatum aut alicujus praepeditionis omnia fieri possunt." Passage qui, décidément, devait susciter bien des gloses à l'abbaye: dans son regeste de l'acte, en 1706, Dom Michel Félibien (*Histoire de l'abbaye royale de Saint-Denys...*, lib. 2, p. 94) expliquait, plus clairement encore que ses lointains prédécesseurs: "Dans les temps où toutes choses ne pourront pas se faire en plein jour selon le précepte de la règle de saint Benoist, le doyen fournira trois chandeliers de cinq lumières chacun au réfectoire pour éclairer les religieux pendant le souper..."

et establi que sor les rentes de cele vile fussent pris[33] li despens de VII lampes qui ardent continuement et en toutes saisons devant l'autel de la Trinité. La premiere establi pour l'ame de l'empereur Loys son pere, la seconde pour l'ame de la roine Judith sa mere, la tierce pour lui, la quarte pour la roine Hermentruz sa premiere fame, la quinte pour la roine Richeut se presente fame, la sisiesme pour toute sa lignie presente et trespassee, et la VIIme pour Boson et pour Gui et pour tous ses autres familiers.

ita tamen quod pro hiis ardeant tam die quam nocte ante altare sancte Trinitatis VII lampades

Aprés establi XV cierges en refetor a metre seur les tables **en yver pour ce que li covent i vet trop tart aucunes foiz a collation, pour le service qui pas ne puet estre acompliz par jor, et mesmement aus granz festes.**

et quindecim cerei in refectorio **hyberno tempore quando conventus tarde bibit vel comedit,**

et quod qualibet mense conventus habeat refectionem aliquam ex predictis. Debet autem villa ista et omnia que supra memorata sunt esse in providentia atque dispositione decani.

Du treizième au dix-huitième siècle, l'atelier historiographico-archivistique de l'abbaye s'est ingénié à expliquer la raison de la présence des luminaires au réfectoire, et moins en se recopiant qu'en puisant manifestement à une inspiration commune. Il y a fort à parier que cette insistance, témoin d'une vivace tradition interne, trouve son origine dans le domaine para-liturgique: l'Ordinaire de l'abbaye, compilé entre 1234 et 1241, révèle que, seul apparemment à s'attirer un tel traitement, l'acte de Charles était lu chaque

[33] Méprise: l'acte disait que les lampes devaient brûler en contrepartie du don; c'est la réfection du convent, ici tue, qui était assignée sur les revenus du domaine. Cette erreur n'est pas reprise par l'ancien inventaire noir, plus précis, ce qui montre, si besoin était, que les deux compilateurs travaillent indépendamment.

année aux moines réunis en chapitre, la veille de l'anniversaire du souverain, célébré le 6 octobre.[34] C'est à la répétition séculaire de cette lecture (et, pourquoi pas, des commentaires qui l'accompagnaient) qu'il faudrait attribuer, de Primat et Nangis à Dom Félibien, la reprise séculaire de la glose.

*

* *

Jusque dans ce modeste mais tenace souci de mise en lumière—ce que l'approche philologique appellera, à juste titre, une interpolation—, les archivistes non professionnels de Saint-Denis dévoilent l'irréductible, et féconde, tension entre écriture de l'histoire et gestion du chartrier, entre service du saint (ou du prince) et défense de ses serviteurs, qui promet une belle moisson à l'histoire, à venir, des archives médiévales.[35]

[34] Comme il ressort de la belle étude et édition d'Edward B. Foley, *The First Ordinary of the Royal Abbey of St-Denis in France*, Spicilegium Friburgense 32 (Fribourg, 1990), 626: "In precedenti die recitetur carta Karoli imperatoris in capitulo." Les attestations croisées sur l'importance de la fausse bulle d'or ne laissent pas de doute sur l'identification du document.

[35] Sur l'insertion de documents dans des textes historiographiques ou hagiographiques, voir désormais les deux contributions très suggestives de Morelle, "La mise en œuvre des actes diplomatiques," et de Dominique Boutet, "Hagiographie et historiographie: La *Vie de saint Thomas Becket* de Guernes de Pont-Sainte-Maxence et la *Vie de saint Louis* de Joinville," *Le Moyen Âge*, 106 (2000): 277-93. Plus largement et plus récemment encore, noter les thèses (2001) de Laurent Morelle sur Saint-Bertin (à paraître à l'École des chartes) et de Sébastien Barret sur les archives de Cluny.

Originaux et copies: La reproduction des éléments graphiques des actes des Xe et XIe siècles dans le cartulaire de Cluny

Hartmut Atsma et Jean Vezin

Les cartulaires constituent souvent la source unique permettant de connaître des documents administratifs dont les originaux ont disparu. Les diplomatistes se sont toujours demandé quel degré de confiance on pouvait légitimement accorder à ces recueils d'actes, la première question étant de savoir si leurs compilateurs avaient fidèlement transcrit les actes qu'ils réunissaient dans un souci de bonne gestion.[1] Bien entendu, nous écartons d'emblée de cette étude les recueils d'actes faux ou falsifiés comme ce cartulaire factice réuni à Saint-Denis dans la première moitié du onzième siècle dans le dessein évident de défendre les prétentions du monastère qui reposaient en grande partie sur des forgeries.[2]

Nous nous intéressons ici aux recueils d'actes sincères. Une étude d'ensemble des problèmes posés par leur réalisation, de ce point de vue, nous semble prématurée, faute de recherches systématiques, aussi préférons-nous étudier seulement un cartulaire tout à fait exceptionnel par son ancienneté, par son importance historique et par le grand nombre de docu-

[1] Voir Olivier Guyotjeannin, Laurent Morelle, et Michel Parisse, éd., *Les cartulaires: Actes de la table ronde organisée par l'École nationale des chartes et le G.D.R. 121 du C.N.R.S. (Paris, 5-7 décembre 1991)*, Mémoires et documents de l'École des chartes 39 (Paris, 1993).

[2] Paris, BnF, nouv. acq. lat. 326; cf. Hartmut Atsma et Jean Vezin, "Les faux sur papyrus de l'abbaye de Saint-Denis," dans *Finances, pouvoir et mémoire: Hommages à Jean Favier*, éd. Jean Kerhervé et Albert Rigaudière (Paris, 1999), 674-99; Hartmut Atsma et Jean Vezin, "Le dossier suspect des possessions de Saint-Denis en Angleterre revisité (VIIe-IXe siècles)," dans *Fälschungen im Mittelalter: Internationaler Kongreß der Monumenta Germaniae historica, München 16-19 Sept. 1986*, t. 4, *Diplomatische Fälschungen*, MGH Schriften 33.4 (Hanovre, 1988), 211-36, en particulier pp. 225-27; Rolf Grosse, "Remarques sur les cartulaires de Saint-Denis aux XIIIe et XIVe siècles," dans *Les cartulaires*, 279-90.

ments qu'il contient, nous voulons parler du cartulaire de Cluny compilé sous l'abbatiat de saint Hugues (1049-1109). Cet ouvrage, actuellement relié en trois volumes, communément distingué comme «Cartulaire A»,[3] «Cartulaire B»[4] et «Cartulaire C»,[5] contient plusieurs milliers d'actes. Son édition par Auguste Bernard et Alexandre Bruel est bien connue et mérite l'admiration pour son ampleur, bien qu'elle ne réponde plus à tous les critères scientifiques actuellement exigés d'une telle publication.[6] On peut regretter en particulier que les travaux sur les index de noms de personnes et de lieux n'aient pas abouti presque un siècle après la publication. Il faut cependant relativiser ces réserves en se demandant ce que seraient les études clunisiennes si nous ne disposions pas de cet extraordinaire instrument de travail.[7]

Le cartulaire, dont le projet est dû à saint Odilon (994-1049), a été réalisé à notre avis en deux étapes au cours du long abbatiat de saint Hugues. Il se compose de deux parties: une série d'actes copiés en suivant l'ordre des différents abbatiats (Paris, BnF, nouv. acq. lat. 1497 et 1498) et un volume de format plus grand (Paris, BnF, nouv. acq. lat. 2262) qui contient les documents les plus importants pour l'administration de Cluny et pour son histoire, en particulier l'acte de fondation de 910 et les documents émanés, dans l'ordre, des papes, des empereurs et des rois, puis les actes concernant les biens possédés par Cluny en Italie et en Espagne.

Dans ce dernier volume, qu'on désigne sous le nom de «Cartulaire C», les copistes ont transcrit les documents en s'attachant à donner une idée de l'original en imitant certaines particularités graphiques: écriture curiale, *rotae*, et *Bene valete* des bulles pontificales, *litterae elongatae* et monogrammes des privilèges impériaux ou royaux et certaines caractéristiques, surprenantes pour un moine bourguignon de la seconde moitié du onzième

[3] Paris, BnF, nouv. acq. lat. 1497; cf. Léopold Delisle, *Inventaire des manuscrits de la Bibliothèque nationale: Fonds de Cluni* (Paris, 1884), no. 134, pp. 229-31.

[4] Paris, BnF, nouv. acq. lat. 1498; cf. Delisle, *Fonds de Cluni*, no. 135, pp. 231-32.

[5] Paris, BnF, nouv. acq. lat. 2262; cf. Delisle, *Fonds de Cluni*, no. 136, pp. 232-33.

[6] Auguste Bernard et Alexandre Bruel, éd., *Recueil des chartes de l'abbaye de Cluny*, 6 t., Collection de documents inédits sur l'histoire de France (Paris, 1876-1903).

[7] Cf. Jean Richard, "La publication des chartes de Cluny," dans *A Cluny: Congrès scientifique: Fêtes et cérémonies liturgiques en l'honneur des saints abbés Odon et Odilon, 9-11 juillet 1949* (Dijon, 1950), 155-60; Dominique Iogna-Prat et Christian Sapin, "Les études clunisiennes dans tous leurs états: Rencontre de Cluny, 21-22 septembre 1993," *Revue Mabillon*, n.s., 5 [66] (1994): 233-65; Joachim Wollasch, "Zur Erforschung Clunys," *Frühmittelalterliche Studien* 31 (1997): 32-45.

siècle, qu'on observe dans les actes notariés italiens ou dans ceux des rois de Castille et de León.

L'ensemble des cartulaires de Cluny a retenu l'attention de plusieurs savants au cours de ces dernières années.[8] Le Professeur Barbara Rosenwein a consacré une analyse particulièrement détaillée au «Cartulaire C».[9] Contrairement à Bruel qui pensait que le cartulaire avait été réalisé en deux étapes principales, elle estime qu'il a été rédigé pendant une période relativement brève, probablement au début du douzième siècle.

Pour notre part, nous pensons que l'ensemble des trois volumes qui composent ce cartulaire a été copié en deux étapes situées toutes les deux à l'intérieur de l'abbatiat de saint Hugues. L'étape la plus récente doit se placer, croyons-nous, autour de 1095-96, c'est à dire au moment du périple du pape clunisien Urbain II (1088-99) en France. Nous estimons que la partie la plus ancienne, remonte au début de l'abbatiat d'Hugues, comme le montrent les dates de plusieurs documents appartenant à ce groupe, bien que le style de l'écriture et de la décoration aient incité plusieurs auteurs à penser qu'on pouvait y voir un produit du deuxième quart ou du deuxième tiers du onzième siècle.[10]

Malgré les destructions de l'époque révolutionnaire, dont les copies prises par le feudiste Louis-Henri Lambert de Barive de 1770 à 1790 permettent de se représenter l'ampleur, la Bibliothèque nationale de France conserve dans ses fonds latins et des nouvelles acquisitions latines ainsi que dans la Collection de Bourgogne un nombre important de documents originaux.[11] Ces actes appartiennent à des catégories différentes et fournissent

[8] Dominique Iogna-Prat, "La confection des cartulaires et l'historiographie à Cluny (XIe-XIIe s.)," dans *Les cartulaires*, 27-44; Maria Hillebrandt, "Les cartulaires de l'abbaye de Cluny: Aspects d'une conception monastique," *Mémoires de la Société pour l'histoire du droit et des institutions des anciens pays bourguignons, comtois et romands* 50 (1993): 7-18. Voir toujours l'introduction de Bernard et Bruel, éd., *Recueil des chartes de Cluny*, 1:xiv-xxxi.

[9] Barbara H. Rosenwein, "Cluny's Immunities in the Tenth and Eleventh Centuries: Images and Narratives," dans *Die Cluniazenser in ihrem politisch-sozialen Umfeld*, éd. Giles Constable, Gert Melville, et Jörg Oberste, Vita regularis 7 (Münster, 1998), 145-63.

[10] Hartmut Atsma et Jean Vezin, "Gestion de la mémoire à l'époque de saint Hugues (1049-1109): La genèse paléographique et codicologique du plus ancien cartulaire de l'abbaye de Cluny," *Histoire et archives* 7 (2000): 5-29.

[11] Il subsiste 267 documents remontant aux gouvernements des cinq premiers ab-bés Bernon, Odon, Aymard, Maïeul et Odilon (910-1049); Paris, BnF, lat. 11826,

un panorama très large de la production documentaire pendant les deux premiers siècles de l'histoire de Cluny. Ils comprennent des bulles pontificales, des privilèges émanés d'empereurs, de rois de France et de Bourgogne transjurane. Une place à part doit être faite à l'original de l'acte de fondation de Cluny par le duc d'Aquitaine Guillaume Ier le Pieux (886-918) daté du 11 septembre 910.[12] La majorité des documents appartient à la catégorie improprement appelée «actes privés» dans laquelle on trouve des actes d'évêques et de seigneurs territoriaux, mais aussi de simples particuliers.

L'expansion de Cluny au delà des Alpes et des Pyrénées est matérialisée par la présence d'actes notariés italiens et de privilèges des rois de Castille et de León. Le fonds de Cluny présente ainsi pour les dixième et onzième siècles un ensemble de données graphiques variées, soit selon la qualité des autorités d'où émanent ces actes, soit selon les commanditaires, les lieux ou les circonstances de la réalisation en faisant abstraction des données rédactionnelles.

La confrontation entre le cartulaire et les originaux permet d'illustrer concrètement le propos de ce recueil. Nous le ferons en concentrant notre attention sur les aspects graphiques en examinant la manière dont les rédacteurs du «Cartulaire C» ont compris et interprété les particularités des documents qu'ils transcrivaient.

Pour suivre l'ordre, en quelque sorte hiérarchique, adopté dans le cartulaire, nous commencerons par examiner des documents pontificaux et précisément une bulle du pape Benoît VII (974-83) en date du 22 avril 978 conservée dans les archives de Cluny sous la forme d'une copie en écriture

---

11829, 11834, 17715; nouv. acq. lat. 2154, 2163, 2281; Collection de Bourgogne, vols. 76 à 79; cf. Delisle, *Fonds de Cluni*, pp. 237-47 et 253-64. Nous avons entrepris avec Sébastien Barret la publication de ces documents en fac-similé à grandeur d'original avec transcription et commentaire dans la collection des *Monumenta palaeographica Medii Aevi.* Trois volumes sont déjà parus: Hartmut Atsma, Jean Vezin, et Sébastien Barret, éd., *Les plus anciens documents originaux de l'abbaye de Cluny*, t. 1 (Turnhout, 1997), t. 2 (Turnhout, 2000), t. 3 (Turnhout, 2002). L'ensemble devrait comprendre huit ou neuf tomes: cf. Hartmut Atsma, "Les plus anciens documents originaux de l'abbaye de Cluny conservés à la Bibliothèque nationale de France: Bilan et perspectives d'un projet d'édition en fac-similé," dans *Les ateliers de l'Institut historique allemand* (Paris, 1994), 33-43; Hartmut Atsma et Jean Vezin, "Une nouvelle collection de fac-similés: Monumenta palaeographica Medii Aevi," *Francia* 24.1 (1997): 141-45.

[12] Atsma, Vezin, et Barret, éd., *Les plus anciens documents*, t. 1, no. 4, pp. 33-39.

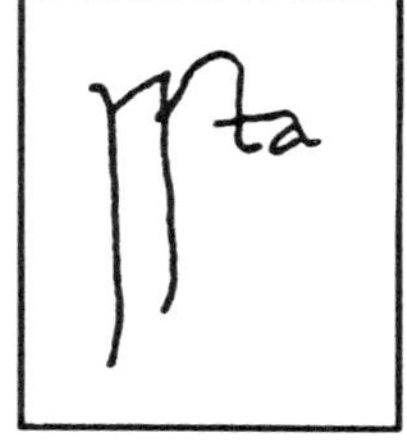

Figure 1

livresque du dixième ou du onzième siècle.[13] A la fin du document original, aujourd'hui disparu, se trouvait une abréviation de l'adjectif *suprascripta* que le copiste n'a pas comprise et dont il a donné une représentation figurée fidèle (Fig. 1). Le scribe du «Cartulaire C» l'a reproduite,[14] soit d'après l'original lui même, soit, plus vraisemblablement, d'après la copie figurée. En revanche, il a omis les croix tracées en tête de l'acte et devant la ligne de date.

Les particularités graphiques d'une bulle du pape Alexandre II (1061-73) fulminée le 10 mai 1063[15] sont soigneusement reproduites dans le «Cartulaire C».[16] On observe en particulier que la première ligne et la *rota* sont transcrites avec soin. Par contre, le scribe du cartulaire introduit des variantes dans le dessin du *Bene valete* (Fig. 2). Dans la bulle originale, le texte est, comme c'est la règle, copié en écriture curiale. Le copiste clunisien, lui, utilise la minuscule caroline qui lui était plus familière; mais, en plusieurs endroits, il imite la curiale avec un talent certain. C'est ainsi qu'il emploie notamment le *a* oncial typique de la minuscule caroline, mais aussi le *a* en forme d'ω de la curiale. Il imite d'autres lettres de la curiale, *q* et *t*, par exemple ou des ligatures comme *et, gi, ri, ti*. Il dessine fidèlement l'abréviation pour *episcopi* (Fig. 3). On remarque aussi la reproduction soigneuse des deux mots *et anathematis* (Fig. 4) et de la terminaison *-gatione* (Fig. 5).

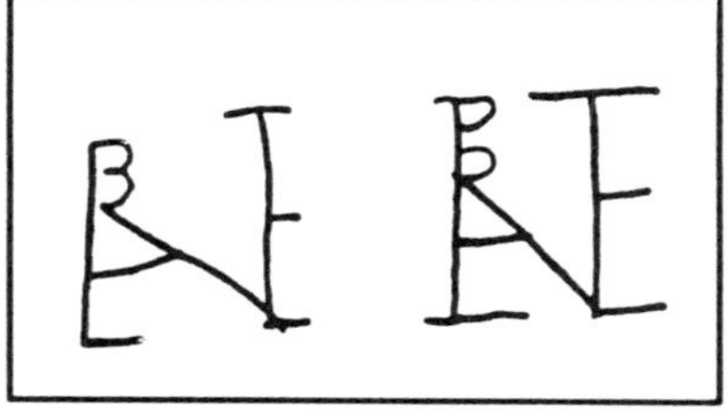

Figure 2: Original et copie

Figure 3

L'original d'une bulle du pape clunisien Urbain II, datée de Plaisance le 16 mars 1095, est écrit avec une

[13] Atsma, Vezin, et Barret, éd., *Les plus anciens documents*, t. 2, no. 43, pp. 68-71 = JL 3796 (2906).

[14] Paris, BnF, nouv. acq. lat. 2262, no. 21, p. 19.

[15] Paris, BnF, Coll. de Bourgogne, vol. 78, no. 115 = JL 4513 (3387).

[16] Paris, BnF, nouv. acq. lat. 2262, no. 40, p. 39.

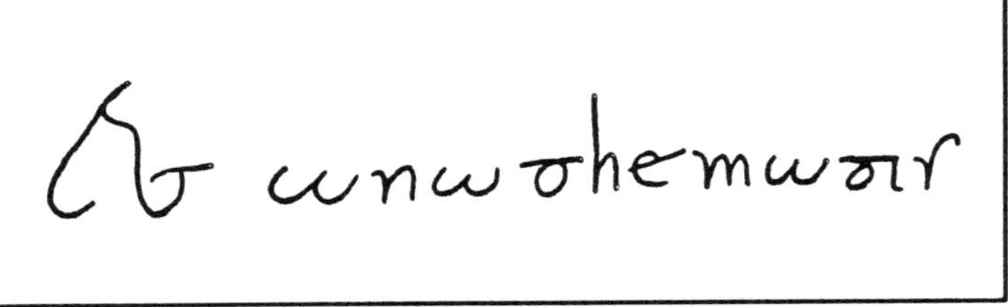

Figure 4

minuscule très régulière, sans trace de curiale.[17] La première ligne, qui contient l'adresse, est tracée en *litterae elongatae*. La transcription dans le cartulaire[18] a été réalisée au moyen d'une minuscule caroline de caractère livresque; les *litterae elongatae* de la première ligne n'ont pas été reproduites. Seul, le dernier mot du texte proprement dit de la bulle, *amen*, fait l'objet d'une représentation figurée assez fidèle (Fig. 6). La *rota* et le *Bene valete* sont dessinés à l'emplacement convenable; mais il ne s'agit pas de reproductions fidèles, comme c'était le cas pour la bulle précédente d'Alexandre II. Le dessin de la *rota* est conforme à son modèle, à cette différence près que les boules qui terminent les extrémités des bras de la croix n'ont pas été reproduites. La mention qui occupe le pourtour de la *rota* «Benedictus deus et pater domini nostri Iesu Christi» est tracée en minuscule, sauf les mots «N(ost)RI IHU XPI» qui sont en capitales rustiques, dans l'original. Dans la copie, cette invocation est entièrement tracée en capitales. Les invocations

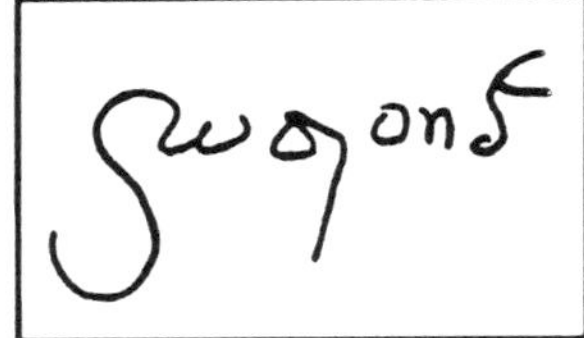

Figure 5

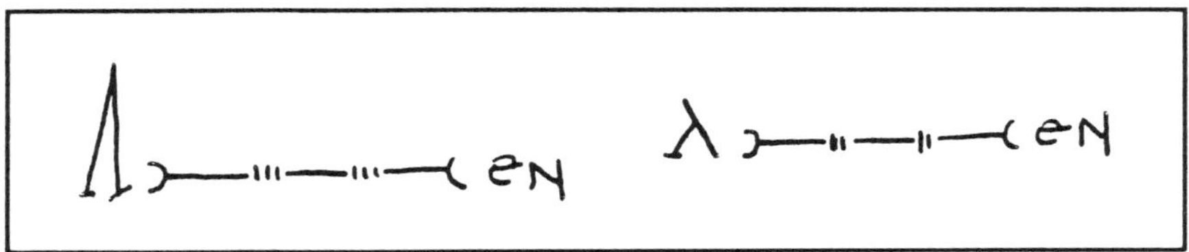

Figure 6. Original et copie

[17] Paris, BnF, Coll. de Bourgogne, vol. 79, no. 161 = JL 5551 (4157).

[18] Paris, BnF, nouv. acq. lat. 2262, no. 45, pp. 46-47.

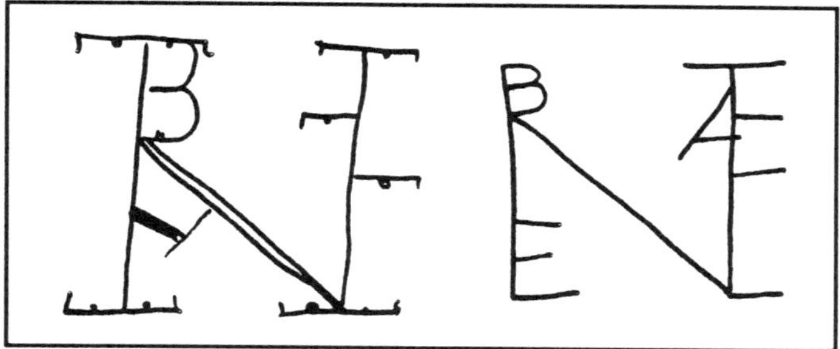

Figure 7. Original et copie

«Sanctus Petrus, Sanctus Paulus» sont conformes au modèle dans le cartulaire; mais l'inscription «Urbanus papa secundus» n'est pas tracée de la même manière dans la bulle et dans le cartulaire.

En ce qui concerne le *Bene valete*, le copiste du cartulaire n'a pas compris la forme assez complexe du modèle (Fig. 7). Il n'a pas remarqué notamment le trait horizontal de *A*, très fin, tracé entre le premier jambage vertical de N et le trait oblique de cette même lettre, non plus que le *V* tracé dessous. Il a ajouté en bas du premier jambage de *N* un *E* qui ne figure pas dans l'original. Le *A* accolé au second trait vertical de *N* est une invention de sa part. On doit voir dans son dessin une interprétation du modèle et non sa reproduction exacte.

La première ligne d'un précepte du roi de France Raoul (923-36), daté du 21 juin 932 à Anse, près de Lyon,[19] est entièrement tracée en *litterae elongatae*, qu'il s'agisse de l'invocation initiale, de la titulature du roi et des premiers mots de l'acte proprement dit. Le reste du texte est écrit en cursive diplomatique. Sur la ligne 15, le «signum Rodulfi regis gloriosissimi» est suivi d'un monogramme et d'un sceau plaqué (Fig. 8).

Dans le cartulaire,[20] la première ligne, qui contient seulement l'invocation initiale et le début de la titulature royale, est transcrite en *litterae elongatae* qui reproduisent fidèlement le tracé de l'original. Le scribe a toutefois omis de reproduire le chrismon placé en tête de l'acte et il a tracé le *I* initial à l'encre rouge en lui donnant des proportions beaucoup plus fortes que dans le modèle. Ce *I* fait penser aux initiales de paragraphes ou de cha-

[19] Paris, BnF, Coll. de Bourgogne, vol. 76, no. 13; Atsma, Vezin, et Barret, éd., *Les plus anciens documents*, t. 1, no. 11, pp. 62-66.

[20] Paris, BnF, nouv. acq. lat. 2262, no. 49, pp. 49-50.

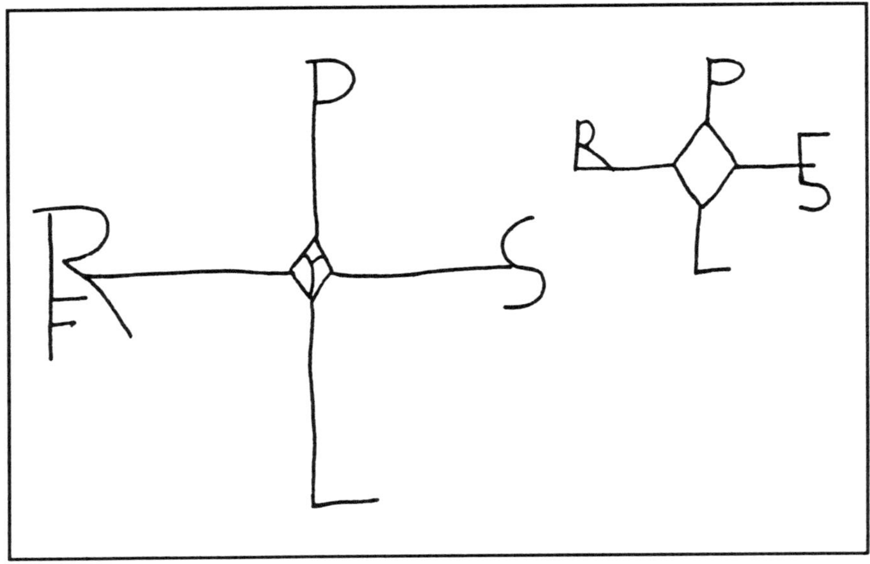

Figure 8. Original et copie

pitres dans les livres contemporains. Le reste du texte est entièrement copié en minuscule caroline livresque, sans trace d'écriture diplomatique.

Le sceau plaqué sur la ligne 15 de l'original n'est ni mentionné, ni reproduit sur la copie (Fig. 8). Comme dans le *Bene valete* de la bulle d'Urbain II que nous venons de commenter, la reproduction du monogramme royal n'est pas exactement conforme à l'original. Le *Vollziehungsstrich*, un trait qui exprime normalement l'achèvement de la transcription de l'acte juridique, a disparu. A gauche, le *R* est placé sur l'extrémité du trait horizontal et le *F* est transféré à l'extrémité du trait de droite, au dessus de *S*, alors que seul *S* se trouve à cette place sur le modèle.

Des observations comparables peuvent être faites à propos d'un précepte du roi de Bourgogne transjurane et de Provence Conrad le Pacifique (937-93) daté du 18 mai de l'année 943, 945 ou 946.[21] Ni le chrismon placé en tête de l'acte, ni celui qui précède le *signum* royal n'ont été reproduits. La première ligne de la copie[22] est écrite en *litterae elongatae* dont le tracé

[21] Paris, BnF, Coll. de Bourgogne, vol. 76, no. 20; Atsma, Vezin, et Barret, éd., *Les plus anciens documents*, t. 1, no. 18, pp. 79-81.

[22] Paris, BnF, nouv. acq. lat. 2262, no. 55, p. 54.

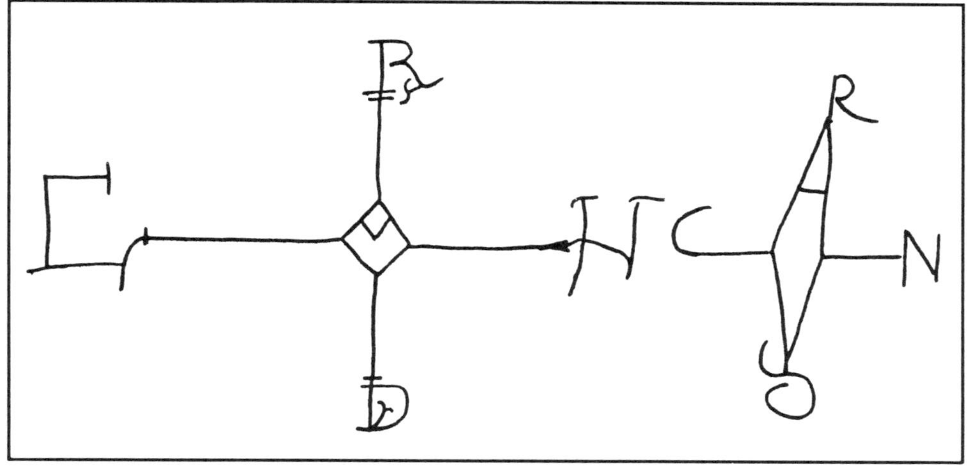

Figure 9. Original et copie

diffère sensiblement de celui des *litterae elongatae* du modèle. Tout le reste de l'acte a été copié dans le cartulaire en minuscule caroline livresque, sans trace d'écriture diplomatique. Les *litterae elongatae* du *signum* royal et de la souscription du notaire *Einricus* sont transcrites en minuscule caroline livresque comme le reste de l'acte. Il n'y a aucune mention du sceau plaqué de l'original. La reproduction du monogramme n'est pas très fidèle (Fig. 9). Le *C* «carré» et le *D* capital du précepte sont transcrits par un *C* capital ordinaire et par un *d* oncial. Comme dans le document précédent, le *Vollziehungsstrich* est également omis. La forme du losange central est différente; elle est très allongée dans le cartulaire. On peut donc penser que le copiste cherchait seulement à donner une idée de la présentation du document orginal plutôt que de reproduire fidèlement ses particularités graphiques.

Un autre document royal, un précepte émané de l'autorité de Louis IV d'Outremer (936-54) daté du 3 février 951 à Pouilly-sur-Loire,[23] se prête exactement aux mêmes observations que les actes précédents: omission du chrismon tracé en tête de l'original, première ligne de la copie en *litterae*

[23] Paris, BnF, Coll. de Bourgogne, vol. 76, no. 27; Atsma, Vezin, et Barret, éd., *Les plus anciens documents*, t. 1, no. 25, pp. 100-103.

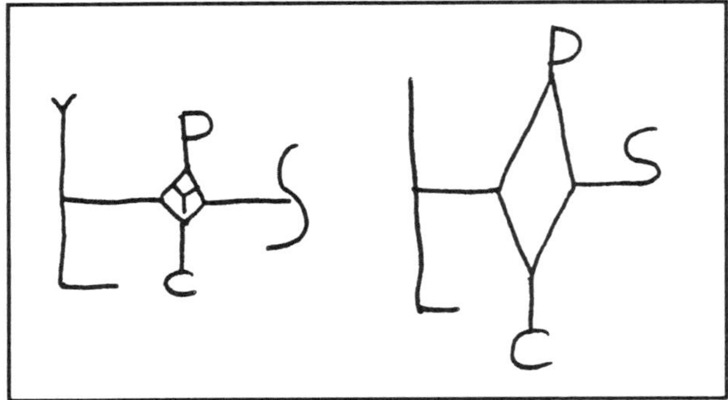

Figure 10. Original et copie

elongatae reproduisant à peu près celles de l'original, transcription de tout le reste de l'acte en minuscule caroline livresque.[24] Le monogramme royal a été imité plus fidèlement que précédemment (Fig. 10); toutefois, le *Vollziehungsstrich* a été omis, de même que le *V* placé dans le modèle au dessus de la lettre *L*. La position de *S* par rapport au trait horizontal de droite est différente sur le modèle et sur la copie. Le losange central est très allongé dans la copie.

Les archives de Cluny conservent deux actes notariés italiens du 16 juillet 967 concernant des possessions de l'abbaye situées à Pavie.[25] Ces actes, par leur forme, mais surtout à cause de leur écriture cursive caractéristique du notariat dans le nord de la Péninsule, ont dérouté les copistes du «Cartulaire C».[26] Les deux actes ont été copiés l'un à la suite de l'autre entièrement en minuscule caroline, sous une forme très modifiée, et insérés dans le texte d'un jugement daté du 18 juillet 967, en corrigeant le latin et en abrégeant les formules.

Le numéro 40 de notre édition, *Les plus anciens documents originaux de l'abbaye de Cluny*, a été transcrit une seconde fois dans le cartulaire.[27] Cette

[24] Paris, BnF, nouv. acq. lat. 2262, no. 70, p. 63.

[25] Paris, BnF, Coll. de Bourgogne, vol. 77, nos. 42 et 43; publ. dans Atsma, Vezin, et Barret, éd., *Les plus anciens documents*, t. 2, nos. 40 et 41, pp. 54-58 et 59-63.

[26] Paris, BnF, nouv. acq. lat. 2262, nos. 85 et 86, pp. 75-76 et 76-78; Atsma, Vezin, et Barret, éd., *Les plus anciens documents*, t. 2, nos. 41, 40, pp. 59, 54.

[27] Paris, BnF, nouv. acq. lat. 2262, nos. 85 et 86, pp. 75-76 et 76-78; Atsma, Vezin, et Barret, éd., *Les plus anciens documents*, t. 2, nos. 41, 40, pp. 59, 54.

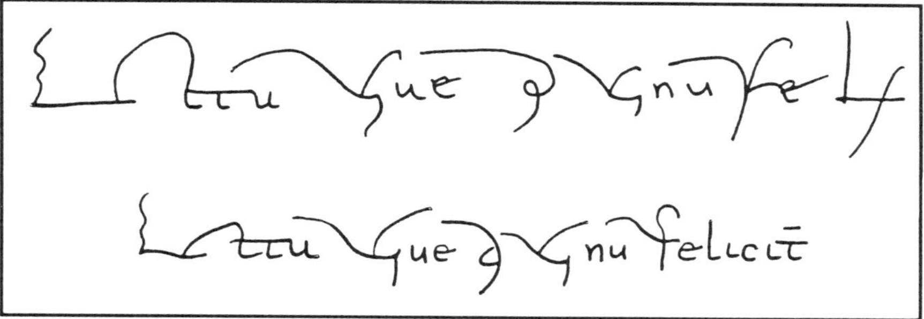

Figure 11. Original (en haut) et copie (en bas)

seconde copie a été, comme précédemment, écrite en minuscule caroline; mais le scribe a dessiné un véritable fac-similé de la mention de lieu: «Actu(m) cive(tate) Ticinu(m) fel(iciter)», à une exception près: il a développé le dernier mot du modèle: *fel* en *felicit* (Fig. 11). La manière dont il a dessiné les lettres montre à notre avis qu'il avait compris son modèle; cependant il a mal reproduit la ligature *ti* marquée par une sorte de boucle dans l'original.

On sait combien étroites étaient les relations de Cluny avec le royaume de Castille et de León pendant le onzième siècle. Ceci explique la présence dans les archives de l'abbaye de plusieurs documents d'origine espagnole dont le plus ancien conservé en original est daté de l'année 1033.[28] Ces documents ont présenté plusieurs difficultés aux scribes de Cluny. Les premières provenaient de l'écriture traditionnelle des scribes de la Péninsule, l'écriture dite «wisigothique», qui recelait plusieurs pièges pour un copiste qui avait appris à lire et à écrire la minuscule caroline: problèmes de déchiffrement des abréviations et confusion entre les lettres *a* et *u* notamment. La forme diplomatique des actes aussi pouvait leur paraître étrange et surtout la manière d'indiquer la date suivant l'ère d'Espagne, qui, comme on le sait, a son point de départ trente-huit ans avant l'ère de l'Incarnation.

Un bon exemple des problèmes posés par les actes provenant d'Espagne est constitué par une *Carta testamenti* d'Alphonse VI (1040-1109), roi de Castille et de León, en date du 10 juillet 1077.[29] Dans le cartulaire, l'acte est entièrement transcrit en minuscule caroline. On ne voit pas de trace d'imi-

[28] Paris, BnF, Coll. de Bourgogne, vol. 77, no. 90.

[29] Paris, BnF, Coll. de Bourgogne 78, no. 135; copie dans le «Cartulaire C», no. 106, pp. 100-101.

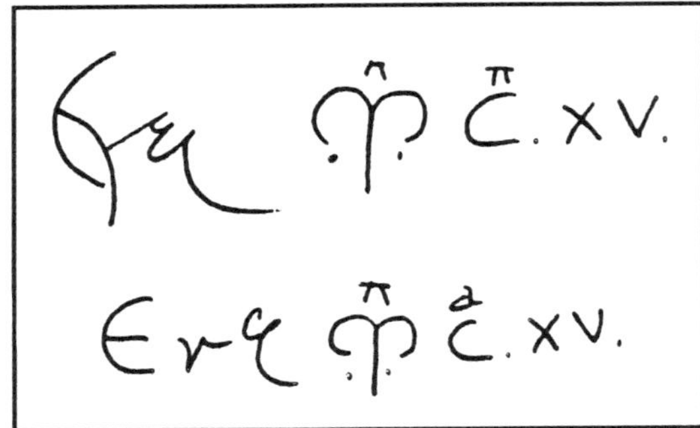

Figure 12. Original (en haut) et copie (en bas)

tation de l'écriture wisigothique du modèle. Alors que l'original est entièrement écrit à l'encre noire, sur la ligne 8 de la copie, la formule «Ego Adefonsus gratia dei rex Leonum» est transcrite à l'encre rouge, ce qui la fait ressortir et en fait une sorte de titre. Dans la formule de date, les mots «regnante rege Aldefonso» sont également transcrits à l'encre rouge dans le cartulaire.

Le copiste du cartulaire a rencontré quelques difficultés pour transcrire la formule de date qui se présente dans le modèle. Le *k* de *kartula* a été remplacé par un *c* de même que celui de *Kastella* et le mot *testamenti* a été omis. Le scribe du cartulaire a été induit en erreur par la ligature *te* du nom *Kastella* qu'il a dû prendre pour un simple *e* et il a transcrit ce mot *casella*. Il a commis en outre la confusion classique entre *a* et *u*, écrivant *Gonsulviz* au lieu de *Gonsalviz* dans une souscription. Probablement par crainte de commettre une erreur, il a réalisé une sorte de fac-similé de la formule de date (Fig. 12). Il a en revanche modifié la mise en page des souscriptions car il ne possédait pas assez de place en largeur pour reproduire celle de l'acte. Au lieu de transcrire trois colonnes parallèles avec, dans l'ordre, de gauche à droite, les souscriptions des comtes, celles des abbés et celles des évêques, il a inscrit ces souscriptions les unes à la suite des autres en commençant par les comtes qu'il a fait suivre par les évêques enfin par les abbés.

Les quelques exemples que nous venons de passer en revue montrent, au moins en partie, comment les copistes du «Cartulaire C» de Cluny ont procédé. Il s'agit d'un cartulaire exceptionnel dans lequel les scribes ont donné des indications plus ou moins exactes sur les principales particularités graphiques des documents qu'ils reproduisaient. Dans certains cas, comme celui de l'abréviation de *suprascripta* dans le privilège de Benoît VII, on peut penser que le scribe, ne sachant pas développer cette abréviation ou craignant de mal l'interpréter, a préféré dessiner ce qu'il avait sous les yeux, selon une technique bien connue. Le même phénomène a dû se produire quand il s'est agi de reproduire le chiffre *mil* dans les documents espagnols dont la minuscule wisigothique les a gênés pour la transcription de noms propres auxquels des scribes bourguignons n'étaient pas habitués. Une motivation différente semble avoir animé le scribe qui a transcrit l'acte notarié de Pavie du 16 juillet 967. Il a visiblement éprouvé des difficultés pour déchriffer son écriture cursive, ce qui explique les nombreuses erreurs de transcription qu'il a commises. Par contre, nous ne pensons pas que la mention de date «Actum cive(tate) Ticinu(m) felicit(er)» ait présenté pour lui des difficultés de lecture. On peut supposer qu'il l'a reproduite fidèlement parce que sa forme lui semblait jouer un rôle important et pour renforcer l'impression d'authenticité de sa copie.

La transcription des bulles pontificales et des diplômes de souverains soulève des problèmes différents, si l'on met à part les actes d'origine espagnole. Nos scribes paraissent avoir été familiers de ces documents puisque même l'écriture curiale ne semble pas soulever pour eux de problèmes particuliers de lecture et qu'ils sont capables, le cas échéant, de reproduire très convenablement cette calligraphie si particulière alors qu'à peu près à la même époque, en 1075, l'archevêque de Tours Raoul devait s'adresser à l'abbé de Marmoutiers pour déchiffrer une bulle de Grégoire V (996-99) datée du 29 septembre 996 et transcrite, elle aussi, en écriture curiale.[30] Le copiste de la bulle d'Alexandre II reproduit avec soin la *rota* et le *Bene valete*. Il n'en va pas de même dans le cas de la bulle d'Urbain II où des différences, pourtant faciles à éviter, existent entre le modèle et la copie. Le copiste se souciait sans doute seulement de donner une impression d'ensemble du document qu'il transcrivait, sachant que les lecteurs du cartulaire n'avaient pas besoin d'une précision parfaite pour se rendre compte de la nature de l'acte dont ils examinaient la transcription.

On observe le même procédé dans les privilèges des rois Raoul, Conrad le Pacifique et Louis IV d'Outremer. Les copies rappellent que la première ligne de ces actes sont transcrites en *litterae elongatae*; mais la longueur du texte ainsi recopié ne correspond pas à celle de l'original. Comme dans le cas de la *rota* et du *Bene valete* de la bulle d'Urbain II, les monogrammes accompagnant les *signa* de ces souverains ne sont pas exactement reproduits, alors que leur dessin n'offrait pas de difficultés. On peut en outre se demander si ce n'est pas intentionnellement que les copistes n'ont reproduit ni les *chrismon*, ni les *Vollziehungsstriche*.

[30] Donatien de Bruyne, "Scriptura romana," dans *Mélanges d'histoire offerts à Charles Moeller*, t. 1 (Louvain, 1914), 322-23, cité par Jacques Stiennon, *Paléographie du Moyen Âge* (Paris, 1973), 24.

Ainsi, le «Cartulaire C» donne une impression de l'apparence des originaux des documents qu'il contient plutôt qu'une reproduction fidèle. Les diplomatistes qui seraient tentés de l'utiliser pour faire une critique d'authenticité des actes disparus à partir des reproductions des signes graphiques qu'il contient risqueraient de commettre de lourdes erreurs.

Étienne de Gallardon and the Cartulary of Bourges

John Baldwin

"Étienne de Gallardon and the Making of the Cartulary of Bourges," *Viator* 31 (2000), 121-46.

This study pursues the career of Étienne de Gallardon as canon and *prepositus temporalis* at Bourges from 1227 to 1243 after he left the royal chancery. Thanks to a distinctive self-consciousness and scribal hand, his role in creating a new cartulary for the chapter (Paris, BnF, nouv. acq. lat. 1274) can be discerned. By 1230-31 he completed the original redaction to which he contributed a hierocratic organization, transcriptions of charters, running heads, rubrics, numbering of charters, and inventories to the major sections. Afterwards he added other materials to which he appended large black titles in a more cursive hand. Étienne's cartulary also contains an unusual text purporting to be a dialogue over the choice of worthy bishops between King Philip Augustus and Pierre, chanter of Paris. Although not copied in Étienne's book hand, it can be ascribed to him through a large black title in his cursive hand. Transcribed before 1239, the dialogue may be situated in the context of the disputed election of 1232-36 that chose the sainted Philippe Berruyer as archbishop (1236-60).

The Earliest Comital Cartulary from Champagne

Theodore Evergates

The eight cartularies produced by the comital chancery of Champagne in the course of the thirteenth century constitute the largest collection of princely cartularies from medieval France.[1] They were much appreciated by the early historians of medieval institutions who consulted them in the Chambre des Comptes in Paris, and they figured prominently in the well-known treatises on feudal institutions by Louis Chantereau-Lefebvre (1662) and Nicolas Brussel (1727).[2] In the mid-nineteenth century Henri d'Arbois de Jubainville catalogued most of the cartularies in order to establish a secure chronology for his history of the counts of Champagne, but he did not explore the creation, function, or significance of the cartularies themselves.[3] Nor did the other great authority on medieval Champagne, Auguste Longnon, who edited the financial, feudal, and domanial registers of the counts.[4] Today, the comital cartularies remain entirely unedited, and rarely consulted.

The earliest of the eight cartularies was produced in 1211.[5] It is today the earliest extant comital register from Champagne. It also carries the distinction of being the earliest princely cartulary from northern France, predating by over half a century the comparable volumes from the county

[1] Theodore Evergates, "The Chancery Archives of the Counts of Champagne: Codicology and History of the Cartulary-Registers," *Viator* 16 (1985): 159-79.

[2] Louis Chantereau-Lefebvre, *Traité des fiefs et de leur origine* (Paris, 1662); Nicolas Brussel, *Nouvel examen de l'usage général des fiefs en France*, 2 vols. (Paris, 1727; 2d ed. 1750).

[3] Henri d'Arbois de Jubainville, *Histoire des ducs et des comtes de Champagne*, 7 vols. (Paris, 1859-69).

[4] Auguste Longnon, ed., *Documents relatifs au comté de Champagne et de Brie (1172-1361)*, 3 vols. (Paris, 1901-14); Longnon, ed., *Rôles des fiefs du comté de Champagne sous le règne de Thibaut le Chansonnier (1249-52)* (Paris, 1877).

[5] Paris, Archives nationales de France, KK 1064, fols. 238-45, 254-66 (see Evergates, "The Chancery Archives," Tables 2, 3).

of Blois and duchy of Burgundy (both compiled in 1272).[6] Preparatory to an edition of the cartulary, I would like to address two general sets of questions. First: why was the cartulary produced, what does it contain, how is it organized, and how does it compare with contemporary secular cartularies? Second, what does the cartulary reveal about the formation and content of the chancery archive, and what can that archive, in turn, reveal about the governance of a territorial state around 1200?

The cartulary was produced shortly after the appointment of Remi of Navarre as chancellor (January 1211-February 1220). Unlike earlier chancellors recruited from collegiate chapters in Troyes and Provins, Remi was an outsider, the illegitimate son of Sancho VII the Strong, king of Navarre (1194-1234), and thus the nephew of Blanche of Navarre, regent countess of Champagne (1201-22).[7] Blanche had arrived in Champagne a decade earlier, in 1199, to marry count Thibaut III (1198-1201), and at his death she ruled the county for his posthumous son Thibaut (IV) under the protection of King Philip II. She was an active ruler from the very start of her regency. She continued Thibaut III's new castle policies; she exploited every opportunity to increase the comital domain and extend comital influence; and she established close spiritual and economic ties with the region's monastic communities.[8] In 1210, however, she may have been jolted when, at the king's insistence, she surrendered her nine-year-old son for a four-year residence at the royal palace, where he joined his cousins Jeanne and Marguerite, heiresses of Flanders.[9] It is possible that Blanche's need for a familial presence in Champagne led her to seek out her nephew Remi to fill the chancellorship, which had been vacant since March 1207.

[6] Robert-Henri Bautier, "Cartulaires de chancellerie et recueils d'actes des authorités laïques et ecclésiastiques," in *Les cartulaires: Actes de la table ronde organisée par l'École nationale des chartes et le G.D.R. 121 du C.N.R.S. (Paris, 5-7 décembre 1991)*, ed. Olivier Guyotjeannin, Laurent Morelle, and Michel Parisse, Mémoires et documents de l'École des chartes 39 (Paris, 1993), 369-76.

[7] Little is known about Remi, who became bishop of Pamplona (1220-28); see Arbois de Jubainville, *Histoire*, 4:526-27, and José Goñi Gaztambide, *Historia de los obispos de Pamplona*, vol. 1, *siglos IV-XIII* (Pamplona, 1979), 551-66.

[8] Blanche's rule is discussed briefly in Theodore Evergates, "Aristocratic Women in the County of Champagne," in *Aristocratic Women in Medieval France*, ed. Theodore Evergates (Philadelphia, 1999), 81-83, and at greater length in Arbois de Jubainville, *Histoire*, 4:101-97.

[9] Karen Nicholas, "Countesses as Rulers in Flanders," in *Aristocratic Women*, 127-33.

Remi appeared as chancellor in January 1211, and nine months later, in October 1211, the chancery completed its first-ever cartulary.

The cartulary originally consisted of at least five eight-folio quires containing copies of more than two hundred sealed letters received from lay and religious persons, primarily barons and prelates. In view of the cartulary's fragmentary state, and in the absence of earlier cartularies in Champagne that might have served as local models for it, the purpose of the cartulary is difficult to determine.[10] The highly abbreviated nature of the script suggests that the new chancellor had the cartulary made as an in-house finding aid, perhaps for his own convenience. But it is also possible that Blanche requested the cartulary as a record of her rule to date, for it was prepared with great care: the folios are precisely ruled in double-column format; the texts are complete and accurate copies; and space has been left for rubrication.

Between February 1212 and July 1214 additional texts were inserted into the completed folios. The latest ones, letters from Philip II affirming his support for the countess and her thirteen-year-old son, were inserted haphazardly, in hurried hands, reflecting the recent turn of events in Champagne. A local baron, Erard of Brienne, lord of Ramerupt and scion of one of the most prestigious lineages in the county, had challenged young Thibaut's right to succeed.[11] I omit the details here, except to say that, with King Philip's unswerving support, Countess Blanche put down a nasty civil war (1216-18), and after hostilities ended Chancellor Remi created a new cartulary (1218) devoted to the recent conflict and its resolution.

With the accession of Count Thibaut IV (1222-53) and the arrival of a

[10] Montier-en-Der's first cartulary dates to ca. 1127 (Chaumont, AD de la Haute-Marne, 7 H 1); see Laurent Morelle, "The Metamorphosis of Three Monastic Charter Collections in the Eleventh Century (Saint-Amand, Saint-Riquier, Montier-en-Der)," in *Charters and the Use of the Written Word in Medieval Society*, ed. Karl Heidecker, Utrecht Studies in Medieval Literacy 5 (Turnhout, 2000), 190-94. Warin, canon of the cathedral chapter of Châlons-sur-Marne, compiled a small cartulary in the early twelfth century (Châlons-sur-Marne, AD de la Marne, G 462; Paul Pélicier, ed., *Cartulaire du chapitre de l'église cathédral de Châlons-sur-Marne, par le chantre Warin* [Paris, 1897]). Molesme's first cartulary was drawn up ca. 1142 (Jacques Laurent, ed., *Cartulaires de l'abbaye de Molesme*, 2 vols. [Paris, 1907, 1911]). There is no evidence for other twelfth-century cartularies in Champagne, despite substantial monastic archival collections at the time.

[11] Arbois de Jubainville, *Histoire*, 4:101-7, which narrates Countess Blanche's entire regency as a response to Erard of Brienne's challenge.

new chancellor, Guillaume (1222-32), the chancery archive was thoroughly reorganized, as several hundred documents were resorted and copied into two new cartularies. The volume now known as the "Cartulary of Countess Blanche" was a selective record of her entire regency and seems to have accompanied her to Argensolles, the Cistercian convent she had founded for her retirement years. The second cartulary remained in the chancery as a finding aid to a closed archive of documents received before Thibaut's accession. As a result of the archival reclassification, the earlier cartularies of 1211 and 1218 lost their organic ties to the archival collection and, consequently, their utility as finding aids; they had become commemorative volumes. It was at that point, in 1222-24, that a chancery scribe foliated in Roman numerals (I-XXXII) what remained of the cartulary of 1211 and added a descriptive title to one quire: *littere baronum*. Within the next decade, perhaps in 1232, the cartulary of 1211 lost its entire first quire (fols. I-VIII).[12] Only two intact quires and parts of two others remained from the original cartulary.

The surviving folios contain 104 texts copied in 1211 plus 17 others added to July 1214, for a total of 121 texts. The letters are primarily from the great lay and religious personages of the county and concern matters directly of interest to the count or countess. Most of the letters (103, or 84 percent) are dated between 1198 and 1211, that is, from the three-year rule of Thibaut III and the first decade of Blanche's regency. Within the cartulary the letters are gathered pell-mell into two categories, according to whether their authors were lay or religious persons. The quire labelled *littere baronum* consists of secular letters dealing with governance and feudal tenure, primarily homage, fiefs, *mouvance*, and the rendering of castles. A second group of letters deals with economic and lordly rights over rural communities, *pariages*, sales, mortgages, debts, and pledges. A smaller third group relates to the personal affairs of the count and countess, particularly support for Thibaut IV's succession and spiritual benefits for Blanche.

In terms of content, organization, and purpose, the cartulary of 1211 differs fundamentally from the contemporary royal registers. Philip II's Register A of 1205 consists primarily of copies of the royal chancery's own internally generated administrative lists and royal acts, and the texts added

[12] The first quire probably was lost when all the chancery cartularies were disassembled and recopied in 1232; see Evergates, "The Chancery Archives," 169-70.

to it between 1205 and 1211 are in large part copies of the king's own acts. In fact, almost 90 percent of the letters in Register A are outgoing royal letters; in the comital cartulary, by contrast, almost 90 percent of the letters are incoming ones.[13] Closer in spirit to the comital cartulary, in being copies of incoming letters, are the earlier royal cartularies compiled by Abbot Suger of Saint-Denis and Bishop Hugh of Champfleury. Suger collected 164 letters he received or sent as regent for Louis VII in 1147-49,[14] while Hugh amassed over 400 letters during his term as chancellor from 1152 to 1172.[15] Yet those collections contain what can be called "missive letters" or diplomatic correspondance.[16] They are quite unlike the sealed, constitutive letters dealing with oaths, homages, castles, fiefs, lordship, dowers, and *pariages* that make up the comital cartulary.

The comital cartulary most closely ressembles two secular cartularies from the south, both called *liber instrumentorum*. The cartulary of the Trencavel, viscounts of Béziers and Carcassonne, was composed initially in 1186-88. It contains over five hundred texts from the eleventh and twelfth centuries dealing mostly with feudal matters: oaths, grants, recognitions, sales, mortgages, and bilateral accords.[17] Two decades later Guilhem (VIII) of Montpellier collected 570 similar acts.[18] Those two cartulaires stand in the shadow of an even grander collection from Barcelona, the *Liber feu-*

[13] John W. Baldwin et al., eds., *Les registres de Philippe Auguste,* vol. 1, *Texte* (Paris, 1992), 441-512. In the comital cartulary of 1211, only 14 (11.5 percent) of the 121 letters are comital ones.

[14] Suger, "Epistolae Sugerii Abbatis S. Dionysii," ed. Michel-Jean-Joseph Brial, *Recueil des historiens des Gaules et de la France,* vol. 15 (Paris, 1878), 483-532. Michel Nortier has suggested that Suger's collection constitutes the earliest royal cartulary; see his comment in *Les cartulaires,* 377.

[15] Hugh of Champfleury, "Epistolorum Regis Ludovici VII et variorum ad eum volumen," ed. Michel-Jean-Joseph Brial, *Recueil des historiens des Gaules et de la France,* vol. 16 (Paris, 1878), 2-170; Françoise Gasparri, "Manuscrit monastique ou registre de chancellerie: A propos d'un recueil épistolaire de l'abbaye de Saint-Victor," *Journal des Savants* (1976): 131-40.

[16] Giles Constable, *Letters and Letter Collections,* Typologie des sources du Moyen Âge occidental 17 (Turnhout, 1976), 12: a "missive letter" confers no authority or legal right; it simply reports or declares an intention.

[17] Hélène Débax, "Le cartulaire des Trencavel (*Liber instrumentorum vicecomitalium*)," in *Les cartulaires,* 291-99.

[18] Francisco Miquel Rosell, ed., *Liber feudorum maior: Cartulaire des Guillems de Montpellier,* 2 vols. (Montpellier, 1884-86).

dorum maior of the mid 1190s, containing almost one thousand letters and contracts spanning two centuries.[19] The *Liber feudorum* and *libri instrumentorum* are without peer in the north, and one wonders whether Remi of Navarre knew about them in 1211, when he undertook to copy the comital archive shortly after assuming the chancellorship. But his cartulary would be more modest: five eight-folio quires containing perhaps two hundred letters, mostly from 1198 to 1211, that is, within a decade of the cartulary itself. That the comital cartulary lacks the volume and chronological depth of the southern cartularies reflects the more recent formation of the comital archive and the nature of the documents preserved in it.

In Champagne a formal comital chancery existed only since 1157, when Count Henry I founded Saint-Étienne of Troyes to serve as his chancery, treasury, chapel, and necropolis. The sixty or so canons of the chapter drafted almost all of the more than seven hundred comital acts known from the second half of the twelfth century, as well as the earliest rolls of fiefs (1170s) and no doubt financial accounts, now lost. It is not clear when the canons began to store incoming letters in any systematic manner, since the chancery served primarily as a record-producing bureau, rather than as a record-preserving one. The oldest baronial letter still extant from the chancery archive is from the seneschal Geoffroy V of Joinville in 1199.[20] The cartulary of 1211 contains only one baronial letter before that date: the letter from Robert I, count of Dreux, who promised in 1160 to render his fortress of Savignies to Count Henry I.[21] It is possible that similar letters existed in the chancery archive but were destroyed in the fire of 1188 that ravaged Troyes and caused severe damage to Saint-Étienne.[22] A destruction of the archive at that time would explain the absence of early materials in the cartulary of 1211 (it contains only eleven items before 1198, of which

[19] Francisco Miquel Rosell, ed., *Liber feudorum maior: Cartulario real que se conserva en el Archivo de la Corona de Aragón*, 2 vols. (Barcelona, 1945-47). See Adam J. Kosto, "The *Liber feudorum maior* of the Counts of Barcelona: The Cartulary as an Expression of Power," *Journal of Medieval History* 27 (2001): 1-22.

[20] Paris, Archives nationales de France, J 1032, no. 2; edited in A. Teulet et al., eds., *Layettes du Trésor des chartes*, 5 vols. (Paris, 1863-1909), vol. 5, no. 127, p. 44.

[21] Paris, Archives nationales de France, KK 1064, fol. 238r; edited in André Duchesne, *Histoire généalogique de la maison royale de Dreux* ... (Paris, 1631), 236.

[22] Robert of Auxerre reported that Saint-Étienne, with its ornaments and expensive furnishings, perished in the conflagration (*Chronicon*, s.a., ed. O. Holder-Egger, MGH Scriptores 26 [Hanover, 1882], 219-87, at 253).

seven are comital acts). On the other hand, there is no evidence in Champagne for the early bilateral accords and related feudal documents that make up the bulk of the three southern archives, nor is there any evidence that Count Henry I collected sealed letters from his barons. Moreover, it appears that the chancery archive was usable after the fire. Henry's feudal rolls survived the fire, and two years later, in 1190, Count Henry II deposited his own feudal rolls at Saint-Étienne.[23] The chapter of Saint-Étienne's foundation charter of 1157 also survived and later was copied into the chapter's cartulary.[24] Thus, even if the chancery archive suffered some damage in 1188, it appears unlikely that a substantial archive of baronial letters, like the one reflected in the cartulary of 1211, existed before 1190.

The lack of early baronial letters in the comital archive was not unique to Champagne: the princely archives sent to Paris in the thirteenth century and placed in *layettes* in the royal archive contain very few northern materials before the 1180s. Even in the royal archive, the earliest letters dealing with royal-baronial relations date from the 1190s: the earliest is the homage of Ida, countess of Boulogne, in 1191.[25] In Champagne, comparable sealed letters were first collected by Count Thibaut III following the imposition of a number of new restrictions on his barons, such as the licensing and rendering of all castles and fortified residences, and the giving of direct homage by younger sons who held militarily significant fortifications. Each of those negotiated agreements resulted in a self-sealed letter that was deposited in the chancery archive. Before the 1190s, the counts simply did not collect those probative letters; by 1210 the barons routinely sealed letters attesting to homage, feudal tenure, and the conditions of castleholding. It was a remarkable shift in practice: the barons had become accountable for their actions through their own sealed letters.

In Champagne, as elsewhere in the north of France, aristocratic men and women from the middle decades of the twelfth century adopted personal seals that enabled them to validate written instruments in their own

[23] Milo II Breban, chamberlain of the count, reported ca. 1205 that he had been present (in 1190) when Count Henry II deposited his feudal rolls in Saint-Étienne (Longnon, ed., *Documents*, vol. 1, p. xiii, n. 2).

[24] Elizabeth Chapin, *Les villes de foires de Champagne des origines au début du XIVᵉ siècle* (Paris, 1937), Pièces justificatives, no. 1, pp. 279-82.

[25] Baldwin et al., eds., *Les registres de Philippe Auguste*, no. 31, pp. 472-73 (dated from 26 December 1191 to 4 April 1192).

names.[26] The earliest use of those seals was in grants to religious institutions, which may have encouraged that practice in order to strengthen their titles to donated property. In 1155, for example, the monks of Boulancourt asked Simon, lord of Beaufort, to confirm the gift his father and grandfather had made forty years earlier. Simon sealed his confirmation because, he said, "at the time the gift was made, it was not customary to seal charters of donation."[27] In addition to those instruments of benefaction, monastic archives began to store another category of baronial letter: those exchanged between laymen and regarding their private affairs. Some of those secular letters may have been surrendered with property that later passed to religious institutions.[28] But others appear to have been deposited for safekeeping by their recipients who wished to protect their dower lands or inheritances: Elizabeth of Dreux, for example, left her dower letter with the monks of Clairvaux, who later copied it for Countess Blanche.[29] The use of self-sealed letters was already an established practice within the aristocracy by the 1190s, when King Philip II and Count Thibaut III began to require those probative instruments from their barons.

When Thibaut III did homage to King Philip in April 1198, the two men exchanged identical sealed letters attesting to the event, clearly at the insistence of the king.[30] It appears that Thibaut took the king's example to Champagne, for he was the first count to collect sealed letters from his barons. The archiving of baronial letters was a natural consequence of that new practice and, as the later comital cartularies reveal, the chancery in Champagne soon became a vast repository of secular letters dealing with all facets of governance and aristocratic practices. Most of the original letters have disappeared: in the cartulary of 1211, for example, 69 percent of the texts are known only from copies. Yet these letters—the *littere baronum*—deserve a separate place in medieval diplomatics. Originating in the mid-twelfth century as self-sealed instruments, usually without witnesses,

[26] Jean-Luc Chassel, "L'usage du sceau au XIIe siècle," in *Le XIIe siècle: Mutations et renouveau en France dans la première moitié du XIIe siècle*, ed. Françoise Gasparri (Paris, 1994), 61-101. See also Brigitte Bedos-Rezak, *Form and Order in Medieval France: Studies in Social and Quantitative Sigillography* (Aldershot, 1993).

[27] Duchesne, *Histoire généalogique*, pt. 5 (Broyes), Preuves, 20.

[28] Laurent Morelle, "Mariage et diplomatique: Autour de cinq chartes de douaire dans le laonnois-soissonais," *BEC* 146 (1988): 227-28.

[29] Duchesne, *Histoire généalogique*, pt. 5 (Broyes), Preuves, 18 (1197).

[30] Teulet et al., eds., *Layettes*, vol. 1, no. 473, pp. 195-96 (Philip's letter); Longnon, ed., *Documents*, vol. 1, no. 4, p. 468 (Thibaut's letter).

they continued to serve aristocratic interests through the thirteenth century and, after 1230, increasingly in their vernacular form. The edition of extant vernacular letters in the series *Documents linguistiques de la France,* now in progress, suggests their riches as a major unexplored source for the social history of medieval France.[31] The cartulary of 1211 is of great interest precisely because it captures the point at which these secular letters were first exploited as a tool of governance.[32]

[31] Two volumes have appeared for Champagne: Jean-Gabriel Gigot, ed., *Chartes en langue française antérieures à 1271 conservées dans le département de la Haute-Marne* (Paris, 1974); Dominique Coq, ed., *Chartes en langue française antérieures à 1271 conservées dans les départements de l'Aube, de la Seine-et-Marne et de l'Yonne* (Paris, 1988).

[32] M. T. Clanchy, *From Memory to Written Record: England, 1066-1307,* 2d ed. (Oxford, 1993) argues persuasively that the demands of royal government accelerated the use of written records and, by extension, practical literacy among lay persons in the thirteenth century. That seems to be the case in France as well. Yet the baronial class was already sealing letters for their own affairs before being required to do so by their rulers.

Cartularies and the Preservation of Documents in the Archives of the Bohemian Crown before the Hussite Revolution

Ivan Hlaváček

The history of Czech archival practice in the Middle Ages is not an easy subject.[1] The reconstruction of the ways in which documents were preserved for use is possible only in exceptional cases, such as the dioceses of Prague and Olomouc, and a few other, mostly monastic, foundations.[2] And

The author wishes to thank the editors of this volume for their assistance in preparing this article for publication.

[1] Among general works, see: Harry Bresslau, *Handbuch der Urkundenlehre für Deutschland und Italien*, 2d ed., 2 vols. (Leipzig, 1912-32; repr. Berlin, 1958), esp. 1:149-84; Peter Rück, "Die Ordnung der herzoglich-savoyschen Archive unter Amadeus VIII. (1398-1451)," *Archivalische Zeitschrift* 67 (1971): 11-101; and, most recently, Olivier Guyotjeannin, "Les méthodes de travail des archivistes du roi de France, XIIIe-début XVIe siècle," *AfD* 42 (1996): 295-375. See also Julius Ficker, "Instruction für Archivare aus dem vierzehnten Jahrhunderte," *Mitteilungen des Instituts für österreichische Geschichtsforschung* 1 (1880): 121-23, and Marie Bláhová, "Archivy v dílech nejstarších českých kronikářů," in *155 let archivnictví v českých zemích: Sborník příspěvků z konference...v Brně...1994*, ed. Kateřina Smutná and Ivan Štarha (Brno, 1995), 117-24.

[2] For the archives of the metropolitan chapter of Prague in the late Přemyslid period, see Jaroslav Eršil and Jiří Pražák, *Katalog listin a listů kapituly pražské* 1 (Prague, 1956), 3ff., and Jiří Pražák, "Otakarus 29," in Jindřich Šebánek, Jiří Pražák, and Sáša Dušková, *Studie k české diplomatice doby přemyslovské*, Rozpravy Československé akademie věd, řada společenských věd, 69.9 (Prague, 1959), 50ff. For the chapter of Olomouc, see Miroslav Flodr, *Skriptorium olomoucké* (Prague, 1960), 184ff. For the monasteries of the Přemyslid era (to 1306) see Jindřich Šebánek and Saša Dušková, "Česká listina doby přemyslovské," *Sborník archivních prací* 6.1 (1956): 139ff., and Saša Dušková, "Naše listiny doby přemyslovské pro nižší světské feudály a otázka šlechtických archivů," *Sborník prací filosofické fakulty brněnské univerzity*, ser. C, 3 (1956): 56-78. On Bohemia generally in the fourteenth century, see Ferdinand Tadra, *Kanceláře a písaři v zemích českých za králů z rodu lu-*

we should not pass over in silence the efforts of other issuers of documents to ensure their preservation, as is testified by a grant made by Henry of Hradec in 1361, in which it is expressly stated that "de predictis (i.e., a donation to a parish church) fiant quatuor paria literarum eiusdem tenoris de verbo ad verbum, unum reservetur in Pragensi, aliud in Olomucensi sacristiis et reliqua duo per plebanos et capellanos nostros serventur."[3] The monarch's care for the Archives of the Bohemian Crown (ABC), was, as we might expect, far from adequate in this period. In some instances, other institutions or noble families took on the task of preserving royal documents; there is evidence of such activity, albeit in isolated cases, by the bishops of Prague and by the prominent south-Bohemian Rožmberk lineage.[4] On the whole, however, the number of surviving documents for the Bohemian kings is quite small, especially for the Přemyslid era (to 1306). Indeed, even for a right as fundamental to the Bohemian monarchs as the acquisition of their royal title *ad personam*, so politically significant on the international stage, the first surviving written confirmation dates from 1158. It is not at all clear whether any document was issued for the first grant of the royal title, awarded by Emperor Henry IV in 1085.[5]

Despite these unpromising beginnings, however, the ABC represent one of the most important medieval documentary collections of central Europe. Their neglect by scholars outside the Czech lands is highly surprising, given the fact that an extremely high-quality facsimile edition is currently being published, and that the collection also served in its own fashion as—sit venia verbo—imperial archives for a number of decades.[6] From the four-

---

cemburského Jana, Karla IV. a Václava IV. (1310-1420) (Prague, 1892), 194-99. On the Old Town of Prague, see Josef Teige, *Základy starého místopisu pražského*, vol. 3 (s.l., s.d.), 24ff. ("Formulář staroměstský ze XIV. století"), and Božena Kubíčková, "Archiv hlavního města Prahy," *Documenta Pragensia* 15 (1997): 541ff. On the town of Olomouc, see Vladimír Spáčil, *Sbírka listin archivu města Olomouce 1261-1793* (Olomouc, 1998), 7ff. See also Lenka Matušíková, "Menší kopiář archivu Koruny české," *Sborník archivních prací* 41 (1991): 357-416 (with English summary), esp. 358 (a review of cartularies) and 364 (remarks about the oldest Bohemian cartularies).

[3] Clemens Borový, ed., *Libri erectionum archidioecesis Pragensis*, vol. 1 (Prague, 1875), 27, and Tadra, *Kanceláře*, 196.

[4] There are only a few charters in these "unauthorized" archives.

[5] Cf. Josef Žemlička, *Čechy v době knížecí* (Prague, 1997), 104ff.

[6] *Archivum Coronae regni Bohemiae*, 4 vols. to date (Prague, 1978-). The question of the *Reichsarchiv* is very complicated and cannot be analysed in detail here.

teenth century, in fact, the ABC offer excellent evidence for medieval archival practices. The present paper focuses on the reign of Charles IV (1346-78), a period of considerable change in the size of the archives, their personnel, and the means of preserving documents practiced there.

Over the course of time there have been significant losses of documents from the ABC, the extent of which we cannot know. Similarly, it should not be forgotten that not all documents in the ABC today constitute an integral —or, more precisely, original—part of the archives. Some documents appear for irregular reasons, such as the documents of Bohemian rulers issued to their direct subjects but never dispatched because the recipients thought that keeping them in the custody of the issuer would be safer. Other items made their way into the collection at a later date and thus have no relevance to a study of the original composition of the archives. We might mention, for instance, several thirteenth-century documents for the Counts of Luxemburg, known only from cartularies of the latter half of the fourteenth century; or the documents from the archives of the lords of Colditz,[7] which found their way into the archives when the Luxemburgs took over some of the Colditz properties. In some cases, documents may have been acquired later in association with escheats. The Luxemburg and Colditz documents demonstrate that whole or partial archival units of originally foreign provenance were absorbed into the ABC after a change in the possession of certain titles or properties.[8]

If we look at the chronological increase in the material kept at these archives, we obtain a very instructive picture of the internal dynamics of

---

See, generally, Bresslau, *Handbuch*, 1:149-184, esp. 169ff. For the early Middle Ages, see Heinrich Fichtenau, "Archive der Karolingerzeit," *Mitteilungen des Österreichischen Staatsarchivs* 25 (1972): 15-24, repr. in Fichtenau, *Beiträge zur Mediävistik: Ausgewählte Aufsätze*, vol. 2, *Zur Urkundenforschung* (Stuttgart, 1977), 115-25; for the high Middle Ages, Heinrich Appelt, "Die Reichsarchive in den frühstaufischen Burgunderdiplomen," in *Festschrift Hans Lentze*, ed. Nikolaus Grass and Werner Ogris (Innsbruck, 1969), 1-11, and the brief summary in *Lexikon des Mittelalters*, 10 vols. (Munich, 1977-99), s.v. Archiv (by K. Colberg).

[7] Demko Čumlivski is preparing a monograph on the archives of the lords of Colditz, which were incorporated into the royal archives beginning in the fourteenth century.

[8] For basic information, see Rudolf Koss and Otakar Bauer, *Archiv Koruny české*, vol. 1, *Dějiny archivu* (Prague, 1939), though some of its conclusions are questionable. Cf. Ivan Hlaváček, "Žatecký landfríd Václava IV. z března r. 1415," in *Sto let od narození profesora Jindřicha Šebánka* (Brno, 2000), 99-108, especially p. 108.

their growth. This growth in itself is very telling, not just about the archives, but about the political situation in general. Because it is not always possible to know the scope of the losses of documents, described above, estimates of the extent of the holdings of the ABC in any given period are necessarily far from accurate. The figures that follow are only meant to suggest overall trends.[9] It should also be mentioned at this point that because these figures refer only to single-sheet documents (originals or copies), they represent only a fraction of the documentary wealth of the ABC from this era; many other documents have been preserved in cartulary form. From the period before the end of the Přemyslid dynasty in 1306, we have only sixty-nine official documents, of which twenty-seven are copies, and three are originals currently outside the ABC. From before the accession of Přemysl Otakar II in 1253, there are only seven documents of constitutional law, one of which is a copy. Another four original documents from this period were added to the archives only at a later date. With the beginning of the fourteenth century, we find a significant increase in the overall preservation of documents, and in the proportion of documents preserved as originals. From the reign of John of Luxemburg (1311-46), 213 documents have been preserved (an average of 6 documents per year); from the reign of Charles IV, 939 (28/year); from the reign of Wenceslas (1378-1419), 278 (7/year); and from the period of the Hussite Revolution, or the reign (or not) of Sigismund (1419-37), 78 (4/year).

As these figures suggest, the reign of Charles IV is exceptional and can clearly be considered a key period in the development of the ABC. The marked rise in the number of documents from Charles's reign suggests that there must have been changes in archival practice. This applies beyond the ABC, as well, as the growth in diplomatic material in the Czech lands generally led to changes in the filing and protection of documents, especially privileges. We can see this in the appearance during these years, the first half of the fourteenth century, of the earliest cartularies from the Czech lands. This is clearest for the bishopric of Olomouc[10] and, in a way, for the Old Town of Prague. In the latter case, copies of various interesting

[9] For an introduction, see Antonín Haas, *Archiv koruny české: Inventář listin* (Prague, 1961), and more recently the *regesta*-volumes of the facsimile edition, *Archivum Coronae regni Bohemiae.*

[10] Jan Bistřický, "Übersicht über das Kanzlei- und Urkundenwesen der olmützer Bischöfe in den Jahren 1303-1364," *Mediaevalia Bohemica* 1.1 (1969): 30-50, does not discuss the problem of cartularies.

or important municipal documents were included in the oldest town memorial book on different occasions during the fourteenth century, making it a "diffused" cartulary of sorts.[11] Other Church and urban institutions, as well as the most prominent of the noble lines in Bohemia, the Rožmberks, followed suit after a short interval.[12]

The Church and urban environments must be left to one side here, however, and we should return to the ABC. Given that Charles IV was also the Roman Emperor, we might expect to find scholarly discussion of joint imperial and Czech archives, since we know that Charles's court chancery functioned for both "state" entities, and since we know that Karlštejn Castle, near Prague, was built as a depository for the imperial treasures, which included, in a way, the imperial "documentary treasure." Yet neither Czech nor German literature examines this question; works usually state, without providing substantiation, that the imperial archives did not actually exist at this time because the various lines that alternated as Roman Emperors considered archives to be a family matter, and the pertinent material was subject to destruction. Only in the early Renaissance did the situation change.[13] As shown below, however, the veil of mystery surrounding this matter can be at least partly lifted with the assistance of the cartularies from Charles's reign.

In contrast to the "imperial archive" generally, the ABC were subject to relatively stable and consistent care on the part of the Czech kings from the fourteenth century onwards, and later, from the end of the fifteenth century, by the Czech estates.[14] Even before the fourteenth century, however, they must have been in a state that made it possible to locate politically important documents, as is demonstrated by several episodes in which powerful adversaries of the Crown were able to acquire documents from the archives. A sufficient illustration here is the period at the end of the

[11] Prague, Archiv hlavního mesta Prahy, 986 ("Liber vetustissimus Antiquae civitatis Pragensis ab anno 1310"). An edition is in preparation.

[12] For the ecclesiastical milieu, see, e.g., Rostislav Nový, "Studie o předhusitských urbářích 1, Codex Damascus Oseckého kláštera," *Sborník historický* 13 (1965): 19-31, which discusses a *codex mixtus* from the end of the reign of John of Luxemburg; for the Rožmberk family, see Miroslav Truc, "Rožmberský kodex řečený Marientálský," *Jihočeský sborník historický* 32 (1963): 1-24.

[13] Lothar Groß, *Die Geschichte der deutschen Reichshofkanzlei von 1559 bis 1806* (Vienna, 1933), does not discuss the medieval situation in his chapter on the archives of the Imperium.

[14] Cf. Koss and Bauer, *Archiv Koruny české*, 37ff.

Přemyslid era, when a number of official documents were handed over to the Habsburgs, who did not return some of them until the period of the diplomatic and military dominance of the Luxemburgs several decades later.[15] Of course the Přemyslid era was a time when the scope of the entire archives was easy to take in; as noted above, their expansion postdates this period. In fact, the archives were small enough and so little used that they remained closely tied, as elsewhere in Europe, to the royal (and therefore state) treasure, which was deposited in the metropolitan cathedral of the Czech Crown, Saint Vitus in Prague Castle.[16]

Because the archives were so limited under the Přemyslids—due to the great pragmatism employed in the selection of material to be filed permanently—there was no need to pay particularly close attention to their arrangement and to record-keeping. They were filed far away from the locus of the regular administrative routine, but it must have been acceptable for them to be accessible only on special occasions. Under the reign of the first Luxemburg monarch, John, there was still no need (nor perhaps was it possible) to make any significant changes. In this respect, it is well known that, after failing in his attempts to establish autocratic rule, John put all of his energy into international politics, activity reflected only dimly in documentary material.[17]

The increase in documentary material at the ABC under Charles IV, as well as the enlightened policies of that ruler, led to a special measure being taken sometime around the end of the first decade of his reign, a measure that had a considerable impact on all later developments: the appointment of a registrar for the archive. Because Charles's order creating the position has survived only in a formulary, we know neither the exact date nor the name of the person chosen. Still, the nature of the collection, which was produced in the royal chancery, and its fortunes—it achieved wide distribution (in several dozen manuscripts) as the *Summa cancellariae*—allow confidence that the text in question was not a mere exercise in composition, but rather a reflection of a draft copy or registry record of an actual royal document. Because of its inherent interest and its importance for the present discussion, I reproduce it here in its entirety, followed by a rough

[15] Koss and Bauer, *Archiv Koruny české*, 149ff.

[16] Koss and Bauer, *Archiv Koruny české*, 44ff. Jiří Fajt, ed., *Magister Theodoricus: Court Painter to Emperor Charles IV* (Prague, 1998), although excellent, does not discuss the problem of the archives and Karlštejn before 1437.

[17] See Jiří Spěváček, *Jan Lucemburský a jeho doba 1296-1346* (Prague, 1994).

translation:

> Karolus etc. Notum facimus etc., quod dudum siquidem matura consideracione prehabita cordi nobis frequenter existit, litteras privilegiales corone /terre/ et regni Boemie a Romanis pontificibus et...imperatoribus et regibus, predecessoribus nostris, obtentas et alias similiter aliarum principum, baronum, comitum et nobilium pro antedicti regni utilitate hincinde congestas in summam colligere et per ydoneum rectorem et registratorem constituere in locis certis propensius custodiri, ac de legalitatis et circumspeccionis industria honorabilis...de... notarii familiaris etc. obtinentes presumpcionem fiducie singularis, sibi ac sue custodie universa et singula privilegia et litteras, que et quas de presenti habemus aut obtinuerimus annuente domino in futurum, harum serie deputamus, ut easdem sua distinccione previa registret et reponat in ordinem, servet, custodiat et gubernet, ut, quociens de una vel pluribus earum necessitatem habuerimus, nobis possit et valeat expedire celeriter et respondere. Et ut ipse ad prefati laboris onera eo diligencius eo frequencius curet intendere, quo sibi de nostre Celsitudinis gracia senserit habundancius fore provisum, unam marcham reddituum septimana qualibet ab instanti festo...primum incipiendo in et super [urbora] Montis Cutnensis habendam et percipiendam ad vite sue tempora harum serie deputamus, volentes occasione singularis meriti, quo dictus...in officio notarie sue honori nostro pridem curavit intendere et intendit continuato fidelitatis obsequio sollicite de presenti, quod ipse prefatam marcham in quocunque statu consistens, eciam si dimisso prefato officio ad presulatus honorem volente Altissimo perveniret, singulis septimanis sine quavis difficultate et omni impedimento remoto recipere debeat et habere. Mandamus igitur universis et singulis urborariis Moncium Cutnensium, qui pro tempore fuerint, quatenus prefato...familiari, notario nostro, dictam marcham septimanis singulis sine quavis difficultate, contradiccione sive impedimento integraliter administrent, sub indignacionis nostre etc....[18]

[18] See Ferdinand Tadra, ed., *Summa cancellariae: Summa Caroli IV.* (Prague, 1895), no. 116, p. 81. Czech translation and short commentary in Karel Beránek, "K výročí Karla IV.," *Archivní časopis* 28 (1978): 129ff. See also, Koss and Bauer, *Archiv Koruny české,* 80ff.; Otakar Bauer, "Několik slov o nejstarším inventáři českého korunního archivu z roku 1437," in *Sborník prací z dějin práva československého,* vol. 1, ed. František Čáda (Prague, 1930), 27-38; Bauer, "K počátkům organisace archivu České koruny za panování Karla IV.," in *K dějinám československým v období humanismu: Sborník prací věnovaných Janu Bedřichu Novákovi k šede-*

Charles etc....We make known etc....that we have long had it in mind to gather the various privileges of the Bohemian Crown /land/ and Kingdom that our predecessors obtained from the Roman popes, emperors, and kings, and the privileges of other princes, barons, counts, and nobles for the use of the said kingdom, and in order that they might be more efficiently guarded at safe places by a suitable manager and registrar, and, having previously unswerving confidence in his faithful and circumspect diligence, we hereby appoint our servant, the honorable...of..., notary etc., and into his custody we entrust all individual privileges and documents that we now have or that we shall receive in the future, God willing, that he might register, put into order, tend, guard, and manage them with his former proven circumspection, in order that whenever we shall have need of one or more of them, he can and shall be able to find it for us and give a reply. And in order that the more he seeks to devote himself all the more industriously and frequently to the burden of the assigned task, the better he shall become acquainted with the fact that our majesty's favour shall see he is taken care of, we hereby assign (to him) one talent from the revenues of the Kutná Hora mine tithes per week beginning with the next feast of...for the period of his life; wanting, on the occasion of (the) unparalleled merit, which the said...has already demonstrated in his office of notary for our honor and today expends in ceaseless faithful obedience, that he might get and have the said talent weekly with no difficulty and without any encumbrance, in whatever position he might be, even if he were to leave the said office and attain, at the wish of the Supreme Lord, a high Church office. Hence we order each and every Kutna Hora mine-tithe registrar, serving at any given time, to prepare for our said notary the said talent every week with no difficulty, resistance, or encumbrance, under threat of our displeasure etc.

This text focuses our attention more closely on the themes of the present volume, offering clear evidence, as it does, of medieval attempts to pre-

---

sátým narozeninám 1872-1932 (Prague, 1932), 148-58, with important comparative information. More recently, Josef Kollmann, *Dějiny ústředního archivu českého státu* (Prague, 1992), 10ff., esp. 16, follows in this context principally obsolete literature of the nineteenth century, such as Jaromír Čelakovský, *O domácích a cizích registrech zvláště o registrech české a jiných rakouských kancelářích* (Prague, 1890). Neither registers nor cartularies were used in the Bohemian royal chancery in the thirteenth century.

serve and transmit diplomatic texts. There are two relatively autonomous issues here: (1) the creation of functional, independent archives; and (2) an attempt to improve and simplify access to the information contained in the documents in those archives.

As regards the first point, documents preserved in the ABC could only begin to be more useful when they had become readily accessible to competent persons. This was not sufficiently possible under the Přemyslids and John of Luxemburg, nor, indeed, was it particularly necessary: any relevant file was undoubtedly stored, as mentioned above, at the metropolitan cathedral, and rarely was there a need to know its precise content. From the early years of Charles's reign, the rapid growth of the collection by an average of twenty-eight original documents a year (plus a substantial albeit indeterminable number of documents, at least some of which we know from the royal cartularies, discussed below) meant there was a need for more regular access to the collection, if only for the purpose of actually filing the new records. We should assume, then, that the collection, or at least a considerable portion of it, was removed from the cathedral to an independent location in Charles's palace at Prague Castle. We know from surviving accounts that at some point during the reign of Wenceslas IV, the archives were transferred to the more extensive royal court complex in the Old Town of Prague, into the home of a prominent courtier.[19]

The second point—ease of access to the information in the documents—is even more crucial. Charles's order sets out the main duties of the new registrar of the archive, who was obviously different from the registrars at the court chancery. First of all, he had to assemble the collection of constitutional documents, expressly called *litterae privilegiales corone /terre/ et regni Boemie*; the formulation of this duty might seem to be an exaggeration, but the fact that these documents had to be gathered makes clear that the archives were not yet in a state that would permit efficient use. It should be stated clearly that what is at issue here is a collection of documents only, not of codices containing acts or fiscal records; these were the responsibility of the registrar of the chancery and did not make their way into the ABC until a little before 1437.[20]

Although the order does not refer to imperial documents (other than those granted to the Bohemian Crown), there can be no doubt that charters

[19] See also Ivan Hlaváček, "Vratislavská epizoda Českého korunního archivu," *Archivní časopis* 30 (1980): 100-106.

[20] See Bauer, "Několik slov." Two of four boxes contained tax and other registers.

received by Charles IV in his capacity as emperor were in fact stored and filed here alongside texts of a Bohemian nature. The cartularies discussed below show this quite clearly, as they contain many feudal oaths offered by imperial secular functionaries and records of the acceptance of regalia by the imperial bishops, even those from areas west of the Rhine. The only possible explanation is that Charles IV saw these documents as part of his own personal archives. Because his main residence was in Prague and his "archivist" was paid out of the funds of the Kingdom of Bohemia, the fusion of the royal and imperial archives would have been very easy; this is all the more true because only contemporary imperial records were joined to a preexisting Bohemian core. The formulary that contains the decree of appointment of an archivist offers further evidence for this fusion, as it reveals both the royal and imperial aspects of Charles's competence.

The new archivist was given clear instructions to institute written record-keeping; in other words he was told to draw up a cartulary, or perhaps even cartularies. (So far we have not found any evidence for the emergence of inventories at this time.) This instruction itself, of course, is not proof that he in fact did so. Nevertheless, there are documents available that suggest that this was indeed the case. I have already indicated that the cartularies were well known in Bohemia during Charles's reign.[21] Even if this were not the case, the monarch must have known the so-called *Balduinea*, the contemporary set of cartularies of the archdiocese of Trier, named after Charles's granduncle, Baldwin of Trier.[22] These contain around twenty-five hundred documents, and systematic records of this material preceded their creation. Its four independent manuscripts, differing from each other only slightly, were designed for fast record-keeping and the daily use of the different ecclesiastical officers at Trier. In the case of the Trier cartularies, we are fortunate to be able to work with the originals. We are not so fortunate in Prague; we must work with later copies of cartularies, rather than with the original cartularies, edited and perhaps even written by an unknown archivist. Several scholars have already tried to identify this archi-

[21] See also Ivan Hlaváček, "The Use of Charters and Other Diplomatic Documents in Přemyslide Bohemia," in *Charters and the Use of the Written Word in Medieval Society*, ed. Karl Heidecker, Utrecht Studies in Medieval Literacy 5 (Utrecht, 2000), 133-44.

[22] See Johannes Mötsch, *Die Balduineen: Aufbau, Entstehung und Inhalt der Urkundensammlung des Erzbischofs Balduin von Trier*, Veröffentlichungen der Landesarchivverwaltung Rheinland-Pfalz 33 (Koblenz, 1980).

vist, but with limited success. The principal candidates are Johannes Pauli of Pistoia—a canon at Olomouc and at All Saints at Prague Castle, but also a *notarius secretarius domesticus familiaris*, who had *duos subnotarios familiares domesticos*, both also of Italian origin—and Ulricus Schoff, from Silesia.[23]

The fruits of this archivist's labor are relatively clear, as we can reconstitute, at least in part, the original state of the cartularies he produced from an analysis of the surviving material. At the same time, we can imagine the poor state the ABC fell into immediately before, and then after, the Hussite wars, when the original cartularies evidently were removed from the state archives themselves, as testified by unofficial copies preserved outside the ABC,[24] and when additional original material disappeared, either as a result of actual losses or destruction, or as a result of a removal of imperial documents. Sigismund of Luxemburg undoubtedly played a role here, as did the fact that at the time of the Hussite Revolution the archives were removed in their entirety beyond the borders of the state.[25] A clear reconstruction of the form and scope of the imperial jurisdiction as reflected in the documents of the ABC would be a valuable contribution. The great studies on the history of the ABC by Rudolf Koss and Otakar Bauer (1939), on the one hand, and Lenka Matušíková (1991), on the other, lay the groundwork for such an investigation, although they do not address this particular question.

I will not describe at length here the copies, and copies of copies, that emerged in relative abundance between the fifteenth and seventeenth centuries. I will focus instead on what they reveal about the originals. In response to the royal order, the new registrar, who probably had assistants, produced two aids that tried to make more accessible at least part of the wealth of material entrusted to him: the so-called small and large cartularies of the ABC.

The small cartulary has been preserved in four manuscripts of the fif-

[23] Tadra, *Kanceláře*, 37 and 253. Bauer, "K počátkům," 149ff. discusses earlier opinions. The most frequently mentioned other names were Johannes Saxo de Mulle and Johannes Noviforensis, the well-known chancellor of Charles IV.

[24] They appear in fifteenth- and sixteenth-century copies dispersed in many archives and libraries both in Bohemia and elsewhere.

[25] See Koss and Bauer, *Archiv Koruny české*, 156ff.

teenth century.[26] It is relatively limited in scope, containing only sixty-four documents; in one of the manuscripts there are only fifty-five. They were classified into four unequal groups, according to the issuer: documents of the imperial monarchs and princes (thirty-eight); documents of Charles IV as Roman king or emperor (six); papal bulls (eleven); and documents of the French kings (eight); there is also one document of the King of England. The large cartulary has been preserved in at least five late manuscripts, again not entirely identical.[27] Its approximately four hundred texts are again classified into groups; here the arrangement of the cartulary may be seen in more detail. First come documents of Holy Roman kings and emperors, and of kings of France, England, Jerusalem, Sicily, Hungary, and Poland. These are followed by documents issued by German princes: the secular and clerical electors; the dukes of Bavaria, Saxony, and Austria; the margraves of Meissen and landgraves of Thuringia; the margraves of Moravia; the dukes of Silesia; as well as other dukes who need not be enumerated. The hierarchical classification continues with documents of bishops and abbots, counts, and other lower imperial nobles, followed, separately, by documents of the Czech nobility, imperial towns, and towns in the Czech lands. The collection ends with receipts of various sorts and records of feudal undertakings.

At first glance, it is clear that the smaller cartulary offers a very specific selection of documents. But the larger cartulary, too, despite its size, only encapsulates part of the content that had already been gathered at the ABC. (Despite the incomplete nature of these two cartularies, the fact that they offer unique texts for nearly half of the documents they contain [twenty-nine of sixty-four in the smaller cartulary] makes them an extremely valuable resource for historians.) Despite the repetition of some individual

[26] Matušíková, "Menší kopiář archivu Koruny české," the authoritative study, rectified the mistakes of older literature, above all Wolfgang D. Fritz, "Bemerkungen zum Böhmischen Kronarchiv," *Deutsches Archiv für Erforschung des Mittelalters* 18 (1962): 555-58, and to a lesser degree Venceslaus Hrubý, ed., *Archivum Coronae regni Bohemiae*, vol. 2 (Prague, 1928), vi. The promise stated in the foreword of Koss and Bauer, *Archiv Koruny české* by Bedřich Jenšovský, that an eighth volume of the series would contain an exhaustive analysis of all of the cartularies in the royal archive, could not be realized. See also Richard Salomon, "Reiseberichte 1908-1909," *Neues Archiv der Gesellschaft für ältere deutsche Geschichtskunde* 36 (1911): 473-517.

[27] See Hrubý, ed., *Archivum Coronae regni Bohemiae*, vol. 2, vi. The new findings of Tomasz Jasiński have not yet been investigated.

items, there is little overlap between the two cartularies, raising the possibility that another, now lost, cartulary bridged the gap between the two. If this is not the case, and the cartularies were not attempts at comprehensive record-keeping, what was their function? Because of the lack of sources in this respect, there is no point in burdening this issue with rickety hypotheses, and we should return to the documents at hand.

The work of the archivist-registrar in ordering the collection, which amounted to approximately one thousand documents at the time of his appointment, would have had two different phases. First, the documents had to be furnished with abstracts and some type of shelf-marks; only then could he begin devoting his time to copying them. His work cannot be measured by modern standards. He did not put the documents in chronological order, but only into loosely connected groups of documents based on the category of issuer; nor did he make an attempt at completeness, which could have been achieved only after many years of work—time that was not available, even with the assistants that he may have had.[28] Thus the copies of the two different cartularies are testimony to unfinished work during the reign of Charles IV that, nevertheless, indicates a wide scope of interest that included imperial material. We have, for example, evidence from the time of Charles's son relating to the relocation of an important part of the ABC, when the Silesian texts went to Wroclaw, which resulted in the preparation of another partial cartulary.[29]

The ABC were transferred to the new residence of the monarch in the Old Town of Prague at some unspecified time in the latter half of the fourteenth century, probably in connection with the relocation of the residence at the beginning of Wenceslas IV's reign, though explicit information about their location dates only from 1416. This change would coincide with the change in political status of the Luxemburgs. Charles lived at Prague Castle and had the ABC, including the imperial documents, at hand whenever he was in residence. Because he spent a lot of time on journeys outside Prague, outside Bohemia, and even outside the Empire, it is understandable that he was interested in the safe custody of the archives. During these absences, they were under the protection of the archbishops of Prague. But he often needed access to the texts of many of these charters for administrative purposes connected to these frequent voyages. The situation changed with the accession of Wenceslas IV. Because this king changed

[28] See above, text at n. 23.

[29] Hlaváček, "Vratislavská epizoda."

residences he lost immediate contact with Prague Castle, and, in addition, found himself in an ever deepening dispute with "his" archbishop of Prague. His principal interest was in not having his access to the archives restricted in any way, even though the growth of the archives to all intents and purposes halted; he and his advisers thus arranged to have the archives in their immediate care, even though a notion of the rights of the kingdom documented in them could have been conjured up simply from the archival aids created under Charles IV.

After his inglorious coronation, Sigismund of Luxemburg took the entire archives abroad; they spent most of the Hussite period in Vienna. Their return, after Sigismund was accepted as king by the Bohemians, was one of the principal conditions for normalizing the situation. When this happened—the archives had by then, with the odd exception, been deprived of the imperial material—the first act of the estates was to make records. A very general inventory emerges in 1437,[30] combining a territorial arrangement with one based on content.

The goal of this essay has been to show how the most important collection of documents in the medieval Bohemian lands, and indeed one of the most important in central Europe, was treated under Luxemburg rulers. Though much remains unclear, from what has been said it is evident that this archive was not simply a mass of lifeless records; there was an effort to incorporate it into the political and legal life of the Bohemian Crown. The state of the sources means that this history will never be fully illuminated, but there is hope that further detailed study of the surviving records will bring to light additional interesting material to support more profound conclusions.

[30] See above, n. 15.

Documenting the Ordinary: The *Actes de la Pratique* of Late Medieval Douai

Martha C. Howell

The municipal archive of Douai, now in France but during the Middle Ages part of the original county of Flanders, houses an extraordinary collection of what the French call "actes de la pratique"—that is, legal instruments created by individuals, in this case to manage private property.[1] Chief among them are contracts for purchase and sale of real property, preeminently houses and holdings in Douai, although real estate held elsewhere, including land held in fief, is also treated in these documents. Alongside these contracts, there are records of movable property transactions (principally raw materials, livestock, and foodstuffs) and a huge collection of mortgages, quitclaims, testaments, and marriage agreements. For the period between about 1230 (the approximate date of the earliest documents) and 1500 about fifty thousand such records survive. All but a very few early marriage contracts and wills are in Picardese French. All were drafted by clerks in the employ of the city's aldermen, or *échevins*.

Nothing else like this collection is known in the medieval urban North. To be sure, documents of the same genre survive in other archives of the region.[2] There is, for example, a huge collection of property-transfer records in Cologne—the well-known *Schreinsbücher*.[3] Cologne also has a

[1] Douai, Archives municipales, FF.

[2] By the mid- to late thirteenth century, northern cities had institutions in place for registering such transactions, but few cities generated and preserved records as extensive as the Douaisien. For an overview of the documentary record in urbanized Europe, see Walter Prevenier, "La production et la conservation des actes urbains dans l'Europe médiévale," in *La diplomatique urbaine en Europe au Moyen Âge: Actes du congrès de la Commission internationale de diplomatique*, ed. Walter Prevenier and Thérèse de Hemptinne (Leuven, 2000), 559-70.

[3] Hans Planitz and Thea Buyken, eds., *Die Kölner Schreinsbücher des 13. und 14. Jahrhunderts*, Publikationen der Gesellschaft für rheinische Geschichtskunde 44 (Weimar, 1937).

collection of medieval wills, as do several other municipal and ecclesiastical archives from the period, especially in England.[4] Several cities have also preserved small collections of medieval marriage contracts, mostly from the latter half of the fifteenth century.[5] Some cities, medieval Ghent for example, have also left records allowing studies of municipal real estate transactions and estate inventories.[6] The south of Europe, where notaries were widely used much earlier than in the North and where legal culture compelled such registration, also has archives that are in many respects as rich as the Douaisien—Florence, Genoa, Venice, Toulouse, or Montpellier, for example.[7] Thus, what makes the Douaisien collection special is not the

[4] For Cologne, Walther Stein, ed., *Akten zur Geschichte der Verfassung und Verwaltung der Stadt Köln im 14. und 15. Jahrhundert*, 2 vols., Publikationen der Gesellschaft für rheinische Geschichtskunde 10 (Bonn, 1893-95; repr. Dusseldorf, 1993); for other repositories in England and on the continent, see *Actes à cause de mort: Acts of Last Will*, 4 vols., Recueils de la Société Jean Bodin pour l'histoire comparative des institutions 59-62 (Brussels, 1992-94).

[5] Leiden, for example, has preserved a few marriage contracts from the late fifteenth century and a richer collection from the sixteenth: Leiden, Gemeente Archief, Rechterlijke Archief vóór 1811, 76A and 76B. Ghent has similarly registered a few marriage contracts; see Philippe Lardinois, "Diplomatische studie van de akten van vrijwillige rechtspraak te Gent van de XIIIe tot de XVe eeuw" (mémoire, Rijksuniversiteit te Gent, 1975-76).

[6] Marc Boone, Machteld Dumon, and Birgit Reusens, *Immobilienmarkt, fiscaliteit en sociale ongelijkheid te Gent, 1483-1503* (Courtrai, 1981).

[7] Guides to such source collections can be found in: for Genoa, Steven Epstein, *Wills and Wealth in Medieval Genoa, 1150-1250*, Harvard Historical Studies 103 (Cambridge, Mass., 1984); for Montpellier, Jean Hilaire, *Le régime des biens entre époux dans la région de Montpellier du début du XIIIe siècle à la fin du XVIe siècle: Contribution aux études d'histoire du droit écrit* (Montpellier, 1957); for Florence, Julius Kirshner, "Wives' Claims against Insolvent Husbands in Late Medieval Italy," in *Women of the Medieval World*, ed. Julius Kirshner and Susan F. Wemple (Oxford, 1985), Thomas Kuehn, "Law, Death and Heirs in the Renaissance: Repudiation of Inheritance in Florence," *Renaissance Quarterly* 65 (1992): 484-517, and Isabelle Chabot, "La loi du lignage: Notes sur le système successoral florentin (XIVe/XVe-XVIIe siècles)," *CLIO* 7 (1998): 51-72; for Venice, Stanley Chojnacki, "Marriage Legislation and Patrician Society in Fifteenth Century Venice," in *Law, Custom, and the Social Fabric in Medieval Europe: Essays in Honor of Bryce Lyon*, ed. Bernard S. Bachrach and David Nicholas, Studies in Medieval Culture 28 (Kalamazoo, Mich., 1990), and Stanley Chojnacki, "The Power of Love: Wives and Husbands in Late Medieval Venice," in *Women and Power in the Middle Ages*, ed. Mary Erler and Maryanne

nature of the documents, although there are some unusual features about the collection, to which I shall return. What distinguishes the Douaisien archive, above all, is its richness relative to its northern neighbors.

The archive's size accounts for much of its value. Some 50,000 individual documents survive from a period of about 270 years; over 45,000 of them date from the last 125 years, from about 1375 to 1500. This means that there are almost 200 documents per year for the entire period and about 350 per year for the last 125 years of the Middle Ages. By any medieval standard, these are almost incomparable riches. A rate of 350 documents per year, assuming two parties to each of these agreements and assuming no duplication of names, means that seven hundred different adults were parties to business or real estate contracts or were authors of marriage contracts or wills in any given year. In a population that averaged no more than twenty thousand inhabitants, this figure represents about 7 percent of the adult population per year.[8] This calculation underrepresents the number of people who were actually named in the records, for many business and real estate contracts involved more than two actors, while wills and marriage contracts always listed more people than just the testator or the bride and groom. In addition, the archive contains many serious lacunae —suspiciously spotty runs, even months and years that are entirely missing —so that what we have today is only part of what once existed. In short, the documents that survive represent a statistically significant portion of the population of late medieval Douai—most of them heads of household

---

Kowaleski (Athens, Ga., 1988); for Toulouse, John H. Mundy, *Men and Women at Toulouse in the Age of the Cathars*, Studies and Texts 101 (Toronto, 1990).

[8] In fact, there were surely a number of people whose names appeared regularly in this archive, even several times in a given year. Aside from various officials who might be named as witnesses or references for parties to the contract (who are not included in the counts above), a certain number of prominent businessmen and landlords would have been named as parties to contracts to buy and sell. Although we do not have studies testing this proposition, my own experience with these documents suggests that such people, while present, were significantly outnumbered by buyers and sellers who appeared only once (perhaps to buy or sell a residence) or infrequently (perhaps to pay a small debt, fix terms for delivery of dyestuffs, or sell a horse). Certainly for purposes of the very rough estimate made here, it is fair to assume little name duplication, particularly since, as noted in the text above, the assumption of only two parties to a given contract underrepresents the number of participants, thus offsetting any overrepresentation produced by an assumption of no name duplication.

and most of them therefore male.[9]

The range of these documents is as impressive as is their number, whether considered from the point of view of the property being transferred or from the point of view of the actors to the contract. Just about every kind of property appears in these documents: land, rents, houses, and holdings; equipment, tools, raw materials, foodstuffs, livestock; vehicles such as wagons and boats; manufactured goods such as wine presses, arms, and harnesses; personal property such as clothing, jewelry, books, furs, rugs, tapestries, hollowware, paintings, linens, furniture, and bedding. The actors are as various as the property. All imaginable sectors of the property-owning classes of Douai are well represented. Over 75 percent of the writers of contracts, quitclaims, wills or marriage contracts were artisans or retailers, householders, or even wage earners, not merchants, professionals, minor nobility, or *rentiers*. Nowhere in the late medieval North is there a collection evidencing such economic and social diversity. Elsewhere, even in the South, collections are by comparison pathetically spotty, narrowly focused on one kind of property, on one kind of property transfer, or on one sector of society.[10]

This collection is of significance not just to historians of Douai or of the immediate region, but also to scholars more generally interested in the legal, institutional, socioeconomic, and cultural history of northern European cities in this age. As I shall argue, these documents record a fascinating history of law and legal institutions, but they also allow us to see, much more clearly than we are generally able to see, the relationship between law and its social context.

I

The archive's importance for such an inquiry becomes apparent, however, only after a technical analysis of the documents themselves—their formal properties, the language they employ, and their precise relationship to the city's customary or unwritten laws of property and property relations.

[9] Note, however, that women necessarily appear as frequently as men as principal actors in marriage contracts, and that in Douai women authored as many wills as men did. The gender imbalance thus reflects men's dominance of the "contrats divers," which themselves make up 80 percent of the archive.

[10] Statistics in support of this analysis are provided in Martha C. Howell, *The Marriage Exchange: Property, Social Place, and Gender in Cities of the Low Countries, 1300-1550* (Chicago, 1998), 75-89.

Almost all the documents in the collection are in chirograph, a document familiar to most medievalists, but which in Douai had some slightly unusual characteristics. The chirographs making up the Douaisien archive were originally drafted in the presence of two échevins, in three copies on a single parchment, each transcription being separated from the next by the word—written in large letters across the parchment—C-H-I-R-O-G-R-A-P-H-E.[11] The sheet of parchment was thereafter cut at the place where "chirographe" was written, dividing the word horizontally, and each party to the contract took one copy; in Douai, the middle third was held by the échevins and deposited in their "sac." It is the copies in the échevinal sack that make up the collection now housed in Douai's municipal archive.

Although often compared to notarial documents, chirographs did not technically have the same status at law for they were not public acts or records of them; they were simply evidence of acts done privately.[12] It is perhaps for that reason that public authorities tried—sporadically and largely without success—to suppress the chirograph and to substitute for it the sealed act or charter. Such an effort was undertaken between 1368 and 1373, while Douai was still under the French crown.[13] The effort failed, however, and after the city's incorporation into the Burgundian realm, the chirograph was taken up again, with vigor. It is from the Burgundian period that most of the documentation under consideration here comes. Another break occurred between 1422 and 1427, when the chirograph was again suppressed, this time by ducal authorities in Lille, but that effort also failed.

The collection of chirographs as a whole thus breaks down into two distinct chronological periods, before and after 1368, the latter being eight to ten times larger than the first. From the first period, precisely dating

[11] On the three-part chirograph, see M. T. Clanchy, *From Memory to Written Record: England 1066-1307*, 2d ed. (Oxford, 1993), 68-69.

[12] On the (vernacular) chirograph as an alternative to the traditional (Latin) sealed charter, see Prevenier, "La production," 58. Prevenier also points out that, although unsealed, the chirograph acquired the authority of the sealed charter by virtue of its having been safeguarded by the échevins: place substituted for the formal symbols of authority.

[13] In 1305, after the French-Flemish wars, Douai was formally ceded to the French crown. With the marriage of the Valois Duke Philip to Marguerite of Male in 1369 and Philip's later assumption of the title of Duke of Burgundy, Douai was joined to the Burgundian domain. Although part of Burgundy until 1667, Douai was administered as a distinct entity within the dukedom, and retained much of its independence at the cost of paying enormous taxes to the crown.

from 1228 to 1368, we have about 2,000 chirographs "ordinaires" (that is, "contrats divers"), another 150 testaments, and 157 marriage documents, of which only 75 date from the period before 1300. Starting in 1374, the first year the chirograph was resumed after the 1368-73 break, we have, in contrast, several hundreds of documents per year, every year that the chirograph was in use, of which about thirty to forty are marriage documents. Supplementing the chirographs are register entries of two kinds: first, marriage agreements and "contrats divers" recorded when the chirograph was not used; second, deathbed testaments taken by priests and thereafter registered with the échevins in six folio volumes, dating from 1419 to 1495 (with breaks).[14]

The chirograph, then, played a leading role in regulating property transfers in Douai, for it was the principal means for documenting gifts of property, whether made inter vivos or post mortem, and for registering property sales. So often was this instrument used, by so many different people, that legal scholars have credited it with changing Douaisien customary law, especially law concerning marital property relations and inheritance, for a great many of the property transfers recorded in the chirographs were part of marriage agreements or estate settlements.[15]

II

In this regard, the most important of these documents, and by far the best studied, is the collection labeled "contrats de mariage," which number about five thousand, thus accounting for about 10 percent of the pre-1500 archive under study here. Alone of the documents in this archive, the marriage agreements are beautifully indexed in a *fichier* made during the 1970s by the former archivist.[16] Thanks to this index, legal historians have in the

[14] Douai, Archives municipales, FF 393-411, 444-50.

[15] In particular, see Robert Jacob, *Les époux, le seigneur et la cité: Coutume et pratiques matrimoniales des bourgeois et paysans de la France du Nord au Moyen Âge* (Brussels, 1990); Jean Yver, *Egalité entre héritiers et exclusion des enfants dotés: Essai de géographie coutumière* (Paris, 1966); Yver, "Les deux groupes de coutumes," *Revue du Nord* 35 (1953): 197-220, and 36 (1954): 5-36; Philippe Godding, *Le droit privé dans les Pays-Bas méridionaux du 12e au 18e siècle*, Mémoires de la Classe des lettres, Collection in 4°, 2d ser., 14.1 (Brussels, 1987).

[16] See Monique Mestayer, "Les contrats du mariage à Douai du XIIème au XVème siècle: Reflets du droit et de la vie d'une société urbaine," *Revue du Nord* 61 (1979): 353-79.

past decade been able to analyze the marriage agreements, and social and cultural historians exploring the socioeconomic and cultural history the documents record have closely followed these scholars.[17]

Although the marriage agreements are all inventoried as "contrats de mariage," in fact only about 75 percent of them are marriage contracts in the technical sense; the remainder are mostly what Douaisiens and others in the region called *ravestissements par lettre.* Although the contract and the ravestissement par lettre would eventually have very different effects on marital property relations and inheritance, they are correctly catalogued together because both served to modify the terms of marital property relations, succession, and inheritance prescribed by Douaisien custom and because, as I will argue, the latter literally evolved out of the former. I will return to the latter point about the development of the marriage contract, but let me begin by relating the two instruments to custom.

Both the contract and the ravestissement par lettre modified customary rules about marital property relations, succession, and, thus, inheritance. According to that custom, the survivor of any fertile marriage (that is, any marriage that had produced a live birth), whether man or woman, was the full and absolute possessor of all the property in the household, no matter its kind, its provenance, or the date at which it had been acquired. In the language of Douai, such couples had achieved a *ravestissement par sang.* During the marriage, the husband had full and absolute control over this

[17] In addition to the classic study by Georges Espinas, *La vie urbaine de Douai au Moyen-Âge*, 4 vols. (Paris, 1913), which employs some of these documents (without benefit of Mlle. Mestayer's modern index), the recent work on Douai's social history includes Jean-Pierre Deraugnecourt, "Autour de la mort à Douai: Attitudes, pratiques et croyances, 1250-1500" (Ph.D. diss., Université Catholique de Lille, 1993); Deraugnecourt, "Le testament: Un reflet de la conjoncture sanitaire, individuelle et collective: L'exemple de Douai au bas Moyen-Âge," *Revue du terroir* 24 (1985): 117-29; Alain Derville, "Les échevins de Douai (1228-1527)," in *La sociabilité urbaine en Europe du Nord-Ouest du XIVe au XVIIIe siècle: Actes du Colloque, 5 février 1983*, Mémoires de la Société d'agriculture, sciences et arts de Douai, 5th ser., 8 (Douai, 1983); Mestayer, "Les contrats du mariage à Douai"; Michel Rouche and Pierre Demolon, eds., *Histoire de Douai*, Collection d'histoire des villes du Nord/Pas-de-Calais 9 (Dunkirk, 1985); Walter Simons, "Begijnen en begarden in het middeleeuwse Dowaai," *De Franse Nederlanden: Jaarboek* 17 (1992): 180-97; Catherine Dhérent, "Abondance et crises: Douai, ville frontière 1250-1337," 3 vols. (Ph.D. diss., Université de Paris, 1993). Also see Jacob, *Les époux*, and Howell, *Marriage Exchange*.

property, but if his wife survived him, she assumed all these rights upon his death. If the marriage had been infertile, the property (again, all of it, of any kind) was split fifty-fifty between the survivor of the marriage and the "next of kin" of the deceased—parents, then siblings. Radical as the Douaisien system seems in its preference for the conjugal household, it was not unique. Other cities in the region, including Orchies and Hesdin, adhered to such a custom, and all cities in the Picard-Walloon region similarly, if not quite so radically, privileged the conjugal couple and the unitary property fund created by their marriage.[18]

The chirographs that Douaisiens issued in such numbers served to modify this regime, as I have noted, in one of two very different ways. One kind of change was accomplished by the earlier mentioned ravestissement par lettre, a document that intensified the terms of custom. It provided that the surviving spouse of an infertile marriage would have the same property rights as the survivor of a fertile marriage: thus the aptly named ravestissement par lettre accomplished by convention exactly what the customary ravestissement par sang accomplished by biology. Most of the chirographs stored in the municipal archive as "contrats de mariage" that survive from before 1300 and over 35 percent of those dating from 1374 to 1400 are, in fact, ravestissements of this kind. After about 1400, the ratio of ravestissements to true contracts declines rapidly, but the ravestissement never disappeared from medieval Douai. As late as 1500, about 5 percent of the chirographs stored in the collection of "contrats de mariage" were in fact ravestissements.

The ravestissment par lettre was, thus, a written statement of custom's rules about marital property relations, different from custom only in that it extended to infertile couples the same privileges custom allowed fertile couples. It was a simple document, ostensibly produced by husband and wife alone, who together had it drafted in the presence of two échevins. It positioned the husband and wife as one by treating them as exactly identical partners in the marriage, even using precisely parallel language to describe their respective donations:

> Let it be known to all that Jacquemart de Lommel, who resides in Douai, has made and makes a ravestissement to Jehanne de Sanchy his wife and spouse of all he has, will have and might acquire, whether or

[18] See Jacob, *Les époux*, 319, 242; Jacob, "La Charte d'Hesdin (1243) et la vocation successorale du conjoint survivant dans les pays picard et wallon," *Tijdschrift voor Rechtsgeschiedenis* 50 (1982): 351-70.

not there is an heir, according to the law and custom of Douai. And likewise, the said Jeanne de Sanchi makes and has made a ravestissement to Jacquemart her husband of all she has and will have or might acquire, whether or not there is an heir (of the marriage), according to the law and custom of the city of Douai....[19]

The ravestissment par lettre thus inscribed a vision of marriage as economic unity, positioning both husband and wife as interchangeable successors of one another and treating each, during life, as entirely and equally competent to decide about the disposition of marital property after his or her death. This did not mean, however, that custom imagined husband and wife to have equal powers over property during marriage; in fact, in keeping with its notion that marriage formed a single, indissoluble unit, custom clearly gave husbands all authority over conjugal property during their lives, formally denying wives any control over conjugal property during marriage, including property that they had themselves brought to the marriage or earned during its course. As husbands, men married under Douaisien custom could transfer, sell, and even destroy all property in the conjugal fund, including the property their wives had brought to it. Everything a wife earned, every debt she incurred, was the property of her spouse, her "baron" or "seigneur," as the sources commonly named him.

Obviously, then, custom and the ravestissement par lettre that tracked custom created a contradiction in gender relations—wives were on the one hand successors to their husbands and competent to choose to write a ravestissement par lettre establishing their husbands as their full heirs even if there was no live birth during the marriage but, on the other, they were under complete *couverture* during marriage. The contradiction was not lost on Douaisiens, and beginning about 1400, the ravestissment par lettre expressed this problem in a strange but revealing clause added to the standard text of the document itself:

Let it be known to all that before the aldermen of the city of Douai have personally come Pierre Hardi and Jacque Huquedieu, his wife and spouse, to whom Pierre has made a ravestissement and by virtue of this document makes a mutual donation to Jacque, his wife, of all he has or will acquire during their marriage whether in goods, movables, chattels, or inheritable immovables, to enjoy after his death by his wife and her representatives. And likewise, this woman, *being suffi-*

[19] Douai, Archives municipales, FF 616/2374 (27 December 1442).

> *ciently empowered by Pierre, her husband, whose empowerment she accepts as agreeable*, has made and makes a ravestissement to Pierre, her husband, of all she has or will acquire during their marriage whether in goods, movables, chattels, or immovables for him and his representatives to enjoy after her death, all according to the custom of Douai....[20]

The nonsensical provision underlined in the text thus perfectly captures the contradiction imbedded in Douaisien custom: women were suppliers and potential managers of property but they were also, simultaneously, wives in a marital unit represented solely by husbands; contained by their husbands, they could have no independent claims to wealth. As potential successor to her husband (literally, as successor to the household that contained her), a woman could, however, transfer the property rights thus implied, but as a wife she could do so only with her husband's permission, even if she was giving the property to him; to complete the absurdity, he needed her to agree to accept the permission he granted.

Although also a response to or a commentary on custom, the marriage contract, in the form it had achieved by around 1430, accomplished a very different form of marital property relations than did the ravestissement. The centerpiece of the marriage contract was the *portement*, the term Douaisiens used for the properties each spouse brought to the marriage, and the clauses regulating its disposition during and after marriage. These provisions created what the ravestissement had explicitly refused: a separation of conjugal goods into his and hers and, as will become evident, a marked distinction between male and female succession rights.

Almost all marriage contracts specified the contents of the bride's portement, and in those few that did not, the grooms usually acknowledged the portement's existence by pronouncing himself "content" with it. In contrast, grooms typically did not list their portements, for the good reason that their succession rights did not depend on the size or composition of their portements, but many brides nevertheless declared themselves "contente" with the portement their grooms promised but did not list.[21] It became increasingly rare to omit these details from the contract, either for brides or grooms, as the fifteenth century gave way to the sixteenth. Typi-

[20] Douai, Archives municipales, FF 616/2346 (26 November 1441); emphasis mine.

[21] Or the bride and her father (or other representative of her family) together declared themselves "contents."

cally, the contract distinguished personal property in the portement from cash and from household goods, and it listed immovables and rents individually. For example, Jehanne Caterent who married Lyon Regnart, a cloth finisher, in 1441, brought "in goods, movables, and tools...the sum and value of 150 *livres parisis monnaie de flandre*" along with "approximately 3 *rasières* and 1 *couppre* of tillable land."[22] Jehenne Herbert, who married Collard Le Grant, a "laboreur" (yeoman farmer), in 1441, had considerably fewer worldly goods, but she nonetheless specified a portement consisting of "many goods and movables such as clothing, jewels, and adornments."[23]

The principal reason for listing the bride's portement was to guarantee her rights as a widow, for the portement was the basis of the *reprise*, the property a woman took back from the estate when widowed. Often, the reprise was expressed simply as return of the portement, as in the marriage contract written in 1441 for Jehanne Henemere, whose 110 *livres parisis* would be returned to her at her husband's death "freely and entirely, without difficulty and without liabilities," whether or not children had been born of the marriage.[24] In other cases, the reprise was expressed in somewhat different goods: Jehenne Dymont's portement consisted of two (attached) houses in Douai plus one garden lot and "many shares in goods, movables, and in jewels, clothing and adornments, and a furnished bed set."[25] If her husband died first, she was to take, as her reprise, "all the *héritages* which she had brought to the marriage" plus 3 *francs* of "rentes viagères" (life rent), along with her "furnished bed set, all her clothing, jewels, and adornments which she might have on that day, no matter their value."

In addition to their reprise (or return of their portement), women were almost always granted an "increase," called in Douai the *douaire, douaire conventionnel,* or, more often and more precisely, the *douaire, assene et amendement.* Most such douaires were expressed in cash, although some included real estate, sometimes real estate that would be held only in usufruct (making this property claim more like the dower typical of other northern regimes). There appears to have been no fixed ratio between the douaire and the portement in Douaisien marriage contracts. Jacke De Bimy,

[22] Douai, Archives municipales, FF 616/2326 (15 May 1441).
[23] Douai, Archives municipales, FF 616/2324 (11 May 1441).
[24] Douai, Archives municipales, FF 616/2331 (9 June 1441).
[25] Douai, Archives municipales, FF 616/2347 (25 November 1441).

who married a carpenter in 1362, was promised a douaire exactly equal to her portement of 40 florins d'or.[26] Marie D'Estree, a widow with two daughters who married a brewer in the same year, however, received only 30 *florins d'or* as her douaire, although her portement was 120 *florins d'or* plus seven houses in Douai.[27]

The douaire or increase, along with the reprise, thus functioned as (and was evidently intended as) an alternative to the customary ravestissement. Contracts from the later fifteenth and sixteenth centuries often expressly gave the choice, as did that written for Colle Brouche dit Caillet, from 1521; it provided that she could take 900 *livres parisis* out of the marriage as her reprise and douaire, assene et amendement, plus her clothing, her "chambre," and her jewels, or, alternatively, she could "hold to the goods and liabilities which the said Jacques [her husband] had left."[28] Scholars have not been sure, however, just what phrases such as "hold to the goods and liabilities" of the deceased meant, whether they implied full ownership, as had the old ravestissement, or whether they intended only usufruct of the entire estate. Court cases before about 1450 suggest the former interpretation: that widows who refused their reprise and douaire, choosing to "rester" or "demeurer" (as the texts usually expressed it) in the estate, were, in effect, beneficiaries of the ravestissement—full owners of the estate. Thereafter, however, some evidence indicates that the right to "stay" was understood to grant only usufruct, that widows who "stayed" were holding the property for the next-in-line of the husbands' kin (his children, or his parents and siblings), and that they could not alienate or encumber the property during their life.[29] Beginning around 1500, Douaisiens made themselves clearer. It was then that they introduced the term *douaire coutumier* to refer to the widow's right to "stay" in the estate, and that term seems to have been consistently interpreted to mean only usufruct rights to the entire estate. The contract written for Marguerite De Farbus in 1548, for example, provided that, as widow, De Farbus could take a reprise and douaire or she could "hold to her right to the douaire coutumier, of which she has the choice and option."[30] Still relatively rare at the end of the fifteenth century—only one contract in four then specifically

[26] Douai, Archives municipales, FF 585/153 (25 July 1362).
[27] Douai, Archives municipales, FF 585/154 (12 August 1362).
[28] Douai, Archives municipales, FF 649/5127 (12 April 1521).
[29] See Howell, *Marriage Exchange*, 8, and Jacob, *Les époux*, 165-66, 181-89.
[30] Douai, Archives municipales, FF 654/5541 (5 July 1548).

named the douaire coutumier—the clause regularly appeared in contracts written fifty years later; 80 percent of the contracts in one sample from the 1550s included the clause.[31]

The mature marriage contract accomplished very different ends from the ravestissement. By guaranteeing a widow return of her portement (or its rough equivalent) and an increase, it shielded her from the risks of losses her husband may have incurred during the marriage and from debts he might have left when he died. Ysabel Le Dent's and Jean De Temple's marriage contract, for example, specifically expressed this goal:

> If it happens that after the marriage Jean De Temple dies before Ysabel without a living heir in existence or expected on the day of his death, the said Ysabel will have and can freely take, without obligation of any kind, all the héritages she brought to the marriage and all that came to her in its course, whether by gift, succession, inheritance, or any other way if it was from her natal kin, with the rents and revenues well and sufficiently attached. And she takes without obligation as her portement in money and as douaire, assene et amendement of the marriage the sum of 500 *francs*, at 33 Flemish *gros* for the *franc*.[32]

Simultaneously, however, particularly by the time the right to "stay" in the estate had been clearly defined as usufruct alone, the marriage contract eliminated widows' claims to succession rights. No longer could they share in the gains of the marriage; no longer could they assume full managerial control over the conjugal fund when their husbands died, for the property was now explicitly marked for heirs and thus unavailable for sale or mortgage without the approval of those heirs.

In addition to protecting and restraining widows, the contract also served as an explicit guarantor of children's inheritance rights. Contracts written by widows or widowers with children commonly included clauses setting aside monies from the new conjugal fund for these children when they reached majority or married, or they simply labeled certain immovables as the children's after the death of their natural parent. More common still were clauses protecting the inheritance rights of children to be born of

[31] For the figure of one in four, see Jacob, *Les époux*, 187-88; the figure of 80 percent is based on contracts sampled in Douai, Archives municipales, FF 914 (contrats en papier); fifteen of nineteen contracts contained a clause explicitly granting the douaire coutumier. See Howell, *Marriage Exchange*, Appendix A, for a fuller discussion of the property rights of widows who refused their reprise and douaire.

[32] Douai, Archives municipales, FF 616/2321 (23 April 1441).

the present marriage. Gillette Cardron's marriage contract of 1549, for example, provided that the house, garden, and tenement with 12 *couppres* of land she would bring to the marriage, as well as an orchard, would go to her husband at her death (as custom would have dictated), but only for his life (a limitation foreign to custom); thereafter it would pass to their children, or to her "nearest kin."[33]

The marriage contract, thus, imposed a marital property and succession regime quite different from old custom's. Under it, husband and wife were not treated as common owners of all conjugal property and the equal survivors of one another, as they had been under custom. Now, widows had ownership only of specified assets—those they had brought to the marriage (or their equivalent) and those pledged as an increase. Alternatively, they could claim life use, but not ownership, of all marital property. Under this new regime, men did not suffer so costly a decrease in their survivors' rights as did women, for if men survived their wives, they acquired full ownership of all property in the marital estate except that which had been specifically marked for others by the terms of the marriage contract. Typically, those reserves included only a small provision for testamentary bequests and return of immovable property to the woman's natal line, in the absence of living descendent heirs. Although the possessor of relatively favorable succession rights, a man was, as husband, constrained by special clauses which labeled specific items as the property of his bride, forbade their sale without her consent or that of her *avoués* (men assigned by the marriage contract to look after her financial interests), and required their return to her "lez et coste" at her death if there were no children born of the marriage. In effect, the new marital property regime in Douai was "separatist" in spirit, rather more like those of the south of Europe, while the old ravestissement was "conjugal" in intent.[34]

Although the ravestissement and the marriage contract thus came to provide very different conceptions of marital property relations and succession, they had not begun life as such radically different conceptions of marital succession. In fact, in their early days, that is until about 1380 or 1400, marriage contracts—or *convenances de mariage* as they were then usually called—were much closer to the ravestissements that they eventually came to replace, some of them appearing to be little more than modified ravestissements par lettre. Typically, they mixed elements of the

[33] Douai, Archives municipales, FF 654/5542 (2 May 1549).

[34] Jacob develops this comparison more systematically in *Les époux*, 207-15.

mutual donation characteristic of the ravestissement with elements of a separatist marital property arrangement common to later marriage contracts. Just what was intended in such texts is not entirely clear, but it seems that they allowed widows the option of choosing the customary ravestissement or, alternatively, a settlement rather like the reprise of the marriage contract, an option, as discussed, that was more specifically indicated in later contracts.

The pre-1400 so-called "contrats" or "convenances" were odd in other ways as well, archaic in form and unstable in language. These characteristics long confused scholars, leading them to conclude that the legal history recorded by these documents was as confused as the scholars were themselves. Thus, they argued, the marriage agreements Douaisiens left—their ravestissements catalogued as "contrats," their couvenances that looked like ravestissments, their ravestissements that gave women property rights with one hand and took those same rights away with another—were evidence of how difficult medieval Douaisiens had found their transition to modernity. In this telling, the Douaisien archive was the trace of the archaic, the proof of Douaisiens' discomfort with modern legal concepts and the instruments inscribing them. Thanks to the recent work of legal historians, Robert Jacob principally among them, this story has been rewritten, and the peculiarities of the early marriage contracts rendered comprehensible.[35] Now it is clear that the marriage contract emerged as a modification of the old, radical, ravestissement, in effect began life within it. Thus, the inconsistencies and contradictions evident in the archive and in the language of the documents were products of that intertwined history; rather than evidence of Douaisien ineptitude, they serve as measures of Douaisien creativity—and of their determination both to preserve custom *and* to adapt it as needed. While the contract and the ravestissement would come to stand in clear opposition to one another, they had not begun that way—and could thus not have been written as what they had not yet become.

By the mid-sixteenth century, marriages among propertied Douaisiens were more often made by contract than by old custom. This practice had become so firmly a part of Douaisien culture that when Douaisiens first wrote their custom down around 1550, they included the rules associated with the marriage contract alongside those of custom, even going so far as to describe both the ravestissement and the douaire coutumier as "custom-

[35] Jacob, *Les époux.*

ary."[36] Although both systems—which by then were utterly different in effect—could hardly be "customary," their juxtaposition in this text reveals that in sixteenth-century Douai chirographs had served to remake custom. The result was the odd situation in which two different ways of managing marital property relations and inheritance existed side-by-side, one being the default regime, the regime of the ravestissement, and the other the conventional regime, the regime of the written contract.

III

Testaments and "contrats divers" played as key a role in the reform of customary "family" law in Douai, although the role of each lessened as the Middle Ages drew to a close, for the marriage contract came to assume many of the functions these documents once played.

Of the two, the will was indisputably the more important in this long process of change. The Douaisien testaments are among the earliest we have from the urbanized Low Countries—there are seventeen surviving from the period before 1270, for example—and the collection in the municipal archive, if we include both wills in chirograph and those in register, is almost as large as the collection of marriage documents. In addition, there is a collection of wills in the hospital archives of Douai, now closed to scholars.[37]

Following a tradition of scholarship inaugurated by scholars such as Vovelle and Ariès, the Douaisien wills have been approached as windows into the religious culture of the age. Thus, we have studies of burial practices, funerary rites, and charitable or pious gifts based on these documents.[38] These studies have shown that the Douaisien wills of this period,

[36] See Howell, *Marriage Exchange*, Appendix B.

[37] Historians permitted access to these documents in the past have reported that the hospital archives by and large duplicate the municipal archives, the former having surely been created to document the institution's claim to property bequeathed to them in the testament.

[38] For examples of such studies: Jean-Pierre Deregnaucourt, "La piété et son décor à Douai du XIVe au XVe siècle," *Amis de Douai*, 5th ser., 8 (1980-83): 175-78; Philippe Godding, "La pratique testamentaire en Flandre au 13e siècle," *Tijdschrijft voor Rechtsgeschiedenis* 58 (1990): 281-300; Monique Mestayer, "Testaments douaisiens antérieurs"; Simons, "Begijnen en begarden in het middeleeuwse Dowaai"; Ahasver von Brandt, *Mittelalterliche Bürgertestamente: Neuerschlossene Quellen zur Geschichte der materiellen und geistigen Kultur*, Sitzungsberichte der Heidelberger

like wills from urbanized areas elsewhere at the time, were powerful and widely used vehicles for religious expression. Few scholars have, however, focused on what is generally the longest and most elaborate portion of Douaisien wills, the part where the testators arranged their estate, making mostly secular gifts to mostly secular people.

This portion of the will worked, as the marriage contract would later work, to revise Douaisien custom regarding succession and inheritance. In this regard, it is noteworthy that none of the seventeen wills that survive from Douai before 1270 contained a single gift for pious purposes or arranged a single funeral.[39] All, instead, were written by people using the will to ensure that their principal assets devolved as they wished. Ansel Pererin, for example, wrote a short testament in 1259 that gave his residence and all of his income-producing real estate in Douai, rented or empty, to his son, thus bypassing his widow who would have been his customary heir.[40]

Even those wills in chirograph that do include pious gifts—as almost all of those dating from the fourteenth century forward do—also usually contain elaborate provisions for property distribution to secular beneficiaries. This property consisted both of personal goods, such as jewelry and arms, and of wealth normally considered patrimonial, such as houses, rents, and land. For example, the 1364 will of Nicaise De La Desous (dit Dou Pont), after having bestowed token gifts to the clergy officiating at his death, to the poor tables, and to the maintenance fund of his parish church, continued with a much longer list of bequests:

To the six children of his brother Jehan De La Desous, and to the two children of his other brother Pierot, he gives 1 *rasière* of land, to be distributed among them equally;

To the two children of Jacquemart De La Desous and to the daughter of Gillon De La Desous (who is deceased), he leaves 2 *couppres* of land, to be divided among the three;

To Jaquemart De La Desous, his brother, he leaves a gown, his best ("une reube toute le meilleur que le dis Nichaises ara au jour de son trespas"), and two pairs of draperies;

Akademie der Wissenschaft, Philosophisch-historische Klasse, Jahrg. 1973, Abh. 3 (Heidelberg, 1973), 5-32.

[39] See Howell, *Marriage Exchange*, 132-38; Howell, "Fixing Movables: Gifts by Testament in Late Medieval Douai," *Past and Present* 150 (1996): 3-45.

[40] Douai, Archives municipales, FF 861 (March 1259), in Mestayer, "Testaments douaisiens antérieurs," 64-77, 68-69.

To Jehan De Le Desous, son of Jacquemart, he leaves a featherbed ("une keute"), a pair of linens, and a copper pot;
To his godson, he leaves his best bed "tout estoffe" (fully furnished), but without pillows, one copper pot, and his best bronze frying pan;
To Hanotin Le Ticulier, his cousin, son of Jacquemart Le Ticulier, he leaves his house and holding;
To Esthievenart De La Desous, his nephew, he leaves a featherbed, a pair of linens, his best after those already named;
To Katherine, sister of Esthievenart, he leaves a copper pot and a bronze frying pan with a pair of linens;
To Jehane, sister of Esthievenart, two decorated pillows;
To Katherine, daughter of Jacquemart De La Desous, he leaves a pot with two handles, and to Jehane, daughter of Katherine, a bronze frying pan, the best after that mentioned earlier;
The surplus of his estate he leaves to his executors to distribute to Douai's poor, on behalf of the souls of his relatives named in the will....[41]

Although De La Desous probably chose to distribute his personal effects so widely because he was childless, his decision to parcel out his property was in no way uncommon. In fact, in most Douaisien testaments of the late Middle Ages these kinds of provisions make up the most extensive part of the text.

The wills not in chirograph, that is, those deathbed testaments taken by a priest and later registered by the échevins, are more typical of wills elsewhere in northern Europe in that they always devote space to pious gifts, and many of them have that as their exclusive purpose. But a large part of these hastily made testaments also include distributions of secular gifts to secular people, frequently working just like the wills in chirograph, to restrict the succession rights of widows. For example, Jacquemart Le Libert, a prosperous butcher, made a testament in the 1440s leaving all his property to his wife but only on the condition that she not remarry; if she did, she was to pass the estate on to the children.[42]

Thus the Douaisien will, particularly the will in chirograph, was a dual-purpose document, written not just in compliance with ecclesiastical injunc-

[41] Douai, Archives municipales, FF 862 (20 December 1364).

[42] Douai, Archives municipales, FF 448, fols. 29v-30 (23 June 1439). Le Libert's wife did remarry within a few years. She had her adult children witness the new marriage contract to confirm that she had complied with her husband's wishes; Douai, Archives municipales, FF 617/2410.

tions to leave wealth to the church and the poor, to care for the soul, but also composed in an effort to regulate the terms of succession and inheritance. In fact, the will was used for this purpose long before Douaisiens regularly wrote marriage contracts (recall that the first real marriage contracts date from about 1300 and that it is not until after 1373 that we have meaningful numbers of marriage contracts). It is also true, as can be judged from a survey of the medieval wills in Douai, that the wills gradually abandoned their concern with succession and inheritance, becoming more and more like wills elsewhere, exactly during the period that the marriage contract came into greater use. It seems, then, that Douaisiens early adapted the will, using it to alter custom's rules of succession and inheritance, but then switched to the more efficient marriage contract when that document had been fully developed. Douaisiens did not then cease writing wills, of course, but they then used them more often as people elsewhere in northern Europe had long been using them—to divert a portion of their wealth to the church and its causes.

Finally, let us turn to the "contrats divers," the least well studied and by far the largest collection of sources (containing approximately forty thousand chirographs from the pre-1500 period) of the three major collections making up the "actes de la pratique" in Douai. This collection is totally unindexed, and has scarcely been touched except by scholars mining it for anecdotes. It is an incoherent collection, made up of documents of different character—quitclaims, mortgages, sale contracts for everything from houses to horses to dyestuffs to wine.

Although so diverse a collection of documents cannot be imagined to have had a single purpose, it is clear that these contracts often once served, as the will and marriage contract would later more aggressively serve, to record property transfers that intervened in Douaisien customary law concerning marital property relations, succession, and inheritance. A sampling of these documents, taken from five different periods from the late thirteenth century into the early sixteenth, reveals these purposes.[43]

The earliest sample, taken from years in the later thirteenth century when the collection begins, contains a great many quitclaims—documents attesting to the fact that a debt had been settled or an obligation satisfac-

[43] These results are summarized in Martha Howell, "Weathering Crisis, Managing Change: The Emergence of a New Socioeconomic Order in Douai at the End of the Middle Ages," in *La draperie ancienne des Pays-Bas: Débouchés et stratégies de survie (14ᵉ-16ᵉ siècles)*, ed. Marc Boone and Walter Prevenier (Leuven, 1993).

torily met. Typically, the document does not identify the reason for the debt, but instead simply lists the payer, the payee, the sum or property transferred, and the date. Some, however, are more forthcoming, and those frequently explain that the debt was incurred as part of a marriage agreement or that the payment being registered was made to settle an estate, such evidence suggesting that many similar documents that were silent about their origin were also prompted by such prior agreements. In contrast, samples taken from later years, especially after about 1400, contain very few quitclaims as such. Instead, they are made up of records of real estate transactions—almost always of houses and holdings in Douai or in nearby cities—or of sales and purchases of movable goods. For example, forty-four of the fifty-seven contracts taken in one sample from 1497-98 treated sales or mortgages of houses. Many of them were like that written by a certain Jehan De Hem (dit Petit), a butcher, who sold a quarter share in a house and adjoining residence, which he had presumably inherited but could not use in this form.[44] Other real estate contracts proved more complicated and dealt not solely with issues of use but also of succession and sentiment. For example, Eurade Piquette and her husband ceded their half share in a manor to the widow of Piquette's brother, Agnus Artus, now the wife of Hermin De La Pappoire, for the course of her life. Artus had acquired the half share in the manor as her douaire on the property, but it is clear that her former sister-in-law did not want to share use of it (even financial use) during their lives. So De La Pappoire rented the sister-in-law's share, agreeing to pay Piquette and her husband a rent of 4 *livres parisis* per year; each of the parties also agreed to pay half the 4 *livres parisis* of perpetual rents due on the manor, but Artus and De La Pappoire would collect all revenues from the property while they held it. The deal was made, as the document explained, "to assure good relations among the parties and avoid questions" (that is, to disentangle the financial affairs of the separate families) and had the ultimate effect of returning the property to the male line that had acquired it in the previous generation.[45]

These patterns suggest that this section of the Douaisien archive—a section, let us not forget, containing some forty thousand documents—is in part at least the repository of records produced in an effort to manage certain aspects of marital property relations, succession and inheritance. Like the wills and marriage agreements they supplemented, these records

[44] Douai, Archives municipales, FF 796, 26166-234, excluding 26223-32.
[45] Douai, Archives municipales, FF 740 (21 June 1441).

were generated when a Douaisien father or mother, husband or wife, thought that these matters should not be left to custom. In the early days of their use, these contracts played a key role in this management task, sometimes even substituting for a written marriage agreement or will, but more often probably evidencing the satisfactory execution of such a prior document that has not survived in the archive, or perhaps of an oral agreement. As the marriage contract and will acquired more secure status in Douaisien legal culture, however, the "contrats divers" were put to other purposes. They were deployed to record arrangements peripheral to the marriage contract or will, such as the Picquette–De La Pappoire deal just described or, more simply the sale of real estate interests that were obtained by succession and inheritance.

While these later contracts seem not to have served to regulate succession and inheritance, they serve historians in another way, for they help reveal the market's penetration of Douaisien culture. They show that, while in late medieval Douai property changed hands by succession and inheritance, just as it has always been thought to have been the dominant medieval tradition, this was not the end of the story. Having passed in this way, property was often re-transferred in order to render it manageable or to transform it into a more useable asset. The market was the means for the transformation, and it is this step that the later contracts record.

*

* *

The astonishing archive of "contrats divers," wills, and marriage agreements that survives in late medieval Douai thus eloquently records a social and cultural history as well as an institutional history, for to explain why the archive existed, we must invoke more than law and legal capacities. We must consider as well why Douaisiens would have worked so energetically to manipulate the laws of marital property relations and succession they inherited—why they would have preserved a custom that required constant modification, why they would have tolerated the expense and the time required to produce, store, and register written interventions in that custom, why they would have willingly lived with the legal confusion that frequently resulted. While there is no simple answer to that question, the sources themselves reveal a great deal about the sociocultural and political context within which these decisions were made, pointing us towards some of the reasons Douaisiens behaved as they did.

First, the system allowed Douaisiens enormous flexibility in managing their wealth; it gave them choices. One choice was to do nothing. If nothing was done, custom ruled: husbands had absolute control over all family assets, the widow of a fertile marriage assumed that control at his death; property stayed in the household—and with its survivor—at the death of either spouse and moved with that survivor as he or she remarried and had new children. In this way, the rights of the living dominated those of the dead, and the needs of the household superseded those of the family line. Another choice, however, was to issue a document such as a ravestissement par lettre, a will, or a marriage agreement so that all or a part of household property was not subject to custom's rules. For its part, the ravestissement par lettre intensified custom's preference for the household. In contrast, the will and marriage contract invariably served to disestablish the household, grant new rights to the line, and give priority to the deceased.

Different as these choices were, they shared one quality: they provided Douaisiens a wide range of options, a cornucopia of choices about how to manage their property. In effect, Douaisiens were beneficiaries of a kind of paradox—they were subject to a custom so radically privileging the head of household that he or she could undermine custom's logic. Douaisien heads of household, whether male or female, could intervene in custom to fashion ad hoc arrangements about particular pieces of property or about the entire estate, arrangements that seemed to them to suit their particular circumstances.

Thus, probable reason number one for the archive's existence is that Douaisiens thought it was to their advantage to retain customary law while manipulating it as needed, to "customize custom," as it were. Reason number two has to be, however, that they had the institutional means to do so: that, in effect, the échevins could and did support the citizens' efforts. Although we have no direct evidence about why the échevins might have wanted to retain this system, the indirect evidence is suggestive: the échevinage as a body collected a fee for serving as registrars for writing contracts and wills, and the two individual échevins who typically witnessed a document received personal fees as well. Moreover, the system elaborated échevinal authority, for it positioned them as arbitrators in disputes about custom and about the documents' meaning. Finally, it helped legitimate local autonomy, positioning Douai and Douaisiens as makers of their own law.[46] It is worth noting in this regard that very few cases concerning private financial interests of the kind treated in these documents were ap-

[46] On this feature of échevinal registration, see Prevenier, "La production," 566-68. On Douai's échevins, see Alain Derville, "Les échevins de Douai (1228-1527)."

pealed from Douai to Paris or Lille, and among the few surviving, none ruled against local custom, the échevins' interpretations of it, or the validity of the marriage contracts, testaments or "contrats divers."

Third, there were somewhat less instrumental reasons that reflect aspects of Douaisien culture itself. The Douaisien archive was self-evidently the creation of a people deeply invested in the authority of the written word. Surely, the Douaisiens who paid so much to have these documents written and spent so much time in court defending their interpretations of them were not fully literate. But they were just as surely semi-literate—used to dealing with literate people, willing to entrust their financial affairs to the written word, eager to deploy the document to manage their fortunes.[47] In addition, the archive was the creation of people profoundly committed to the market. The merchants and entrepreneurs, shopkeepers, artisans, and laborers who populate the Douaisien archive were, all of them, surprisingly aggressive managers of their wealth, no matter how modest their fortunes, and they were evidently confident of their ability to make good decisions about their property—or better decisions than traditional custom, if unfettered, would have made. The thousands of chirographs they left are witnesses, then, not just to an unusual legal and institutional history; they are also witnesses to a rarely viewed social history.

[47] For a thoughtful discussion of "literacy" and its significance in medieval Europe, see Rosamond McKitterick, "Introduction," in *The Uses of Literacy in Early Medieval Europe*, ed. Rosamond McKitterick (Cambridge, 1990). My thanks to Adam Kosto for bringing this essay to my attention.

Observations on Entry and Copying in the Cartularies with Charters of the Province of North Brabant

Geertrui Van Synghel

"Observations on the Entry and Copying in the Cartularies with Charters of the Province of North Brabant," in *Secretum Scriptorum: Liber alumnorum Walter Prevenier*, ed. Wim Blockmans, Marc Boone, and Thérèse de Hemptinne (Leuven, 2000), 77–92.

This study examines charters copied in cartularies among the 668 charters which were published in M. Dillo and G. A. M. Van Synghel, eds., *Oorkondenboek van Noord-Brabant tot 1312*, vol. 2, *De heerlijkheden van Breda en Bergen op Zoom* (The Hague, 1999). The emphasis is placed on explicit or unusual issues arising during this process, such as the selection of charters in general and in the case of forgeries, double expeditions, and versions that strongly resemble each other. Cartularies always exclude some of the charters available to the compiler, even if he strove to reproduce almost all texts. Since copyists performed their work in different ways, depending on the goals of the instigator, it is impossible to generalize about which charters were passed over. Some cautious conclusions are, however, possible. Many monastic cartularies have simply incorporated forged charters among the genuine charters. There is also a tendency to record both originals of a double expedition in cases with divergent *datatio* or *corroboratio*. Seals, graphic symbols, and notes are often left out. The incorporation into cartularies of forgeries, wrong versions, and translations highlights how critical the scholar must be when dealing with such transcriptions.

Papal Letters to Scandinavia and Their Preservation

Anders Winroth

In 864, Pope Nicholas I sent a letter to King Horik II of Denmark thanking him for gifts that he had sent.[1] This is, as far as I know, the first time that the papacy had direct contact with anyone in Scandinavia. Horik was a pagan, and in this letter the pope admonished him to relinquish his old idols for the one and only God. Horik was never baptized, but Scandinavia eventually became a part of Latin Christianity. From this time until the Reformation in the sixteenth century severed the ties between the Scandinavian countries and Rome, thousands of papal letters were transmitted from Rome and Avignon to Scandinavia.

My interest in the papal letters of Scandinavia focuses on the period before 1198. This is the year when the unbroken series of papal registers begins, and for that reason Philipp Jaffé's calendar of papal letters ends with Celestine III's papacy (1191-98). Just over a hundred years ago, Paul Kehr started the work on a geographically organized replacement of Jaffé, which has already produced several volumes of *Italia* and *Germania pontificia* and in 1998 the first volume of *Gallia pontificia*.[2] I am the editor of *Scandinavia pontificia* and in that capacity am charged with collecting what information there is about correspondence between the popes and Scandinavians before 1198.[3] In the present paper, I address how the letters that these correspon-

[1] *Diplomatarium Danicum*, vol. 1.1 (Copenhagen, 1975), no. 118, p. 50 = JL 2761. The text of this letter was preserved in a manuscript in Hamburg which later was in the library of the Jesuits in Cologne but now is lost. Philippus Caesar edited the letter in *Triapostolatus septentrionis* (Cologne, 1642), 189.

[2] Paul Kehr, *Regesta pontificum Romanorum: Italia pontificia*, 10 vols. in 12 to date (Berlin and Göttingen, 1906-); Albert Brackmann et al., *Regesta pontificum Romanorum: Germania pontificia*, 7 vols. in 9 to date (Berlin and Göttingen, 1906-); Bernard de Vregille, René Locatelli, and Gérard Moyse, *Regesta pontificum Romanorum: Gallia pontificia*, vol. 1, *Diocèse de Besançon* (Göttingen, 1998).

[3] About the progress of the project, see Theodor Schieffer, "Der Stand des Göttinger Papsturkunden-Werkes," *Jahrbuch der Akademie der Wissenschaften in Göt-*

dents sent to each other have been preserved.

The Christianization of Scandinavia brought with it European culture of all kinds, including diplomatic skills. It is probably significant that the pope in 864 was responding to gifts that King Horik had sent, not to a letter. Horik's court was probably not capable of producing a letter in Latin or in any other language.[4] Horik was probably not in the habit of saving in his archives the letters which he received, either. The text of this letter was preserved not in Denmark, but in cartularies at the cathedral of Hamburg-Bremen, the archepiscopal see whose province included Scandinavia until 1104.

Fortunately, the filing habits of Scandinavians changed. For the period before 1198 ten original papal letters survive in Scandinavian archives, five from Sweden, three from Denmark, and two from Norway. A much larger number of papal letters survive in copies of one kind or another. Altogether, *Scandinavia pontificia* will list some two hundred known letters.[5] This is not a great number in comparison with other parts of Europe. The first volume of *Gallia pontificia* lists 321 letters for the diocese of Besançon alone; 183 letters are known to have been sent to the archbishops of Hamburg-Bremen before 1198.[6] I do not think that the paucity of letters directed to Scandinavia illustrates shortcomings in the preservation of such documents there. Rather, it simply illustrates the fact that Scandinavia is an area on the periphery of Europe far away from Rome. The popes had plenty of problems to handle much closer at hand, and they seldom had reason to write to the sparsely populated Scandinavia.

---

tingen (Göttingen, 1971): 68-79, and the yearly reports of its leader, e.g., Rudolf Hiestand, "Bericht über die Tätigkeit der Pius-Stiftung für Papsturkundenforschung im Jahre 1996/97," *Deutsches Archiv für Erforschung des Mittelalters* 54 (1998): 433-43.

[4] According to the Life of Ansgar, chapter 12, in 831 King Björn of the Swedes sent a letter to Emperor Louis. It is, however, likely that Ansgar himself formulated and wrote this letter. See Alf Uddholm, "Till Ansgarsproblematiken: Sveakungen Björns brev till kejsar Ludvig den fromme 831," *Kyrkohistorisk årsskrift* 90 (1990): 109-14.

[5] As of June 2000, I had noted about two hundred letters. More will almost certainly be added, and a few may be deleted. This total includes a few letters concerning Estonia and (for practical reasons) a couple of letters directed to Russian princes.

[6] Vregille, Locatelli, and Moyse, *Gallia pontificia*, vol. 1; Brackmann et al., *Germania pontificia*, vol. 6.

Some papal letters to Scandinavia are, naturally, preserved in archives outside Scandinavia, for example in Gregory VII's register or in the archives of the archbishops of Hamburg-Bremen.[7] With one important exception, I will not discuss here this aspect of the problem, but instead will concentrate on the letters that survive in Scandinavia.

As indicated, five original papal letters from before 1198 survive in Sweden. One of them comes from the Cistercian nunnery of Gudhem. The archives of this monastery are in general well preserved, but include only charters, no cartularies.[8] More interesting are the remaining four originals, which all come from the metropolitan cathedral of Uppsala. Its archives are also well preserved, and they include a medieval cartulary known as the *Registrum ecclesie Upsalensis*, which was compiled in 1344.[9] The *Registrum* contains three of the four papal letters conserved in the original, and it contains two additional pre-1198 papal letters which do not survive in original. One of these actually survived until the eighteenth century. It is a letter written in 1164 by Pope Alexander III to the bishops of Sweden collectively, exhorting them henceforth to obey the newly created archbishop of Uppsala.[10] This letter was not originally copied in the *Registrum*; it is found (twice) on a loose parchment leaf that was inserted into the cartulary at a later point.[11] This was sufficient to start a debate among Swedish historians of the seventeenth century about whether this letter was a forgery. However, the archivist Claudius Örnhielm (d. 1695) managed to dig up the original letter, complete with the leaden bull, from the vast and clearly not very well organized collections of the Royal Archives of Antiquities. A few years later this letter was in the collection of the well-known collector Nils Rabenius (1648-1717), and after his death it disappeared without a trace.[12] Before its disappearance, several historians had, fortunately, been able to

[7] *Diplomatarium Danicum*, vol. 1.2 (Copenhagen, 1963), no. 28, p. 62.

[8] Lars Sjödin, "Kanslistilar och medeltida arkiv, I," in *Meddelanden från svenska riksarkivet för år 1939* (Stockholm, 1940), 129-30. The letter is edited in *Diplomatarium Svecanum*, vol. 1 (Stockholm, 1829), no. 72, p. 97 = JL 12672.

[9] Sjödin, "Kanslistilar och medeltida arkiv," 125-26, and Göran Dahlbäck, *Uppsala domkyrkas godsinnehav med särskild hänsyn till perioden 1344-1527*, Studier till Det medeltida Sverige 2 (Stockholm, 1977), 6-10.

[10] *Diplomatarium Svecanum*, vol. 1, no. 50, p. 72 = *Diplomatarium Danicum*, vol. 1.2, no. 154, p. 289 = JL 11048.

[11] Stockholm, Riksarkivet, A 8, pp. 179-80.

[12] Nils Ahnlund, *Nils Rabenius (1648-1717): Studier i svensk historiografi* (Stockholm, 1927), 145.

make good copies of it, so its text can be reconstructed easily.

We are less fortunate when it comes to the other missing original, which is no less a document then Alexander III's solemn privilege from 1164 raising the bishop of Uppsala to the rank of archbishop.[13] The privilege survives in the *Registrum*, but it is incomplete there. The scribe who copied it was probably flustered or perhaps intimidated when he came to the end of the text and encountered the signatures of the pope and the cardinals, and the peculiar symbols accompanying them, the *rota* and the *bene valete*. So he stopped copying there, omitting also the date line at the bottom of the privilege. The exact date for the foundation of the Swedish church is, thus, unknown, although the date cannot be many days before that of Alexander's letter informing the other bishops of their colleague's exaltation.

It is perhaps to be expected that the originals of some letters included in the *Registrum* are lost, although it is perhaps surprising that as important a document as the privilege of 1164 was lost when so much else is preserved.[14] More significant in the context of the theme of the present volume are the letters that survive in the original but were not included in the *Registrum*. One such document is a letter sent by Alexander III in 1174, 1176, or 1178 to the clergy of the diocese of Uppsala. The letter was in the archives of the cathedral during the Middle Ages, as is evident from an archival *signum* written on its back in the fourteenth century.[15] It is very likely that the letter would have been available when the *Registrum* was compiled, but that the compiler chose not to include it. His reasons can be deduced by considering which documents actually were included in the *Registrum*.

The *Registrum* contains three sections devoted to papal letters, not in the beginning, but in the middle of the volume.[16] The first one has the heading *bullate littere*, the second *bulle de confirmacionibus bonorum et*

[13] *Diplomatarium Svecanum*, vol. 1, no. 49, p. 70 = *Diplomatarium Danicum*, vol. 1.2, no. 153, p. 285 = JL 11047.

[14] Fewer than 30 percent of the letters copied in the *Registrum ecclesie Upsalensis* have been lost (100 out of 353); see Dahlbäck, *Uppsala domkyrkas godsinnehav*, 23.

[15] *Diplomatarium Svecanum* I, no. 853, p. 705 = JL 12998.

[16] See the medieval table of contents in the *Registrum ecclesie Upsalensis*, edited in *Diplomatarium Svecanum*, vol. 5 (Stockholm, 1858-65), no. 3849, pp. 349-62. Papal letters are listed on pp. 358-61, listing the contents of fols. 108-31. The *Registrum* contains 182 folios.

libertatum ecclesie Upsalensis, and the third *bulle indulgenciarum*. The third group is straightforward enough. It contains the papal bulls of indulgence that had been issued for the cathedral of Uppsala, usually granting indulgences of a specified number of days to pilgrims who visit the cathedral on the feast day of either of its patron saints, Lawrence and Eric. The other two groups are more problematic. It is often difficult to imagine why a specific papal letter was copied in one group and not in the other. Alexander III's letter from 1174 confirming the cathedral's ownership of three specific villages[17] is not found under the second heading, as could have been expected, since this heading expressly talks about bulls concerning ownership of goods. Whatever the basis for dividing the bulls in two groups, it is, however, quite clear which kind of papal letters were copied into these sections of the *Registrum*. These were letters that in one way or another confirm or establish some right, privilege, or possession belonging to the church of Uppsala. Suitably, the very first papal letter to be transcribed is the one I have already mentioned from 1164, establishing the archbishopric of Uppsala. There follows a letter of Pope Alexander IV from 1258 allowing the cathedral to be moved to another city and admonishing the king and the Swedish bishops to support this enterprise financially.[18] Other letters confirm for example specific gifts of goods to the cathedral, and prohibit the Swedish crown from levying taxes from the clergy. The overall purpose of the *Registrum* must have been to preserve a record of the goods and rights that the church of Uppsala owned and to prevent the originals from being destroyed by too frequent use.

Programmatic statements to this effect can be found from late medieval Sweden. At a provincial synod in the Swedish city of Arboga in 1396, it was decided that every cathedral ought to have a cartulary in order to minimize the risk that the original documents were destroyed when used.[19] This implies that the cartulary could have legal force on its own. Indeed, when

[17] *Diplomatarium Svecanum*, vol. 1, no. 852, p. 704 = JL 12997.

[18] *Diplomatarium Svecanum*, vol. 1, no. 451, p. 391 = August Potthast, *Regesta pontificum Romanorum inde ab a. post Christum natum MCXCVIII ad a. MCCCIV* (Berlin 1874-75), no. 17372.

[19] Ernst Nygren, "Registra ecclesie Lincopensis," *Linköpings biblioteks handlingar*, ny serie, 3 (Linköping, 1941), 82, 152. Nygren quotes the council's decision: "Ne maculentur Originalia Privilegiorum, seu per Sigillorum ruptionem destruantur, mandetur, ut quælibet ecclesia cathedralis habeat speciale Registrum Privilegiorum, de quo copiæ eorum recipi poterunt, quoties fuerit oportunum et necessarium."

in 1433 a notarized copy was made from the *Registrum ecclesie Upsalensis* and not from the original, the notary then stated that it was indicated to him that this cartulary "is authentic and owns the same force as notarial instruments or original letters with attached seals."[20]

Returning to the papal letter of 1174 against this background, it is easy to imagine why this letter was not included in the cartulary. In it, Pope Alexander III admonished the priests of the diocese of Uppsala to set an example to their parishioners and not participate in feasts or indecent drinking bouts. They should not allow themselves to be judged by a secular court, they should not baptize without using chrism, and so forth. In other words, this papal letter does not deal with the rights of the Uppsala church, but with the duties of its clergy. It would therefore not be of great interest to the compiler of the *Registrum*. In fact, in the *capitulatio* or index which he put at the beginning of the *Registrum*, he indicates that the archives contained some specific further bulls which were omitted in the *Registrum*. These concern various other duties imposed on the Uppsala church, including the summons to the council of Vienne and the order to pay to the papacy the taxes that were decided at that council.[21] Again, these are letters documenting the duties of the Uppsala church and not its rights, and they were hence of little interest to the compiler of the *Registrum*.

The only other among Sweden's seven medieval cathedrals whose archives preserves pre-1198 papal letters is the cathedral of Linköping. Here no originals have survived, but its cartulary from 1391 contains seven papal letters from this period.[22] The Linköping cartulary, which like its Uppsala counterpart bears the title of *Registrum ecclesie*, contains the text of the earliest papal letter that has been preserved in Sweden. This is a bull issued by Innocent II at some time between 1133 and 1136. Unfortunately, the beginning of this bull was lost when a leaf was cut out of the *Registrum* at some point before 1670. Incidentally, historians overlooked this letter frag-

[20] John Granlund, ed., *Kulturhistoriskt lexikon för nordisk medeltid*, 22 vols. (Malmö, 1956-78), s.v. Fides publica (by Jan Liedgren): "notabilem librum in pergameno scriptum, quem registrum predicte ecclesie Vpsalensis appellauerunt, quemque asseruerunt esse autenticum et habere parem vim cum instrumentis publicis seu litteris autenticis sigillis sigillatis."

[21] *Diplomatarium Svecanum*, vol. 5, no. 3849, p. 360.

[22] Nygren, "Registra ecclesie Lincopensis," and Herman Schück, *Ecclesia Lincopensis: Studier om Linköpingskyrkan under medeltiden och Gustav Vasa* (Stockholm, 1959), 3-6.

ment until Albert Brackmann discovered it when he visited Stockholm in 1902 to collect materials for the *Scandinavia pontificia*.[23]

Two of the papal letters in the Linköping *Registrum* were not addressed to the bishop or the diocese of Linköping, but to the king of Sweden.[24] Neither of these letters concerns the diocese of Linköping specifically; rather, they ask the king to make his people obey canon law. One of them was also included in collections of decretals and came ultimately into Gregory IX's *Liber extra*.[25] It is not difficult to explain how the documents from 1154 and 1172 came to be transcribed in the cartulary of Linköping cathedral. Until the fifteenth century, the kings of Sweden did not have their own chanceries. Instead one of the bishops would serve as chancellor, and his episcopal chancery would write the king's letters and also file received documents in the archives of the cathedral.[26] It is known that the bishop of Linköping served as the king's chancellor in 1230, but this does not explain why these two much earlier letters were archived in Linköping. When the second of them was sent, the bishop of Linköping was named Kol. Two sources from the fourteenth century claim that he was the king's chancellor. Both sources are problematic, and the historian of the medieval Swedish royal chancery Herman Schück has, therefore, not trusted their information about Kol.[27] The fact that the letter from 1172 came to be archived in Linköping constitutes, however, new support for their assertion that Kol was the king's chancellor.

Two cartularies written before 1400 survive in Denmark, from the cathedrals of Ribe and Aarhus, respectively. The Ribe cartulary, written

[23] Albert Brackmann, "Papsturkunden des Nordens, Nord- und Mittel-Deutschlands: Zweiter Bericht der Wedekindischen Preisstiftung für Deutsche Geschichte," *Nachrichten von der Gesellschaft der Wissenschaften in Göttingen: Philologisch-historische Klasse* 11 (1904): 125-26 = Nygren, "Registra ecclesie Lincopensis," 204. Claudius Örnhielm noticed this fragment and identified it as a papal letter already in the seventeenth century, but his identification remained unpublished and did not influence later historians.

[24] *Diplomatarium Svecanum*, vol. 1, nos. 38, 41, pp. 61, 72 = JL 9938, 13546.

[25] *Liber extra* X.3.45.1; Emil Friedberg, ed., *Corpus iuris canonici*, 2 vols. (Leipzig, 1879-81), vol. 2, col. 650.

[26] Herman Schück, "Kansler och capella regis under folkungatiden," *Historisk tidskrift* 83 (1963): 133-187, and Schück, *Rikets brev och register: Arkivbildande, kanslivåsen och tradition inom den medeltida svenska statsmakten*, Skrifter utgivna av Svenska riksarkivet 4 (Stockholm, 1976).

[27] Schück, "Kansler och capella regis," 141-43.

around 1290, is known by the delightful title of *Ribe Oldemoder* ("Ribe Great-grandmother," *Avia Ripensis* in Latin).[28] Since this is the oldest Scandinavian cartulary that has survived, the name is perhaps suitable. *Ribe Oldemoder* contains two pre-1198 papal letters.[29] Two such letters are also found in the cartulary from Aarhus, which was written around 1313.[30] I do not know of any other papal letters that would have been available to the compilers of these cartularies.

In fact, very few original papal letters from any part of the Middle Ages are preserved in Denmark. Only the cathedral archives of Roskilde contain any pre-1198 originals at all. There are three originals there, all of which concern the bishop's rights in the harbor that he had built and which he called Hafn (modern Cophenhagen).[31] There was a fourth original in the Roskilde archives in the sixteenth century, but it has since been lost.[32]

The medieval archives of Denmark are in general poorly preserved. This is not due to any single large catastrophe, as one might have suspected, except that many archives were destroyed during the 1320s and 1330s when the kingdom of Denmark fell apart in civil strife. For this reason, the preserved archives of the kings of Denmark go back only to Denmark's second founder Valdemar Atterdag, who reconstituted the kingdom in the middle of the fourteenth century. Various explanations for the poor state of transmission apply at the different institutions that should have received papal letters. Large parts of the archives of the metropolitan see, Lund, were destroyed in the great fire of Stockholm Castle in 1697. They had been moved there after Sweden had conquered the diocese in 1658. The archives of the bishops of Roskilde were likewise largely destroyed by fire, when the city of Copenhagen burned in 1728. The archives of the bishops of Odense were destroyed during the war of succession to the Danish

[28] Niels Skyum-Nielsen, "Haandskriftet 'Ribe Oldemoder': En kritisk studie," *Scandia* 19 (1948-49): 126-56, and Granlund, ed., *Kulturhistoriskt lexikon*, s.v. Ribe Oldemoder (by Erik Buus).

[29] *Diplomatarium Danicum,* vol. 1.3 (Copenhagen, 1976-77), nos. 191, 219, pp. 298, 348 = JL 16951, 16958.

[30] *Diplomatarium Danicum,* vol. 1.3, nos. 220-21, pp. 349-50 = JL 17524-25. Cf. Granlund, ed., *Kulturhistoriskt lexikon*, s.v. Brevbog, Danmark (by Erik Kroman).

[31] *Diplomatarium Danicum,* vol. 1.3, nos. 137, 190, 194, pp. 211, 297, 307 = JL 15682, 16953, 16967.

[32] *Diplomatarium Danicum,* vol. 1.3, no. 91, p. 139 (not in JL).

throne in 1534.[33]

Perhaps surprisingly, the Danish section of *Scandinavia pontificia* will list more papal letters than will the Swedish section, despite the scarcity of originals and texts transmitted through cartularies. The reasons for this are twofold. First, Denmark is closer to Germany, and many documents survived in the archives of northern Germany. The second reason is more important. Several literary sources surviving in Denmark contain copies or summaries of papal letters. In addition to two saints' lives, the most important such source is the so-called *Exordium monasterii qui dicitur Cara Insula*.[34] This is an account of the foundation of the Cistercian monastery of Øm written around 1205. The anonymous author inserted the texts of documents illustrating the history of his monastery. No fewer than eight papal letters are here reproduced in full. In other words, this single monastic chronicle contains more pre-1198 papal letters than do all more traditional diplomatic sources surviving from Denmark.

The situation is similar in Norway. Here, only two original pre-1198 papal letters survive, both directed to the archbishop of Trondheim.[35] They must have been preserved in the archives of that cathedral. No medieval cartulary is known from Norway. The *Brevbog* ("Letter book") of the bishop of Bergen from the early fourteenth century is not a cartulary, but rather a collection of contemporary letters of importance for the bishop's day-to-day political engagements.[36]

The reasons for the scarcity of papal letters preserved in Norway are similar to those in Denmark. Several specific cathedral archives were destroyed at separate occasions in the early modern period. The archives of

[33] Kr. Erslev, *Repertorium diplomaticum regni danici mediævalis: Fortegnelse over Danmarks breve fra middelalderen* 4 (Copenhagen, 1906-12); Granlund, ed., *Kulturhistoriskt lexikon*, s.v. Arkiv (by Jan Liedgren).

[34] Ed. M. Cl. Geertz, *Scriptores minores historiæ Danicæ medii ævi* (Copenhagen, 1918-20), 153-64; cf. Granlund, ed., *Kulturhistoriskt lexikon*, s.v. Klosterkrøniker (by Herluf Nielsen).

[35] Christian C. A. Lange and Carl R. Unger, eds., *Diplomatarium Norvegicum: Oldbreve til kundskap om Norges indre og ydre forhold, sprog, slægter, sæder, lovgivning og rettergang i middelalderen*, vol. 2 (Christiania, 1852), no. 1, p. 1 = Erik Gunnes, ed., *Regesta Norvegica*, vol. 1 (Oslo, 1989), no. 191, p. 84 = JL 16379; Lange and Unger, eds., *Diplomatarium Norvegicum*, vol. 1 (Christiania, 1847), no. 1, p. 1 = Gunnes, ed., *Regesta Norvegica*, vol. 1, no. 236, p. 98 = JL 17343.

[36] Granlund, ed., *Kulturhistoriskt lexikon*, s.v. Bergens kopibok (by Bjarne Bjerulfsen).

Hammar, for example, were annihilated when a Swedish army burned the city in 1567.[37]

That the section for Norway in *Scandinavia pontificia* is not as small as this might suggest is again thanks to another type of source. The source is this time canonical and legal. Eleven letters from Alexander III to the archbishop of Trondheim are found in an English decretal collection, the *Cottonian Collection*.[38] This twelfth-century collection also contains a letter directed to the king of Sweden.[39] What could have been the source used by the compiler of the *Cottonian Collection*?

We know that collectors of decretals in the twelfth century could have found their texts either in the papal registers in Rome or collected them from the addressees. Many English collections, including the *Cottonian Collection*, contain a large number of decretals directed to English addressees, suggesting that they were the result of collecting activity in England.[40] It is thus tempting to imagine that the authors of the *Cottonian Collection* somehow got the eleven Trondheim letters and the one Swedish letter from Trondheim. Did a Norwegian collector of decretals share his collection with an English colleague? After all, Norway had long-standing close contacts with the British Isles. The bishops of the Hebrides and Orkneys were suffragans of the archbishop of Trondheim until the end of the fifteenth century. The fact that the *Cottonian Collection* also contains some decretals issued for addressees in France, Hungary, and even the Crusader States, tends to contradict this hypothesis. However, it would still be quite remarkable if a decretalist happened to select eleven Trondheim letters from a papal register.

To summarize, the preservation patterns of papal letters are different in the three Scandinavian countries. Medieval originals and cartularies are

[37] Granlund, ed., *Kulturhistoriskt lexikon*, s.v. Arkiv.

[38] Walther Holtzmann, "Krone und Kirche in Norwegen im 12. Jahrhundert (Englische Analekten III)," *Deutsches Archiv für Geschichte des Mittelalters* 2 (1938): 341-400; Holtzmann, ed., *Decretales ineditae saeculi XII*, ed. Stanley Chodorow and Charles Duggan, Monumenta iuris canonici, Series B: Corpus collectionum, 4 (Vatican City, 1982), nos. 86-89, pp. 149-157.

[39] *Diplomatarium Svecanum*, vol. 1, no. 41, p. 61 = JL 13546. Stephan Kuttner, "La réserve papale du droit de canonisation," *Revue historique de droit français et étranger*, 4ᵉ série, 17 (1938): 172-228; repr. in Kuttner, *The History of Ideas and Doctrines of Canon Law in the Middle Ages* (London, 1980), VI.

[40] Charles Duggan, *Twelfth-Century Decretal Collections and Their Importance in English History* (London, 1963), 103-10.

best preserved in Sweden, while early papal letters issued for Denmark and Norway are best known through non-diplomatic sources. Why is the diplomatic material best preserved in Sweden? It is dangerous to generalize, but I want to draw attention to the fact that Swedish ecclesiastical archives were centralized earlier than in Norway and Denmark. In connection with the Swedish Reformation of the 1520s and 1530s, ecclesiastical institutions had to deliver their archives to Stockholm. They seem to have been safer there, despite the catastrophic castle fire of 1697, than were Danish and Norwegian ecclesiastical archives remaining in their respective cathedrals until the sixteenth or seventeenth centuries.

Scandinavia pontificia will list not only letters from the popes to Scandinavia, but also letters and gifts sent from Scandinavia to the popes. The earliest such communication that is known are the gifts that King Horik sent to Pope Nicholas in 864. I do not know what kind of gifts Horik sent, but I know what gift one of his successors thought was suitable for His Holiness. At some point around the middle of the eleventh century, King Sven Estridsen of Denmark sent messengers to Pope Leo IX. They presented him with a talking parrot. I have no idea where Sven might have been able to acquire a parrot; no talking birds are indigenous to Denmark. Nor did the parrot speak Danish; it spoke good Latin, greeting the pope with "Papa Leo" and "Ad papam vado."[41] I am sure Leo IX was delighted.

[41] Johann Matthias Watterich, ed., *Pontificum Romanorum qui fuerunt inde ab exeunte saeculo IX usque ad finem saeculi XII vitae*, 2 vols. (Leipzig, 1862), 1:153-54. Cf. Niels Skyum-Nielsen, "Den ældste pavebulle til Danmark," in *Runer og rids: Festskrift til Lis Jacobsen 29. Januar 1952* (Copenhagen, 1952), 172-73.